SHRINK!
SHRANK!
SHRUNK!

SHRINK! SHRANK! SHRUNK!

MAKE STYLISH SHRINK PLASTIC JEWELRY

by KATHY SHELDON

LARK CRAFTS

Asheville

LARK CRAFTS

An Imprint of Sterling Publishing
387 Park Avenue South
New York, NY 10016
If you have questions or comments about
this book, please visit: larkcrafts.com

Art Director

SUSAN WASINGER

Photographer

CYNTHIA SHAFFER

Cover Designer

SUSAN WASINGER

Library of Congress Cataloging-in-Publication Data

Sheldon, Kathy.
  Shrink! Shrank! Shrunk! : Make Stylish Shrink Plastic Jewelry /
Kathy Sheldon. -- First Edition.
    pages cm
  Includes index.
  ISBN 978-1-4547-0349-5
  1. Plastics craft. 2. Plastic jewelry. I. Title.
  TT297.S36 2012
  745.594'2--dc23
                                    2012002240

10 9 8 7 6 5 4 3 2 1

First Edition

Published by Lark Crafts
An Imprint of Sterling Publishing Co., Inc.
387 Park Avenue South, New York, NY 10016

Doodles by Aimee Ray
can be found on pages
27, 28, 31, 38, 44,
47, 56, 61, 63, 68, 71,
82, 90, and 97.

Distributed in Canada by Sterling Publishing
c/o Canadian Manda Group, 165 Dufferin Street
Toronto, Ontario, Canada M6K 3H6

Distributed in the United Kingdom by GMC Distribution Services,
Castle Place, 166 High Street, Lewes, East Sussex, England BN7 1XU

Distributed in Australia by Capricorn Link (Australia) Pty Ltd.,
P.O. Box 704, Windsor, NSW 2756 Australia

ISBN: 978-1-4547-0349-5

For information about custom editions, special sales, and premium and corporate purchases,
please contact Sterling Special Sales Department at 800-805-5489 or specialsales@sterlingpub.com.

Requests for information about desk and examination copies available to college and university professors
must be submitted to academic@larkbooks.com. Our complete policy can be found at www.larkcrafts.com.

CONTENTS

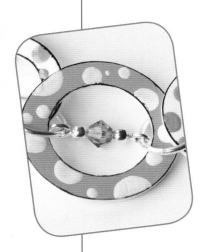

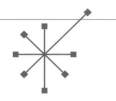

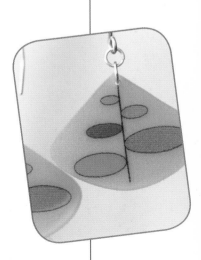

INTRODUCTION

Tell someone you're writing a book on shrink plastic jewelry and you'll get one of two responses: "Oh, I love that stuff!" or "Huh?"

When I get the huh response, I say, "Remember Shrinky Dinks—those plastic cartoon characters you decorated and then baked in the oven?" That usually gets an "Oh, right….But shrink plastic jewelry?" Translation: Wouldn't that be, well, kind of tacky? So I pull out my tablet and show the doubters photos of the projects in this book, and they can't believe the fresh, stylish, and even elegant jewelry you can make with shrink plastic. You won't believe it either.

And you're in for another surprise: Crafting with shrink plastic is super fun. There's something just plain magical about taking a very thin flexible sheet of plastic, cutting and decorating it, popping it in the oven, and then watching it transform into something about a third its original size and nine times as thick. Serious artists and jewelers now employ shrink plastic, but making things with the material still feels like play.

Kids first discovered shrink plastic back in 1968 when the Wham-O toy company introduced the Shrink Machine, which used the heat from a 40-watt light bulb to shrink plastic cutouts. Then in 1973, Brookfield, Wisconsin, housewives Betty J. Morris and Kathryn Bloomberg heated plastic container covers as a Cub Scout project. The boys were so excited with the results that the women knew they were onto something and started selling the material at the local mall. Soon Shrinky Dinks were born. Jewelry makers rediscovered the material in the past few years, and now different brands and kinds of shrink plastic are sold in craft stores, art supply shops, and online.

In this book, I'll teach you everything you need to know about making jewelry from the different kinds of shrink plastic, from the differences between the types to the many ways to decorate the material (including printing images straight onto it from your home inkjet computer). I'll show you how to bake the plastic, how

not to freak out when it does its little curling thing in the oven and sometimes sticks together, how to seal your shrunk pieces, and how to use simple findings and basic techniques to turn them into adorable jewelry.

After learning the basics, you'll find more than 30 projects from designers from as far afield as Seattle, Washington; West Yorkshire, England; and Sydney, Australia. I can't say enough about this wonderful group of jewelry makers. Shrink plastic jewelry is a relatively new craft, and these crafters have spent a lot of time experimenting and perfecting their techniques with the medium. They were so generous and willing to share, not just the discoveries they've made about how to use shrink plastic to create fantastic-looking jewelry, but also their original designs. Please thank them by visiting their blogs and shops, which you'll find in About the Designers, starting on page 125. You'll be inspired by what you see.

Along with step-by-step instructions for each project, you'll find templates and graphics in the back of the book that you can trace or print right onto shrink plastic, along with a bonus page of woodland graphics. And Aimee Ray's doodles that grace these pages can be traced or printed onto shrink plastic to make jewelry, too.

Once you've made a few of these projects, you'll see that you can mix and match the techniques and graphics to make any number of pieces of jewelry and get started on your own creative journey from shrink to shrank to shrunk.

There's something just plain magical about taking a sheet of decorated plastic, popping it in the oven, and then watching it transform.

Shrink Plastic BASICS

As you've seen from flipping through the first few pages of this book, you can make beautiful jewelry from shrink plastic. You can even make serious-looking jewelry if you like. But you'll enjoy the process more if, especially at first, you don't take getting from shrink to shrunk too seriously. Remember, this stuff started out as a toy! I guarantee you that the first time you see a project bake and wiggle its way down into a teeny version of its former self, you're going to get a silly grin on your face.

WHAT IS SHRINK PLASTIC?

Well, if you really must know, it's biaxially oriented thermoplastic polystyrene, but I think that takes the magic out of it. Shrink plastic is plastic stock that's been heated and stretched in two directions to form a thin sheet. When your shrink plastic object is baked and shrinks, it's actually just remembering and returning to its original size and thickness. "Biaxially oriented," scandalous as it may sound, simply means the plastic was stretched (and so will shrink) proportionally in two directions. Once heated and shrunk, designs applied to the shrink plastic become more vivid and refined and permanently bonded to the material.

Enough of the science behind the stuff—the basics of making shrink plastic jewelry are quite simple:

+ **Sand the plastic**
  if not purchased pre-roughened

+ **Draw, trace, or photocopy a design onto the plastic**

+ **Cut the plastic out**

+ **Bake it**

+ **Seal it**

+ **Add findings**

When heated, shrink plastic shrinks to approximately one-third of its original size, but because its mass stays the same, it becomes nine times thicker. And as you can see, any design or color added darkens and intensifies once the piece shrinks.

Is It Safe?

I know, heating plastic sounds scary. But the shrink plastic you purchase for craft projects has been tested to meet safety standards even when heated beyond recommended temperatures. Since you don't know for certain whether all the art supplies you might use to decorate your plastic are nontoxic when heated, err on the side of safety and use separate baking equipment and adequate ventilation when heating your projects. If you're very sensitive to fumes, purchase a dedicated toaster oven (thrift stores are full of them) to use outside with an outdoor extension cord (in dry weather, of course).

Shrink Plastic BASICS

SHRINK PLASTIC MATERIALS AND TOOLS

Because you can do so many different things with shrink plastic, the list of materials and tools you might want to use is quite long. But the "what you absolutely need" list is not.

I've put together a Basic Shrink Kit with the essentials to have handy to get started. If you already make jewelry, you probably have a number of the tools and materials needed. Each project will list any additional materials or tools required.

Basic Shrink Kit

Straightedge or ruler

Sandpaper (300 to 400 grit)

Scissors

Small curved scissors

Hole punches (in various sizes)

Oven or toaster oven

Parchment paper

Baking sheet

Potholder or oven mitt

Flattener (smooth heavy object)

Sealer

Round-nose pliers

Flat-nose pliers

Chain-nose pliers

Wire cutters or flush cutters

SHRINK PLASTIC

As more and more jewelers and general crafters discover shrink plastic, it's become easy to find. Big chain craft stores, independent craft shops, and even art supply stores carry it, and you can order it online. Sometimes it's in the kids' section of the chain crafts stores: Ask if you can't find it—I've discovered it in unlikely aisles.

Shrink plastic comes in several different brands, and they all shrink just a bit differently, although the basic instructions for the projects should work for all brands. In addition to different brands, there are various *types* of shrink plastic (see the chart on the following page). And check your recycling bin—some (but not all) #6 plastics are a kind of shrink plastic (see page 23).

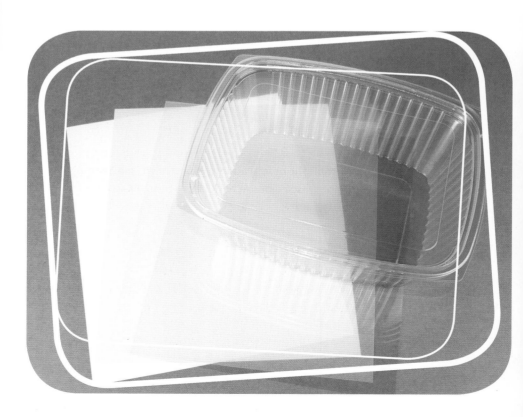

KINDS OF SHRINK PLASTIC

   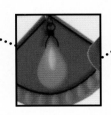 

Clear or Pre-Roughened: Great when you want a translucent look that takes advantage of light coming through the material. Pre-roughened comes with a "frosted" side that's easy to decorate, but the front shrinks down to a nice clear finish.

Matte: Bakes down to a soft, slightly translucent white. I find matte shrink plastic the easiest to cut, so it's good for intricately shaped pieces.

White: Gives crisp lines, bright colors, and high contrast. If your design template is dark enough, you should be able to see through the plastic to trace your design, but white shrink plastic is also good for stamping.

Inkjet: This special shrink plastic is coated for use in inkjet printers, so you can copy images (including photographs) right onto it. Some types allow you to print on both sides of the plastic.

#6 Plastic: Some (but not all) types of #6 plastic can be used as shrink plastic. Look in your recycling bin for pieces with the numeral 6 inside the triangle. The clear containers used for berries and take-out foods are often #6.

SANDPAPER (300 to 400 grit)

If you're not using matte or pre-roughened shrink plastic, you may need to sand your plastic before adding your design (see Sanding, page 17). Sandpaper also comes in handy for sanding away mistakes before baking and smoothing any rough edges after baking.

TEMPLATES AND GRAPHICS

Templates for the projects and extra graphics can be found starting on page 110. For more on decorating the shrink plastic before baking, as well as transferring templates, see page 18.

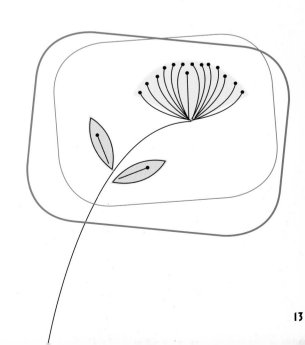

Shrink Plastic BASICS

TOOLS & MATERIALS FOR DRAWING AND COLORING

Permanent markers, colored pencils, permanent stamp ink, and water-based acrylic paints are the art supplies most commonly used to decorate the projects in this book. You can also use other products as long as they will stick to sanded shrink plastic, but keep in mind that not all products are safe to put in an oven.

Pencil: A graphite pencil comes in handy for tracing some designs. If you goof up and erase your pencil marks, the erasure may leave a smudge on the plastic before you bake it, but I haven't had any problem with such marks showing after I've shrunk the piece, as long as I wipe off any eraser residue before baking. Do be careful when you use pencil on inkjet shrink plastic as sometimes the graphite smudges and makes the plastic look a bit dirty.

Colored Pencils: These are some of the best tools to add color to your pieces. On some types of shrink plastic, less-expensive colored pencils seem to work best, and on other types, art-grade ones do. If your colored pencil leaves flecks on the plastic, blow or brush the flecks off before baking.

Permanent Markers: Use these to both outline and to color your designs. Remember that colors will be much more intense when the piece is shrunk, so experiment a bit to figure out the right shades to start with. Nonpermanent markers smear on shrink plastic.

Artist Chalks: Chalks can be used to create beautiful effects on shrink plastic jewelry, especially when you're stamping. Be sure to seal pieces decorated with chalk after baking, so that the color won't rub off.

Stamps and Stamp Ink: If drawing isn't your thing, you can still make wonderful shrink jewelry using stamped images. Just be sure to use permanent stamp ink so that you don't have a problem with smearing. See pages 45 and 66 for jewelry made with stamped shrink plastic.

Paint Markers: These are fun to experiment with—some leave a raised shiny finish on the shrink plastic (see Polka Dots Earrings and Bracelet, page 106).

Acrylic Paint: You can create nice effects by using acrylic paint on the back (rough) side of a clear shrink plastic object that's been shrunk. See pages 36 and 69 for examples.

Inkjet Printer: Some of the projects in this book use inkjet shrink plastic, which can run through an inkjet printer. Do not use shrink plastic in a laser printer: It can melt and ruin the printer.

CUTTING AND PUNCHING TOOLS

Scissors: Use scissors to cut out your shrink designs. Don't ruin your good fabric scissors by using them to cut plastic!

Small Curved Scissors: Curved manicure scissors are great for cutting intricate shapes.

Craft Knife: A craft knife works well for cutting shapes from the center of shrink plastic before you bake it (see Bird Silhouette Bracelet, page 64).

Hole Punches: Use these to punch holes for jump rings, etc., into the shrink plastic before you bake it. Just remember that the size of the hole is also going to shrink.

Large hand punches (especially round and oval ones) are useful if you want to make multiples of the same shape, and they give you more polished-looking and consistently sized pieces, but if you don't have them, just use scissors and remind yourself, as I do all the time, *it's hand-made—it's not supposed to be perfect!*

Large Needle: You can use a large heated needle to make very small holes in your object after you shrink it (see Cutting and Punching Shrink Plastic, page 19).

BAKING EQUIPMENT

You don't need special equipment to bake shrink plastic, but once you get hooked making jewelry from this material, you'll probably want to have separate items that you use just for shrink plastic. You can find almost everything you need at thrift stores or yard sales.

Oven: Electric and gas ovens are fine for baking shrink plastic. You'll enjoy the process more if your oven has a light that works and a window in the door. (Of course, whether or not your door is clean enough to see through is another matter.) Shrink plastic cannot be baked in a microwave oven.

Toaster Oven: This is a handy way to shrink plastic. Since I travel a lot, I have a dedicated shrink plastic toaster oven from a thrift store that I toss in the back of my car so I can shrink while I'm away from home!

Heat Gun: A heat gun (available in the stamping section of most craft stores) is another handy, portable way to bake your shrink plastic. You may need to use something to hold your piece down so that it doesn't blow around as you heat it.

Baking Sheet: Make sure your baking sheet has a flat, smooth surface. Avoid insulated baking sheets with a layer of air in the middle. I use the little baking sheet that came with my toaster oven and it's perfect.

Glass Baking Dish: If you want to try fusing projects (which requires reheating pieces of shrunk plastic at very high temperatures—see Fusing, page 23), you'll need an oven-proof glass baking dish.

Parchment Paper: This paper keeps your shrink plastic item from sticking to a surface while baking. (Fold one edge over to make a little handle for quick pulls out of the oven.) You can also place parchment on top of the piece so that it doesn't stick to itself if it curls up while baking (as shrink plastic is wont to do). You can use cardboard or a paper bag instead, but be careful when mixing any paper product and heat sources—never put paper in the oven while it's preheating: Temperature spikes can cause it to ignite. You can also use a dedicated silicon baking mat in place of the bottom piece of parchment paper.

Chopstick or Skewer: Larger pieces of shrink plastic curl and sometimes stick to themselves while shrinking. If they don't unstick, use one of these tools to gently separate the pieces. (For more on unsticking, see Oh No! It's Curling!, page 20.)

Potholder or Oven Mitt: Make sure you've got one handy when it's time to remove your object from the oven.

Gloves: Shrink plastic is hot when it comes out of the oven, so thin gloves will protect you when handling or shaping fresh-from-the-oven projects.

Flattener: You need something to flatten your item as soon as you remove it from the oven. For small objects, I use a flat lid or the back of a metal measuring cup and a fair amount of pressure. Many of the project designers use a heavy book—Anna Boksenbaum swears by *Joy of Cooking*. Whatever you use, make sure it has a smooth surface; otherwise, your plastic will take on the texture of your flattener.

Ring Mandrel (or other cylindrical object): Use these to shape your rings as soon as you remove them from the oven. Lip balm tubes, glue sticks, and other items all work well for this.

Sealers: Acrylic sealers, spray sealers, varnish, embossing powder, liquid dimensional adhesive glaze, and clear nail polish can all be used to seal your jewelry once it's baked. It's best to consider even your sealed shrink plastic jewelry non-waterproof, and remove it before showering or swimming the English Channel. (See Sealing Your Projects, page 21.)

Shrink Plastic BASICS

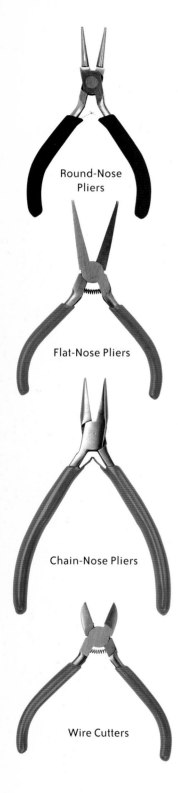

Round-Nose Pliers

Flat-Nose Pliers

Chain-Nose Pliers

Wire Cutters

TOOLS AND MATERIALS FOR JEWELRY MAKING

Almost all the projects in this book require only the most basic jewelry tools and materials.

Jewelry Pliers and Wire Cutters: You need chain-nose, round-nose, and flat-nose pliers to make the projects in this book. (Though in truth, you could probably get away with just two pairs of chain-nose pliers in a pinch.) The Calla Lily Earrings on page 98 call for crimpling pliers— pliers with two sets of notches on their jaws: one to crush the crimp tube and the other to shape it. You also need wire cutters to make some of the projects. If you don't have these tools, they're easy to find and reasonably priced at craft stores.

Findings: Jewelry findings are the small (usually metal) components used to assemble jewelry. It's easy to find clasps, jump rings, pin backs, etc., in a wide variety of finishes online, at bead shops, and in craft stores. You can also find pieces of jewelry at thrift stores and yard sales and take them apart to reuse their findings.

> **Jump Rings:** Wire circles, called jump rings, are a simple way to hold jewelry components together. The rings are split so you can open and close them using flat-nose pliers (see page 24).
>
> **Clasps:** Clasps connect and secure the ends of a necklace or bracelet. They're available in various styles, including box, fishhook, toggle, lobster, S-hook, hook-and-eye, and magnetic.
>
> **Earring Findings:** These include French wires, kidney wires, lever-back wires, and posts (also called studs).
>
> **Pin Backs:** Metal pin backs come in several shapes and sizes. Pin backs can be attached with jewelry glue.
>
> **Ring Blanks:** These are available in many different finishes and are usually adjustable. The ring blanks used for projects in this book have

a flat part where you can adhere your shrink plastic piece with jewelry glue.

Bobby Pin Blanks: These are just what they sound like: metal bobby pins with a flat part where you can adhere your shrink plastic design with jewelry glue.

Head Pins: These thin wires have a head on one end to keep beads or other objects from sliding off.

Bails: Bails are usually used to attach pendants (or in this case, shrink plastic pieces) to a necklace chain or cord.

Chain and Cord: Chain and cord are used in many necklaces and bracelets in this book. You can buy both at craft stores and attach your own clasps. If you're new to jewelry making and want to concentrate on the shrink plastic making, buy plain finished necklaces and bracelets and attach your shrink plastic pieces to them (I won't tell).

Jewelry Adhesive: Use jewelry glue or another strong waterproof glue to attach your shrink plastic pieces to earring backs, ring blanks, bails, etc.

Beads and Crystals: Use these to embellish your shrink plastic pieces.

SHRINK PLASTIC TECHNIQUES

Again, making jewelry from shrink plastic isn't difficult, but there is something a bit unpredictable about it. It's a little like regular baking in that you never know exactly how something will turn out. Test out the following techniques with some shrink plastic scraps before carefully coloring and cutting an elaborate project. I'll admit it: Even though I write instructions for a living, I hate to follow them. I definitely fall into the "blunder on ahead and learn from my mistakes" school of crafting. But even I learned quickly that my shrink plastic projects turned out better if I took the time to follow directions instead of just winging it. Once you're familiar with the material, you can have fun experimenting!

SHRINK … SHRANK … JUST HOW SHRUNK?

Most shrink plastic becomes about one-third to one-half its original size and about nine times thicker when shrunk. Different brands and various types shrink different amounts, though, so it's best to make a shrink plastic ruler when you use a new kind of shrink plastic (see the sidebar at the right). Also, most shrink plastic doesn't shrink the exact same amount vertically as it does horizontally, so if you're making matching pieces (such as earrings), be sure to draw, stamp, or print the designs in the same direction on the sheet before cutting or punching them out.

SANDING THE PLASTIC

This is one of those steps I'm always tempted to skip and almost always regret when I do. If your shrink plastic doesn't come pre-roughened, use very fine (300 to 400 grit) sandpaper to give it "tooth" to grab your drawing or coloring medium and keep it from beading up or smearing when applied to the plastic. If you sand in one direction only, markers and inks will tend to bleed in that direction, so sand in a crosshatch pattern: To do so, sand horizontally (in straight lines, no circular motions), turn the sheet 180°, and sand in straight lines again. Also, it's best to sand on a smooth surface such as a rubber mat; otherwise, texture on your work surface may show up as glossy spots on the sanded shrink plastic. Be sure to wipe any sanding dust off completely before using the plastic. You can skip sanding if you're using permanent markers or permanent ink to make the design on your shrink plastic or using inkjet shrink plastic.

Making a Shrink Plastic Ruler

Since various types and brands of shrink plastic shrink different amounts, getting the jewelry piece to the size you desire can be tricky without experimentation. Solve this problem by making a shrink plastic ruler the first time you use a new type of shrink plastic. It's easy, just:

1. Cut a 2 x 10-inch (5.1 x 25.4 cm) strip lengthwise from your shrink plastic sheet.

2. Use a ruler and permanent marker to mark inches or centimeters.

3. Write the brand and type of plastic on the ruler (you may want to note the direction of your cut—vertical or horizontal—because shrink plastic can also shrink more in one direction than the other).

4. Shrink the plastic. You now have a kind of "reverse ruler": If you compare the approximate size you want your finished piece to be to the marks on this ruler, you'll see how many inches you need the original (preshrunk) piece to be.

Shrink Plastic BASICS

DECORATING SHRINK PLASTIC BEFORE BAKING

The templates and graphics for the projects in this book can be found starting on page 110. They are all at true size, but remember that you may have to make adjustments for different brands and types of shrink plastic. When you're ready to branch out on your own, try using some of the cute Aimee Ray doodles in the book as a design element (see page 4 for a list of pages with the doodles). It's also easy to purchase great digital designs these days: My favorite sources are Etsy shops.

Tracing Templates

Tracing templates and designs onto shrink plastic is easy. Just place the plastic, rough side up, over the design and trace with a permanent marker or colored pencil. You should be able to see most designs through all but colored shrink plastic. (When I'm transferring a faint design onto white shrink plastic, I tape the whole thing onto a sunny window—a light table would work even better!) In order not to waste the shrink plastic, cut a piece to size before tracing larger shapes, or trace as close to the edge of the plastic sheet as possible. If you don't want outlines to show on your finished piece, trace with a pencil so that you can cut inside the lines and then erase any marks that still show. Just be careful: With some kinds of shrink plastic (inkjet especially), smudged graphite will show on your final design.

Remember that most shrink plastic shrinks a bit more in one direction than in the other, which can make your final design a tad distorted. Sometimes this distortion is barely noticeable, but sometimes it's more pronounced (following the manufacturer's directions for baking temperature and time is the best way to avoid this). Because avoiding distortion entirely is nearly impossible, when making matching pieces such as earrings, be sure to trace all pieces in the same direction on the sheet.

Coloring Your Design

Once you've traced your outline (or drawn or stamped it), color in the design with colored pencils or permanent markers—remembering that the color is going to intensify once the piece shrinks. If you plan to use a hand punch to punch out your piece (it's an easy way to get perfect circles), color outside the template lines a bit, so you'll get full coverage on your punched piece.

Going Your Own Way

Once you start making shrink jewelry, you'll notice enticing designs everywhere: linens on your bed, ceramics in your kitchen, or even the pattern on a leaf outside. You can also find wonderfully designed patterns on papers in the scrapbook section of your local craft store or in digital form online. The two key things to remember are that once shrunk, your designs are going to be much smaller and the colors more vivid. Remember, too, that most designs are copyrighted, so you can't use someone else's art, including the graphics in this book, if you plan to sell your jewelry.

CUTTING AND PUNCHING SHRINK PLASTIC

This is yet another area where experimentation helps. I suppose I should be using craft scissors, but I use an old pair of kitchen shears to cut most kinds of shrink plastic. I grabbed them one day, and they worked well. When I'm cutting out small or intricate designs, I use curved manicure scissors, but those don't always provide as smooth a cut as I'd like, so I go back and forth with the scissors depending on what I'm cutting. For smooth lines, cut in a slow, continuous motion that uses the parts of the blades nearest to the base of the scissors, and remember to always turn the plastic, not the scissors.

A craft knife can come in handy when cutting designs out of the inside of a pattern. If cutting tight corners, snip little darts into the piece before making the cut; otherwise, some of the stiffer kinds of shrink plastic can snap. Sharp points become even sharper after shrinking and they can also make pieces uncomfortable to wear. Rounding corners will avoid that and also tends to make shapes shrink with less distortion.

Getting Punchy

When you want very accurate shapes or multiples of a shape, large hand punches are, well, handy. Just remember that not all punches work with shrink plastic (I know, because I ruined a pricey punch that still has shrink plastic stuck in it). The stronger, squeeze types and those with fairly simple shapes tend to work the best. Also, remember that you want the punch size to be about 60 percent larger than the size of your final piece.

Small hand punches are great for making holes to connect findings to your pieces of jewelry. Make sure you punch all holes before shrinking, taking into account, of course, that the hole will also shrink. All the projects in this book had their holes punched with either $1/4$-inch (6 mm), $1/8$-inch (3 mm), or $1/16$-inch (1.6 mm) hole punches. If you wait until the piece is shrunk, you'll have to either drill a hole or use a large, very hot needle to make a hole in the plastic. To use a large needle, care-

fully heat the needle using a soot-free source, such as a butane lighter, and then poke the needle through the plastic. When you're punching holes in a pair of earrings or in two pieces that will be layered (such as the Mexican Oilcloth Necklace on page 48), hold the pieces rough sides together and punch a hole in each piece simultaneously with your hole punch. This ensures that the holes will line up after you shrink your pieces.

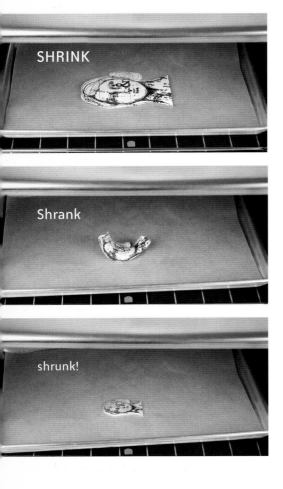

SHRINK

Shrank

shrunk!

BAKING THE SHRINK PLASTIC

✦ Baking temperatures vary for different types and brands of shrink plastic, so always start by reading the manufacturer's instructions—usually temperatures range from 275°F to 325°F (135°C to 163°C). Typically, clearer shrink plastic needs lower temperatures, and more opaque plastic needs higher, but keep in mind that oven and toaster oven temperatures vary, so you may need to make adjustments.

✦ Preheat your oven or toaster oven before inserting the shrink plastic, and do NOT insert cardboard or paper into an oven or toaster oven as it's preheating. Some ovens experience temperature spikes while preheating that are high enough to set the cardboard or paper on fire. If you don't have a heat-proof countertop nearby, use a cooling rack, hot pad, or heavy folded towel to prepare a "landing pad" for the hot baking sheet that will be coming out of the oven, because you'll need to move quickly to flatten (or sometimes form) your pieces as soon as they are done shrinking.

✦ Place your unbaked shrink plastic piece or pieces on brown paper or parchment paper on a flat baking sheet. If you have more than one piece, make sure they aren't touching. (I usually place my pieces between two pieces of parchment paper, but for the photos to the left I wanted the shrink plastic to be easy to see. You may want to leave off the top piece of parchment paper the first few times you experiment, so it will be easy to watch the plastic shrink.)

✦ Now, place the baking sheet into the preheated oven. As the plastic heats up, you'll see the piece come to life and start to curl a bit. Don't panic; instead, read the sidebar Oh, No! It's Curling! below, and then you'll see why I usually use parchment paper on top, too. Once your piece has flattened back down (this usually takes two to three minutes), it's done.

✦ Now you need to move quickly: Using an oven mitt or gloves, carefully remove the baking sheet from the oven, place it on the counter or your landing pad, and press down slightly on the warm parchment-covered piece using a smooth hardcover book or other object.

Oh, No! It's Curling!

That's cool—shrink plastic is supposed to curl. It's contracting back to its dinky "before" size. Just enjoy the show. Sometimes, especially with long pieces, the ends may touch and stick together during the curling stage. Often, the ends will unstick themselves as the piece shrinks and flatten back out. If not, remove the piece from the oven carefully (it's hot!), let it cool a bit so that it doesn't distort, and then gently but firmly pull the stuck ends apart. Put the unstuck plastic back in the oven and let it finish baking. If it doesn't flatten completely when it's done shrinking, use a book or other object to flatten it. If you're baking a long piece, either place it inside a folded sheet of parchment paper (so that the paper is both under and *over* the piece) or sprinkle it very lightly with talcum powder, and you can usually avoid this sticky situation all together.

SHRINKING THE PLASTIC WITH A HEAT GUN

I prefer to use an oven or toaster oven, but you can instead use a heat gun to shrink your shrink plastic. To do so, place your piece on a heat-resistant surface, and hold it gently with the end of a chopstick, spatula, or other long-handled object that doesn't conduct heat. Hold the gun 3 to 6 inches (7.6 to 15.2 cm) above the plastic and turn it on. Move it continuously over the entire piece until the piece has shrunk to one-half or one-third its original size. If the plastic doesn't flatten completely, turn it over and heat the other side.

SANDING OR FILING EDGES

Once your piece has cooled, you may want to gently sand the edges to shave off any irregularities and give the piece a more polished appearance. Some designers use an emery board or small file to do this. You can decorate the edges with permanent markers or metallic markers once they are sanded.

SEALING YOUR PROJECTS

The designs on most shrink jewelry will rub or wash off eventually if you don't seal the piece with some product. (Even sealed shrink plastic jewelry shouldn't be worn in the shower.) Sealers include embossing powder that's added to the shrunk project and then heated back in the oven, liquid clear gloss medium that you squeeze onto the project from a small bottle, clear acrylic spray sealers in matte or glossy finishes, and even clear fingernail polish. For the latter two products, a few light layers work better than one thick one. Some of these products have strong fumes and should be used outdoors.

TIP *Some sealers, when used with certain art materials, can cause your design to run, destroying your piece. And speaking from experience, I can tell you that it will likely be the piece that you spent the most time very carefully tracing, coloring, etc., that will run and be ruined. To be safe, make a little test piece using the same pencils, pens, or inks on the same kind of shrink plastic as your project. Bake it, and then test with your sealer before taking a chance on the real project.*

SPECIAL TECHNIQUES

Each project in the book describes the technique required in a step-by-step fashion, but what follows are instructions for a few special techniques.

Stamping

Stamping is a quick and easy way to apply designs to your projects. Use only permanent inks on shrink plastic—others are likely to bead up and smear or not dry completely. And if you plan to color in the stamped image, remember to use stamps with designs that are mainly outlines. The kind of shrink plastic that comes pre-roughened is perfect for stamping, but you can also use other types as long as you sand first. Always stamp on the rough or sanded side of the plastic and allow the ink to dry before coloring in any stamped outlines. You may want to practice your stamping technique on scrap pieces of shrink plastic first: light pressure usually works best to keep the ink from smearing.

Decorating the Back of the Plastic

One advantage of clear or pre-roughened shrink plastic is that the glossy front of the plastic shrinks clears to provide a kind of "glass" front to enhance your designs. (You can give your piece a three-dimensional appearance if you draw your outline on the glossy side of the clear plastic and add the colors to the rough side.) When using this technique, many crafters like to add a coat of white or light-colored acrylic paint to the back of the piece after it has shrunk to make the colors show better. Remember when you're adding a design that will be viewed through the clear front, to draw, trace, or paint the design in reverse.

Printing on Shrink Plastic

You can make fantastic jewelry using inkjet shrink plastic. The coating on this product allows the water-based inks used in most inkjet printers to adhere, so photos, drawings, and other images can be printed right onto it using an inkjet printer (with some brands you can print on both sides). Never use shrink plastic in a laser printer—it can melt and ruin your printer! Some designers use pre-roughened shrink plastic in their inkjet printers and find it works fine as long as they give the

ink plenty of time to dry. But if you're using an expensive printer, be safe and use the inkjet plastic that's made to go through inkjet printers.

To use the graphics in the back of the book with inkjet shrink plastic, simply scan the images into your computer and then print them on the plastic—they've already been adjusted for size and color (although you may need to adjust the size for your brand of shrink plastic).

If you're using another photo or image, make it two to three times larger

and about 50 percent lighter than your desired final piece. Adjusting the color saturation to just a tad above minimum is usually right. Don't forget that gray areas will also darken (to black) if not sufficiently lightened. In general, photographs without a lot of dark areas work best on shrink plastic. So that you don't waste the inkjet plastic, plan ahead and include as many images as you can fit onto one sheet. Remember to arrange matching pieces (such as earrings) in the same direction so that any distortion will match in the final shapes. Print your images on regular paper first as a test.

Once you're ready to print, remove any paper from the tray and feed the inkjet sheet through the printer just as you would feed paper. If only one side is printable, the manufacturer's instructions should explain how to tell which side it is. (If you're uncertain which side of a sheet your printer prints on, first run a test piece of regular paper with an X drawn on it in pencil through the printer.) Once the inkjet sheet has printed, handle it carefully by its edges and place it on a flat surface to dry. Drying times vary by brand and the amount of ink in your image. Once dry, the plastic is ready to cut and bake.

Shaping Shrink Plastic

Warm-from-the-oven shrink plastic is still pliable enough to shape into rings or other objects. Shaping three dimensional shrink plastic is more of an art than a science: It requires working very quickly with material that's still hot, and you'll be frustrated if you expect to get the exact same results each time. But it's awfully fun to transform a thin sheet of plastic into a tiny little blossom or a unicorn ring. The specific technique required depends on what you're making, so follow the step-by-step instructions for each three-dimensional project in the book.

Using #6 Plastic

You can use many (but not all) types of #6 plastic as shrink plastic. I've found that to-go containers marked #6 often shrink nicely (the centers of the containers' bottoms and lids shrink with the least amount of distortion). If you're at a party or other event, and plastic cups (including colored ones) are about to be thrown in the trash, rinse them out, take them home, and see if they'll shrink. But *only* experiment with plastics marked #6— heating other kinds of plastic can be dangerous. Because #6 shrink plastic gives less consistent results (especially from cups and other curved pieces), use this recycled plastic for projects where symmetry doesn't matter. Also, I've found that #6 plastic in take-out containers tends to shrink a bit thicker than purchased shrink plastic, so I use it for projects where that thickness is an advantage (such as the brooch on page 78).

Fusing

You can get wonderful effects by fusing pieces of shrink plastic together. The necklace, left, was made with this technique. Fusing involves heating the plastic at higher than normal temperatures, and it will let off some fumes, so open a window, turn on a fan, or use a toaster oven (with an outdoor extension cord) outside if the weather is good.

To fuse two (or three) pieces of shrink plastic together, first bake the pieces as you normally would, following the manufacturer's directions. Then raise the oven temperature to 450°F (230°C). Layer the shrunk pieces and place them in an ovenproof glass dish. If you're fusing sanded or pre-roughened plastic, place the pieces so their rough sides are facing down. Sanded plastic will be clear once it's done fusing.

Bake the layered pieces at 450°F (230°C) for 10 to 15 minutes. Every oven is different, so take a quick look at 10 minutes (or even earlier, if your oven cooks hot). Your piece is done when the roughness of the plastic has smoothed out and the edges have rounded but the plastic hasn't melted so much that any holes have closed.

Use oven mitts to take the hot dish out of the oven, and let it cool down. The shrink plastic is much too hot to touch or to remove from the pan.

SUPER SIMPLE JEWELRY MAKING

The pieces in this book use only the simplest of techniques. Refer back to this section as needed.

ADDING JUMP RINGS

Jump rings allow you to make quick and easy connections between jewelry parts. If you open or close a jump ring incorrectly by pulling the ends apart or together, you'll distort its shape and weaken the link. To open a jump ring, use two pairs of pliers to grasp each end of the jump ring. Then pull one side toward you and the other side away from you on the same plane (see figure 1). Open the jump ring only as wide as necessary to insert the objects being joined. To close the jump ring, simply reverse the process by twisting the ends back together.

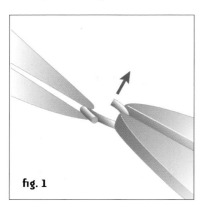

fig. 1

MAKING A SIMPLE LOOP

A simple loop is as simple to make as its name.

1. As shown in figure 2, use pliers to bend the end of the wire 90° to make a right angle, leaving enough wire at the end to make a loop.

2. Using round-nose pliers, grasp the wire close to the bend of the angle, then roll the pliers to shape the loop. Use wire cutters to trim any excess wire.

3. The finished loop is ready for attachment. Once it's in place, gently squeeze the loop with pliers to secure it.

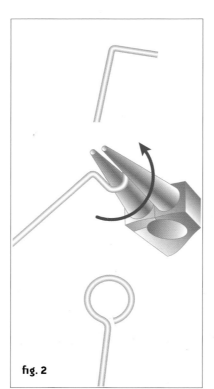

fig. 2

MAKING A WRAPPED LOOP

As shown in figure 3, the wrapped loop is a variation of the simple loop just described. Use an extra length of wire for the 90° bend. Once you've made the loop, reposition the pliers so that the lower jaw is inside it. Using your other hand and keeping the wire at a right angle as you work, wrap the wire tail around the neck of the wire two or three times. Cut the wire, and then tuck the end close to the remaining length.

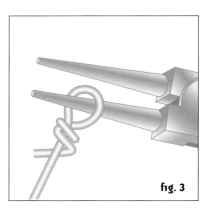

fig. 3

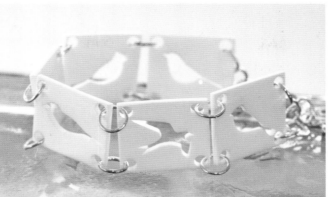

THE PROJECTS

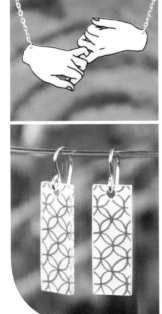

TIGER LILY
Earrings

designer **ELIZABETH BADDELEY**

Templates (page 119)

Basic shrink kit (page 12)

Ultra-thick, misty white
shrink plastic*

Yellow, black, and peach fine-tip
permanent markers (or colored
pencils, see step 3)

Sealer (Elizabeth uses clear
embossing powder.)

Jewelry adhesive

2 stud earring backs

* Elizabeth makes these earrings
with ultra-thick shrink plastic so
they shrink down to a ¹/₈-inch
(3 mm) thickness. You can substi-
tute white or pre-roughened shrink
plastic instead—the end result will
just be a bit thinner.

These earrings look detailed and
complex, but follow the instructions,
and you'll see they're actually simple to create.

① Place the templates under the shrink plastic and use the yellow fine-tip permanent marker to trace the outer circles of the templates onto the rough side of
the shrink plastic sheet.

② Use the black fine-tip permanent marker to trace the inner black lines of the
template onto the shrink plastic. (Don't worry if the traced image looks less
than perfect at this point—shrinking has a wonderful way of smoothing out
imperfections!)

③ Fill in the background around the flower with one coat of peach fine-tip permanent marker, and then go over it with the yellow fine-tip permanent marker.
Feel free to use your own favorite colors, but lighter colors look best after baking. (If you sand the shrink plastic or use pre-roughened plastic, you can use
colored pencils instead, but the end result will look less bold.)

④ Preheat your oven, following the shrink plastic manufacturer's instructions.

⑤ Cut out the circles with scissors, cutting just inside the line.

⑥ Place the plastic circles between two sheets of parchment paper on a baking
sheet, and bake according to the shrink plastic manufacturer's instructions.

⑦ When the circles are fully shrunk (you can tell because they regain their
original proportions), remove them from the oven and let them cool for a few
seconds (you want the ink to dry but the plastic to still be a little warm). Add a
book or other flattener, and let them cool completely. This ensures that your
shrunken earrings harden flat and smooth.

Continued...

⑧ Once the earrings are completely cool, use a sealer to protect them. The earrings shown were sealed with embossing powder (see the Tip).

⑨ Let your sealer dry completely. If some sealer got on the edges, simply sand gently to smooth.

⑩ Use sandpaper to roughen the back of each earring slightly—the sanding will create tiny grooves that will help the jewelry adhesive grab ahold. Wipe off any sanding residue, and then place a small dot of the jewelry adhesive in the middle of each earring back. Attach the back of an earring stud to each and let dry completely. Wear your earrings with style to your next garden party or Monday in the office!

TIP *To use embossing powder, sprinkle a layer of the powder over the surface of your baked object. Be sure that the design is fully covered without any gaps around the edges and that you can't see through the powder. Place the object back on a parchment paper–covered baking sheet and return it to the oven, following the manufacturer's directions for heating the embossing powder.*

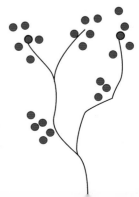

FLOWER POWER
Necklace & Ring

designer **ERIN INGLIS**

FLOWER POWER
Necklace & Ring

Templates (page 114)

Basic shrink kit (page 12)

Matte shrink plastic

Black ultra-fine-point permanent marker

Bright blue, orange, red, green, lime green, and sage green colored pencils

Black fine-point permanent marker

Sealer (Erin uses acrylic spray sealer.)

Jewelry adhesive

6 silver bails (glue-on type)

Silver chain, 16 inches (40.6 cm) in length (see step 9)

6 or 8 jump rings (optional, see step 10)

Lobster clasp set

Adjustable ring blank

M ake a bold statement with this floral necklace and ring set. The extra attention to small details makes the colors really pop.

FOR THE NECKLACE

1. Sand the shrink plastic following the directions on page 17. Place the templates under the sanded shrink plastic and trace the outlines with the black ultra-fine-point permanent marker. If you make a mistake or the marker bleeds a bit, you can erase it with the sandpaper.

2. Referring to the photos, color in the designs with the colored pencils.

3. Go over the outline of the designs with the ultra-fine-point permanent marker a second time to get a darker, cleaner line. Then cut out the pieces.

4. Preheat the oven and bake the pieces according to the shrink plastic manufacturer's instructions. (Erin bakes these pieces at 250°F [130°C] for 3 to 5 minutes.) Because these pieces are large, they may curl. Don't worry—read Oh, No! It's Curling! on page 20. As soon as each piece comes out of the oven, while it's still warm and a little soft, press it with something flat and smooth, such as a hardcover book. Let the pieces cool completely.

5. Sand the edges of both pieces. Doing so is a little tedious with this design, but it will help the black marker adhere, remove all the sharp edges, and make the finished necklace look more polished.

6. Use the black fine-point permanent marker to color the edges you just sanded. You may need to use the ultra-fine point marker to get into some of the corners.

7. Seal your project with the sealer of your choice. (Erin sealed the necklace shown with several thin coats of acrylic spray sealant, with each coat allowed to dry thoroughly before the next was applied.)

8. Once you get the desired shine on your pieces (and they're completely dry), turn them over and use the jewelry adhesive to glue the bails to the areas marked A, B, C, and D on the template. Let the glue dry before attaching the chain in step 10.

9. Cut the chain to the following lengths:

   - two $6^3/_4$-inch (17.1 cm) lengths

   - one 1-inch (2.5 cm) length

   - one $1^1/_4$-inch (3.2 cm) length

10. Use pliers to attach the two pieces of $6^3/_4$-inch (17.1 cm) chain to bails A and B; the 1-inch (2.5 cm) chain to the two C bails; and the $1^1/_4$-inch (3.2 cm) chain to the two D bails. (Depending on the kind of bails you use, you may need to use jump rings to attach the bails to the chain.) Attach the clasp set to the ends of the $6^3/_4$-inch (17.1 cm) lengths of chain.

FOR THE RING

1. Follow steps 1 through 7 for the necklace but use the ring template.

2. Once the sealer has completely dried on the ring's shrink plastic piece, turn over the baked and sealed piece and use jewelry adhesive to glue on the adjustable ring blank. Let dry completely.

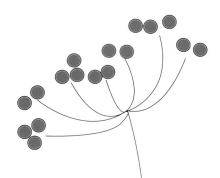

SPRINGTIME FRANCIE
Earrings

designer **DANA HOLSCHER**

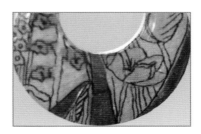

Templates (page 119)

Basic shrink kit (page 12)

Pre-roughened shrink plastic

Brassy green, pink, orange, white, and black colored pencils

2-inch (5.1 cm) circle punch (or scissors)

1-inch (2.5 cm) circle punch (or small scissors)

Sealer (Dana uses dimensional gloss.)

French hook earring findings

nspired by a favorite piece of vintage bed linen, these earrings are made with two circle punches (or a bit of handcutting). They add a touch of spring to any outfit.

1. Place the shrink plastic, rough side up, over the templates, and, referring to the photo, use the colored pencils to fill in the colors only. Go ahead and color slightly outside of the template lines so that when you punch the plastic, you leave an image with an evenly colored surface. Draw the black outlines last to prevent colors from blending and produce a crisp final design.

2. Use the 2-inch (5.1 cm) circle punch to punch out the large circle shape. Use the 1-inch (2.5 cm) circle punch to punch out the small circle window from the design. To do this, place the large punched circle of shrink plastic flush against the back of the 1-inch (2.5 cm) circle punch, center the plastic, and then punch out the center. If you don't have the circle punches, simply trace the circles in pencil and cut them out. Cut the little inside circle first, using small curved scissors. Then carefully cut the larger circle out to create the earring shape.

3. Preheat your oven, following the shrink plastic manufacturer's instructions. (Dana bakes her earrings at 325°F [163°C].) Once the oven is preheated, place both earrings, colored pencil side up, between two sheets of parchment paper on a baking sheet—making sure the pieces aren't touching—and bake according to the shrink plastic manufacturer's instructions. (Dana bakes her earrings for 2 minutes and 45 seconds.)

4. Once the earrings are shrunk and flat, carefully remove the entire baking sheet from the oven, and press down on the parchment-covered pieces with your flattener. Allow the pieces to cool completely.

5. Very gently brush or blow off any colored pencil flecks that may have sprung up while baking (this prevents any unwanted flecks of colored pencil from streaking when the earrings are sealed).

6. Seal your earrings with the sealer of your choice. Test your sealer first on a scrap piece of plastic that has been decorated with the same colored pencils and baked to make sure the two are compatible.

7. Once the sealer has completely dried, attach each loop to one ear wire.

BUCKET AND SHOVEL
Brooches

designer **JODIE ANNA**

Templates (page 121)

Basic shrink kit (page 12)

White inkjet shrink plastic

Computer

Inkjet printer

Sealer (Jodie Anna uses acrylic spray sealer.)

Jewelry adhesive

2 brooch backs

Feel like a kid again with this beachy pair of brooches. Inkjet shrink plastic makes it easy to add playful patterns to your jewelry.

❶ Scan the bucket and shovel templates into a document on your computer. Print the images onto the shrink plastic, using both the slowest and the highest-quality settings possible. (See page 22 for more on printing on inkjet shrink plastic.) The ink will be slightly tacky and can easily smear, so set the freshly printed plastic aside to air dry in a safe place for at least five minutes, preferably longer.

❷ When the ink is completely dry, carefully cut out the bucket and shovel, being sure to leave a white outline around the images.

❸ Preheat your oven, following the shrink plastic manufacturer's instructions. (Jodie Anna bakes her pieces at 250°F [120°C].)

❹ Place both pieces between two sheets of parchment paper on a baking sheet. Follow the shrink plastic manufacturer's instructions to bake and shrink the pieces. Keep a close eye on the oven, because overbaking some brands of white inkjet shrink plastic can cause discoloration. Meanwhile, have something flat and smooth, such as a hardcover book, ready nearby to use as a flattener.

❺ When the pieces are shrunk and flat, carefully remove the entire baking sheet from the oven, and press down on the parchment-covered pieces with your flattener. Allow the pieces to cool completely.

❻ Sand the edges if needed, and then seal the pieces (see Sealing Your Projects, page 21). If you use acrylic spray sealer, apply two or three coats, and remember to allow adequate dry time between each coat.

❼ Use sandpaper to roughen the back of each brooch slightly—the sanding will create tiny grooves that will help the jewelry adhesive grab ahold. Wipe off any sanding residue, apply the jewelry adhesive to the brooch backs, and attach them to the backs of the pieces. Let your brooches sit undisturbed for at least 24 hours as the glue sets.

SEVEN TREASURES
Earrings

designer **JESSICA POUNDSTONE**

Templates (page 118)

Basic shrink kit (page 12)

Pre-roughened shrink plastic

Corner rounder (optional)

$1/4$-inch (6 mm) hole punch

Poppy-orange colored pencil
(see the Tip, page 38)

Small, flat paintbrush

White acrylic paint

Acrylic varnish

Craft knife or razor blade

French hook earring findings

Four 5-mm jump rings (optional,
see step 12)

These earrings give the seven treasures design—
a traditional Japanese motif—a decidedly modern flair.

❶ Trace the plain rectangle template onto the rough side of the shrink plastic twice. Cut the shapes out with scissors or a paper cutter (see the Tip, page 38).

❷ Hold the two pieces rough-sides together, and measure approximately $1/4$-inch (6 mm) below the top edge of the plastic. Use the hole punch to punch a hole at the top center of both pieces simultaneously. (This ensures that the hole is in the same place on each earring so that the earrings hang evenly when you wear them.)

❸ Place each rectangle rough side up on top of the design template. Trace the design using the poppy-orange colored pencil (make sure it's sharp). For best results, use medium to hard pressure to make sure your design is opaque. Hold the piece up to a light when you're finished, and color in any small gaps that you missed.

❹ Remove any flecks of colored pencil (even small specks will look big once a piece has shrunk!). Tap the piece on its edge, blow on it, and use the tip of your craft knife or razor blade to gently flick any flecks away.

❺ Preheat your oven, following the shrink plastic manufacturer's instructions.

❻ Place the earrings rough side up on parchment paper on a baking sheet, and bake according to the shrink plastic manufacturer's instructions.

❼ Once the earrings are shrunk and flat, move the parchment paper and earrings onto a flat, smooth surface, and press down on the warm earrings with a book or other flattener. Allow the pieces to cool completely.

Continued...

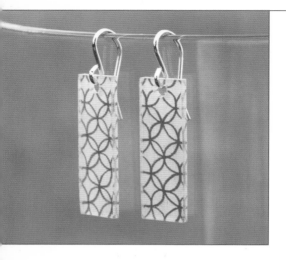

SEVEN TREASURES
Earrings

⑧ Once more, flick off flecks, and blow on the surface to remove any colored pencil dust so that the flecks don't smear when you paint the plastic. (If your piece still has a lot of colored pencil flecks or dust after shrinking, you may not have baked the plastic long enough.)

⑨ Paint a coat of white acrylic paint on the rough side of each rectangle, directly over the circle design. You want the layer of paint to be about as thick as a coat of nail polish for best results. (Don't worry about getting paint on the edges or fronts of the earrings—you'll scrape that off later.) Let the paint dry thoroughly.

⑩ Paint a coat of acrylic varnish over the paint. Let it dry thoroughly.

⑪ Carefully scrape away any paint or varnish around the edges of each rectangle, using a razor blade or craft knife held perpendicular to the edge. If any paint or varnish is on the front (shiny) side of the plastic, scrape it off with a fingernail so that you don't scratch the shiny surface.

⑫ Use flat-nose pliers to open the loops on your earring findings, and place each earring in. (Add two jump rings to the hole for each earring if the loops on your French hook findings are too small to allow the earrings to hang freely.)

 TIP *Jessica uses a sliding-blade paper cutter to cut rectangles from shrink plastic. She's found that quick slices produce the cleanest cuts in the plastic. She also says that less-expensive colored pencils seem to work better than art-grade ones for this project.*

RUSSIAN DOLL
Set

designer **MORGAN SHOOTER**

RUSSIAN DOLL
Set

This adorable Matryoshka set is easy to make using printable inkjet shrink plastic.

Templates (page 123)

Basic shrink kit (page 12)

White inkjet shrink plastic

Computer

Inkjet printer

$1/16$-inch (1.6 mm) hole punch

Sealer (Morgan uses ultra thick embossing powder.)

4-mm jump rings

6-mm jump rings

Toggle clasp set

Ear wires

Bobby pin blanks

Jewelry adhesive

① Scan all of the doll templates into a document on your computer, making sure you scan two extra matching dolls for the earrings and two for the hair clips. Print the images onto the shrink plastic, using both the slowest and the highest-quality settings possible. (See page 22 for more on printing on inkjet shrink plastic.) The ink will be slightly tacky and can easily smear, so set the freshly printed plastic aside to air dry in a safe place for at least 5 minutes, preferably longer.

② Once the ink is completely dry, carefully cut out each image. Select six dolls for the bracelet. For each doll, use the hole punch to carefully punch a hole at about the midway point on each side of the doll. Select two matching dolls for the earrings. Hold the earrings together and carefully punch a hole in the center top of both earrings at the same time. (This will ensure that the holes are in the same place, so the earrings will hang evenly when you wear them.) The two remaining dolls are for the hairpins, so they get to avoid the hole punch.

③ Preheat your oven, following the shrink plastic manufacturer's instructions.

④ Bake a few of the dolls at a time. To do so, place the pieces between two sheets of parchment paper on a baking sheet. Follow the shrink plastic manufacturer's instructions to bake and shrink the dolls. Keep a close eye on the oven, because over-baking some brands of white inkjet shrink plastic can cause discoloration. Meanwhile, have something flat and smooth, such as a hardcover book, ready nearby to use as a flattener.

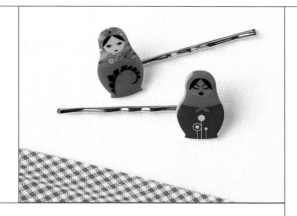

⑤ When the pieces are shrunk and flat, carefully remove the entire baking sheet from the oven, and press down on the parchment-covered pieces with your flattener. Allow the pieces to cool completely. Repeat steps 4 and 5 until all dolls are shrunk, flat, and cool.

⑥ Sand the edges if needed, and then add sealer to each doll (see Sealing Your Projects, page 21). The dolls shown were sealed with ultra thick embossing powder (see the Tip). To use embossing powder, sprinkle a layer of the powder over the surface of each doll. Be sure that the design is fully covered without any gaps around the edges and that you can't see through the powder. Follow the manufacturer's directions for heating and melting the embossing powder.

⑦ Let whatever sealer you've used dry completely. If sealer got on the edges of the dolls, simply sand gently to smooth.

FOR THE BRACELET

❶ Link the six dolls for the bracelet together by attaching a 6-mm, a 4-mm, and then another 6-mm jump ring

between each doll. Once all the dolls are linked together, make a short chain for each end of the bracelet using the 6-mm jump rings and then attach the toggle clasp.

FOR THE EARRINGS

❶ The earrings are super simple to make: Just take the two earring dolls, thread them onto the ear wires, and you're finished!

FOR THE HAIRCLIPS

❶ Take the dolls with no holes and the bobby pin blanks, add a drop of jewelry adhesive to each blank, and attach a doll to each bobby pin. Let the glue dry fully. Now get yourself all dolled up.

TIP *If you see that you've missed some spots when you take your embossed dolls from the oven, you can add more embossing powder and stick the dolls back in. Just be sure to watch them carefully: If left in too long, the embossing powder may yellow and the shrink plastic may warp.*

LIGHTHOUSE
Necklace

designer **JODIE ANNA**

Templates (page 123)

Basic shrink kit (page 12)

White inkjet shrink plastic

Computer

Inkjet printer

$1/8$-inch (3 mm) hole punch

Sealer (Jodie Anna uses acrylic spray sealer.)

16 inches (40.6 cm) of chain (see step 8)

6 jump rings

Lobster clasp

This necklace was inspired by memories of long childhood summers by the sea. You'll almost smell the salt air whenever you wear it.

❶ Scan the lighthouse and seagull templates into a document on your computer. Print the images onto the shrink plastic, using both the slowest and the highest-quality settings possible. (See page 22 for more on printing on inkjet shrink plastic.) The ink will be slightly tacky and can easily smear, so set the freshly printed plastic aside to air dry in a safe place for at least 5 minutes, preferably longer.

❷ When the ink is completely dry, carefully cut out the lighthouse and seagull, being sure to leave a white outline around the images.

❸ Use the hole punch to punch one hole on either side of the lighthouse and one hole at the head and tail of the seagull.

❹ Preheat your oven, following the shrink plastic manufacturer's instructions. (Jodie Anna bakes her earrings at 250°F [120°C].)

❺ Place both pieces between two sheets of parchment paper on a baking sheet. Follow the shrink plastic manufacturer's instructions to bake and shrink the earrings. Keep a close eye on the oven, because over-baking some brands of white inkjet shrink plastic can cause discoloration. Meanwhile, have something flat and smooth, such as a hardcover book, ready nearby to use as a flattener.

❻ When the pieces are shrunk and flat, carefully remove the entire baking sheet from the oven, and press down on the parchment-covered pieces with your flattener. Allow the pieces to cool completely.

❼ Sand the edges if needed, and then apply the sealer to both sides of the pieces. If you use acrylic spray sealer, apply two or three coats, and remember to allow adequate dry time between each coat.

Continued...

8 Cut the chain to the following lengths:

- one 8-inch (20.3 cm) length
- one 5 1/2-inch (14 cm) length
- one 2 1/2-inch (6.4 cm) length

9 Use one jump ring to attach the 8-inch (20.3 cm) length of chain to the hole on the right side of the lighthouse. Use another jump ring to attach the lobster clasp to the other end of this length of chain.

10 Use a third jump ring to attach the 2 1/2-inch (6.4 cm) length of chain to the hole on the left side of the lighthouse. Taking care not to twist the chain, use a fourth jump ring to attach the other end of this chain to the hole at the tail end of the seagull.

11 Almost done! Take a fifth jump ring and use it to attach the 5 1/2-inch (14 cm) length of chain to the head of the seagull. Attach the remaining jump ring to the end of this length of chain to act as the ring for the lobster clasp.

WOODLAND CREATURES
Bracelet & Earrings

designer **KATHY SHELDON**

WOODLAND CREATURES

Bracelet & Earrings

Note: **Glance at the instructions for making the earrings first, because you may want to make the earrings at the same time you make the charms for the bracelet.**

S tamping on shrink plastic is a quick way to create images you can personalize with your own color choices.

Basic shrink kit (page 12)

Matte shrink plastic

Stamps (I combined a few sets to make this bracelet.)*

Black permanent stamp ink

Colored pencils

$1/_8$-inch (3 mm) hole punch

Sealer (I use liquid dimensional gloss.)

7-inch (17.8 cm) silver chain

5-mm silver jump rings (one for each charm)

Two 6-mm silver jump rings

Silver lobster clasp

Jewelry adhesive

Stud earring backs

* If your heart is set on woodland creatures jewelry, but you can't find stamps, use inkjet shrink plastic and the bonus graphics on page 124.

FOR THE BRACELET

1. Sand one side of the shrink plastic sheet (see page 17 for more on sanding). Use stamps and black permanent stamp ink to stamp the images onto the sanded side of the shrink plastic (see page 21 for more on stamping on shrink plastic). When you position the stamp on the plastic, leave plenty of room around the image so that you can easily cut it out, and leave enough room above each image for a $1/_8$-inch (3 mm) hole. Let the ink dry completely.

2. Once the ink is dry, use the colored pencils to lightly color the images. Add a little dot above each image to indicate where you'll punch the hole for the charm, taking into consideration how you'd like the charm to hang. Carefully blow off any flecks of colored pencil left on the plastic.

3. Preheat your oven, following the shrink plastic manufacturer's instructions. (I bake my pieces at 300°F [150°C].)

4. The easiest way to cut an intricate shape from the plastic is to first cut around the image roughly (including the dot for the hole). Use the $1/_8$-inch (3 mm) hole punch to punch out the dot and make a hole. Now, use small curved scissors to carefully cut the image out, being sure to leave a white outline around the image and enough shrink plastic surrounding the hole to make a little loop for hanging the charm. (See the photo below.)

5. Place the pieces between two sheets of parchment paper on a baking sheet. Follow the shrink plastic manufacturer's instructions to bake and shrink the charms. (I baked these pieces for about 2 1/2 minutes.) Meanwhile, have something flat and smooth, such as a hardcover book, ready nearby to use as a flattener.

6. When the charms are shrunk and flat, carefully remove the entire baking sheet from the oven, and press down on the parchment-covered pieces with your flattener. Allow the pieces to cool completely.

7. Sand the edges of the charms if needed, and then apply a sealer to each charm. (I sealed these with one coat of a liquid dimensional gloss. See Sealing Your Projects, page 21.) Let your sealer dry completely.

8. Spread the chain out horizontally. Lay the charms out so that they're evenly spaced in a pleasing order (remembering that they'll be in a circle when the bracelet is worn). Use the 5-mm jump rings to attach them to the chain.

9. Use one 6-mm jump ring to attach the lobster clasp to one end of the chain, and then attach the other 6-mm jump ring to the other end of the chain. Time to make earrings!

FOR THE EARRINGS

1. Follow steps 1 through 7 for the brace-let, except stamp two matching images (such as owls), and skip all the stuff about marking and punching holes.

2. Once your earrings are completely sealed and dry, use sandpaper to rough-en the back of each earring slightly— the sanding will create tiny grooves that will help the jewelry adhesive grab ahold. Wipe off any sanding residue, and then place a small dot of jewelry adhesive in the middle of each earring back. Attach the back of an earring stud to each and let them dry completely.

TIP *You can use pre-roughened shrink plastic (which can be stamped and colored without sanding) instead, but the finished charms will have a slightly different look.*

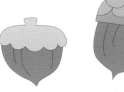

MEXICAN OILCLOTH
Necklace

designer **JALENE HERNÁNDEZ**

Templates (page 115)

Basic shrink kit (page 12)

White inkjet shrink plastic

Clear inkjet shrink plastic

Computer

Inkjet printer

1/4-inch (6 mm) hole punch

Sealer (Jalene uses matte acrylic spray sealer and liquid resin.)

Chain, 18 inches (45.7 cm) in length (The project shown features 2.6-mm antique brass–plated elongated curb chain.)

Two 4-mm jump rings

Two 8-mm jump rings

12 x 7-mm lobster clasp

nspired by travels in Mexico, this necklace is made with both white and clear printable inkjet shrink plastic.

❶ Scan the red and floral circle templates into documents on your computer. Print one floral circle onto the white inkjet shrink plastic and one red circle onto the clear inkjet shrink plastic. (See page 22 for more on printing on inkjet shrink plastic.) To conserve plastic, you can print the templates for other inkjet projects at the same time.

❷ Allow the ink to dry completely.

❸ Cut out each circle. Then use the 1/4-inch (6 mm) hole punch to make a hole at the black dot at the top of each circle.

❹ Because you're using two different types of shrink plastic, bake the two circles individually, following the shrink plastic manufacturer's instructions for pre-heating the oven and baking the circles. Flatten the circles if needed while they are still warm and then allow them to cool completely.

❺ Seal both circles. The pieces in the necklace shown were sprayed lightly with a matte acrylic spray sealer and then given two coats of resin for a glossy, slightly domed surface. If you coat your pieces with resin, take care not to let the resin cover the holes.

❻ Once your sealer is completely dry, sand or file the circles' edges smooth.

❼ To assemble the necklace, attach the two 4-mm jump rings to the ends of the chain. Then attach one 8-mm jump ring to one end of the chain and the lobster clasp to the other.

❽ Attach the other 8-mm jump ring to the circles and the necklace chain, and you're done.

ORIGAMI PLANE
Earrings

designer **TONIA MO**

Template (page 113)

Basic shrink kit (page 12)

Matte shrink plastic

Black ultra-fine permanent marker

Earring backs

Jewelry adhesive

TIP *Be careful not to get the glue on the front of the earrings—some glues react with the permanent marker's ink and will cause images to run.*

O kay, this is my idea of origami—tracing instead of folding. Who doesn't want cute little paper airplane earrings?

❶ Use the template and the black ultra-fine permanent marker to trace two origami plane designs onto the shrink plastic. Cut both earrings from the plastic, taking care to leave just a slight border of plastic around the entire design.

❷ Preheat the oven according to the shrink plastic manufacturer's directions. (Tonia bakes her earrings at 300°F [150°C].)

❸ Place both pieces between two sheets of parchment paper on a baking sheet. Follow the shrink plastic manufacturer's instructions to bake and shrink the earrings. (Tonia bakes her earrings for 4 to 5 minutes.) Meanwhile, have something flat and smooth, such as a hardcover book, ready nearby to use as a flattener.

❹ When the pieces are shrunk and flat, carefully remove the baking sheet from the oven, and press down on the parchment-covered pieces with your flattener.

❺ After the pieces are cool, sand the edges if needed. Because these earrings are decorated with permanent markers, you can skip the sealer or add a coat of sealer if desired. If you add sealer, let it dry completely before moving on to the next step.

❻ Use sandpaper to roughen the back of each earring slightly—the sanding will create tiny grooves that will help the jewelry adhesive grab ahold. Wipe off any sanding residue, and place a small dot of the jewelry adhesive in the middle of each earring back. Attach the back of an earring stud to each and let the glue dry completely.

SIMPLE CIRCLE
Necklace

designer **JESSICA POUNDSTONE**

Template (page 118)

Basic shrink kit (page 12)

Pre-sanded shrink plastic

1¹/₂-inch (3.8 cm) circle punch
(or scissors)

1-inch (2.5 cm) circle punch
(or small, curved scissors)

Craft knife or razor blade

Small, flat paintbrush

Gray-blue acrylic paint

Sealer (Jessica uses acrylic varnish.)

7-mm jump ring

Silver cord with clasp

A simple, perfectly round circle pendant in a subtle shade of gray blue: modern and minimalist, yet playful and fun!

1. Use the 1¹/₂-inch (3.8 cm) circle punch to punch a large circle shape out of the shrink plastic. Next, use the 1-inch (2.5 cm) circle punch to punch a smaller circle in the center of the larger circle you just punched. If you don't have these circle punches, use a pencil to trace the template provided onto the rough side of the shrink plastic and cut it out. Cut the smaller, inside circle first, using small curved scissors (start by cutting a hole in the middle of the small circle with a craft knife or one tip of the scissors). Then carefully cut the larger circle out to create the ring shape. Erase any pencil lines that still show.

2. Preheat your oven, following the shrink plastic manufacturer's instructions.

3. Place the ring shape rough side up on parchment paper on a baking sheet, and bake according to the shrink plastic manufacturer's instructions.

4. When the ring shape is shrunk and flat, remove the parchment paper and ring onto a flat, smooth surface, and press down on the warm ring with a smooth hardcover book or other flattener. Allow the ring to cool completely.

5. On the rough side of the plastic, paint a coat of the gray-blue acrylic paint. You want the coat of paint to be about as thick as a coat of nail polish. (Don't worry about getting paint on the edges or front of the ring; you'll scrape that off later.) Let the paint dry thoroughly.

6. Paint a coat of sealer over the paint. (The earrings shown have a coat of acrylic varnish.) Let it dry thoroughly.

7. Carefully scrape away any paint or varnish on the outer and inner edges of the ring shape with a craft knife or razor blade held perpendicular to the edge. If any paint or varnish is on the front (shiny) side of the plastic, scrape it off with a fingernail so that you don't scratch the shiny surface.

8. Open the jump ring and place the circle in it. Thread the cord through the jump ring, close the jump ring, and you're set. Simple!

BOLLYWOOD
Earrings

d e s i g n e r **DONNA MALLARD**

Templates (page 116)

Basic shrink kit (page 12)

Clear inkjet shrink plastic (the kind that prints on both sides of the plastic)

Computer

Inkjet printer

$1/8$-inch (6 mm) hole punch

Sealer (Donna uses matte acrylic spray sealer.)

Four 6-mm jump rings

2 marquis ear wires

T hese earrings combine a fun play on classic chandelier-style earrings with the bright, colorful palette of Indian textiles, jewelry, and film.

❶ Scan the earring templates into a document on your computer. Print the images onto one side of the shrink plastic, using both the slowest and the highest-quality settings. (See page 22 for more on printing on inkjet shrink plastic.)

❷ The ink will be slightly tacky and can easily smear, so set the freshly printed plastic aside to air dry in a safe place for at least 5 minutes, preferably longer.

❸ Once the first side is dry, load the same sheet into your printer, and print the same images in the exact same place on the other side of the sheet. (Many printers shake a little while printing the shrink plastic sheets, so the two printed sides may not end up perfectly aligned. If the designs don't quite match up, the shrinking process should take care of slight variations. If your printer can't seem to make the two sides match, just make one-sided earrings—they'll still look great.) Follow the instructions in the previous step to let the ink dry completely.

❹ Preheat your oven, following the shrink plastic manufacturer's instructions. (Donna bakes her earrings at 325°F [163°C].)

❺ Once the second side of the printed plastic is completely dry, cut out the earring shapes with a slow, continuous motion, using the parts of the blades nearest to the base of the scissors.

❻ Hold the two earring shapes together. Punch a hole in both pieces simultaneously with the hole punch, centered about $1/4$-inch (6 mm) from the top of the earrings. You can use the top oval in the design, which represents a jump ring, as a guide for the hole placement—see the photo for reference.

Continued…

BOLLYWOOD

Earrings

7 Place both pieces between two sheets of parchment paper on a baking sheet. Follow the shrink plastic manufacturer's instructions to bake and shrink the earrings. (Donna bakes her earrings for 2 to 3 minutes; if your shapes still appear a bit warped after that time, give them another 15 to 30 seconds.) Meanwhile, have something flat and smooth, such as a hardcover book, ready nearby to use as a flattener.

8 Once the pieces are shrunk and flat, carefully remove the entire baking sheet from the oven, and press down on the parchment-covered pieces with your flattener. Mind that hot sheet!

9 Once the pieces are cool, sand the edges if needed, and then apply the sealer to both sides of the plastic.

10 Attach a jump ring to each earring. Then add another jump ring to the first jump ring for each. (These second jump rings keep the designs facing forward.) Attach each assemblage to an ear wire and you're ready for Bollywood, baby!

TIP *Cardboard box lids make great "tents" to protect newly printed shrink plastic sheets from dust, cat hair, etc.*

NOT-YOUR-GRANDMOTHER'S
Cameos

designer **TAMARA BERG**

Templates (page 117)

Basic shrink kit (page 12)

Matte shrink plastic

3 1/2-inch (8.9 cm) diameter
scalloped circle punch (optional)

3-inch (7.6 cm) diameter
circle punch (optional)

Permanent stamp ink or
permanent markers

1/8-inch (3 mm) hole punch
(optional, see step 6)

Jewelry adhesive

Drill with 1/16-inch (1.6 mm) bit
(optional, see step 11)

Large, long needle (optional,
see step 11)

Butane lighter (optional,
see step 11)

3 jump rings

Chain 18 inches (45.7 cm)
in length

Clasp set

Take the old-fashioned charm of cameos and combine it with shrink plastic for necklaces that are both sweet and fun.

❶ Either use the scalloped circle punch to punch the base shape from the shrink plastic, or use the template provided to trace a scalloped circle onto the shrink plastic and then cut it out with scissors.

❷ Either use the plain circle punch to punch a circle from the shrink plastic or use the template provided to trace one onto the shrink plastic and cut the circle out with scissors.

❸ Trace the image of your choice from the templates onto the plastic and cut it out with scissors. The letter T was created using the Lucida Calligraphy font at 140 points. Simple cursive fonts tend to work best for monograms when using shrink plastic.

❹ If you're going to use permanent stamp ink instead of permanent markers to apply color to your plain circle, use sandpaper to roughen one side of the circle (see Sanding the Plastic, page 17). Apply a light layer of the color of your choice. Remember that colors intensify as the plastic shrinks—try out a few test scraps first and shrink them to find the finished color desired. Sometimes the shrunk plastic looks great when viewed from the wrong side—because it's just a circle, using it "backwards" is certainly an option.

❺ Preheat your oven, following the shrink plastic manufacturer's instructions.

❻ It can be tricky to get the holes in both the scalloped and plain circles to align after the pieces are shrunk. Try arranging them as shown in the photos and use the 1/8-inch (3 mm) hole punch to punch a hole through both circles

simultaneously. If this method doesn't work, follow step 11 to make a hole in the circles after the pieces are shrunk and glued together.

7. Place both the plain and scalloped circles on parchment paper on a baking sheet. Follow the shrink plastic manufacturer's instructions to bake and shrink the pieces. Meanwhile, have something flat and smooth, such as a hardcover book, ready nearby to use as a flattener.

8. When the pieces are shrunk and flat, carefully remove the entire baking sheet from the oven, and press down on the parchment-covered pieces with your flattener. Repeat steps 7 and 8 to bake your cameo image.

9. Once all the shrunk pieces are cool, sand the edges if needed.

10. Apply jewelry adhesive to the back of the plain circle and center it on the scalloped circle, taking care to align the holes in the circles if you punched them before shrinking. Apply jewelry adhesive to the back of the cameo's image and center it in the plain circle. Allow the glue to set completely.

11. If you gave up on the hole punch method (hey, sometimes it works!), use one of the following methods to make the hole through both circles. Either drill a hole near the center top of the inside circle with a drill and a $1/16$-inch (1.6 mm) drill bit, or carefully heat a large, long needle using a soot-free source, such as a butane lighter, and poke the needle through both pieces of the plastic to create a hole.

12. Attach a jump ring through the hole and then thread your chain through the jump ring.

13. Connect the clasp set to the ends of the chain with jump rings.

TIP *For a little extra pizzazz, use a colored metal jump ring, or make a bail for the pendant using pearls or crystals and wire wraps (see Making a Wrapped Loop, page 24).*

PINKIE SWEAR
Necklace

designer **STASIA BURRINGTON**

Template (page 115)

Basic shrink kit (page 12)

Matte shrink plastic

Black fine-point permanent marker

Craft knife

1/8-inch (3 mm) hole punch

18-inch (45.7 cm) length of silver chain

Silver lobster clasp

Four 3-mm silver jump rings

This hand-drawn necklace is a reminder of promises made.

1. Place the template under the shrink plastic sheet and trace the outline with the black fine-point permanent marker. If you'd like a reversible necklace, turn the shrink plastic over and trace the design in the exact same spot on the other side, so that both sides of the sheet have an identical image.

2. Carefully cut the piece out, just outside the black outline. Use a craft knife to cut the small gaps between the fingers.

3. Use the hole punch to punch the two holes indicated by the two black dots on the template.

4. Preheat the oven and bake the piece according to the shrink plastic manufacturer's instructions. (Stasia bakes hers at 300°F [150°C] for 3 minutes.) Because this piece is large, it may curl. Don't worry—read Oh, No! It's Curling! on page 20. As soon as the piece comes out of the oven, while it's still warm and a little soft, press it with something flat and smooth, such as a hardcover book. Let it cool completely.

5. Cut the silver chain into two 9-inch (22.9 cm) lengths.

6. Use a jump ring to attach one length of chain to one hole in the baked pendant. Use another jump ring to attach the second length of chain to the other hole in the pendant.

7. Attach one jump ring to the end of one chain. Use another jump ring to attach the lobster clasp to the end of the other chain. Now make a promise to yourself as you put on your new necklace.

HIGH TEA CHARM
Bracelet

designer **JODIE ANNA**

Templates (page 122)

Basic shrink kit (page 12)

White inkjet shrink plastic

Computer

Inkjet printer

$^1/_4$-inch (6 mm) hole punch

Heavy towel

Sealer (Jodie Anna uses acrylic spray sealer.)

7-inch (17.8 cm) bracelet with toggle clasp

10 jump rings

Make this charming bracelet, and you'll feel relaxed and happy each time it jangles on your wrist. Afternoon tea without the calories.

❶ Scan all of the templates into a document on your computer. Print the images onto the shrink plastic, using both the slowest and the highest-quality settings possible. (See page 22 for more on printing on inkjet shrink plastic.) The ink will be slightly tacky and can easily smear, so set the freshly printed plastic aside to air dry in a safe place for at least 5 minutes, preferably longer.

❷ When the ink is completely dry, carefully cut out each image, being sure to leave a white outline around the images. Then use the hole punch to carefully punch one hole in the center top of each image.

❸ Preheat your oven, following the shrink plastic manufacturer's instructions. (Jodie Anna bakes her pieces at 250°F [120°C].)

❹ Place the pieces between two sheets of parchment paper on a baking sheet. Follow the shrink plastic manufacturer's instructions to bake and shrink the charms. Keep a close eye on the oven, because over-baking some brands of white inkjet shrink plastic can cause discoloration. Meanwhile, have something flat and smooth, such as a hardcover book, ready nearby to use as a flattener.

❺ When the pieces are shrunk and flat, carefully remove the entire baking sheet from the oven, and press down on the parchment-covered pieces with your flattener. Allow the pieces to cool completely.

❻ Sand the edges of the charms if needed, and then apply the sealer to both sides of each piece. If you use acrylic spray sealer, apply two or three coats, and remember to allow adequate drying time between each coat.

❼ Spread the bracelet horizontally in front of you. Lay the charms out so that they're evenly spaced in the order shown in the photo (or feel free to change the order—it's your bracelet!). Use the jump rings to attach them to the chain.

BIRD SILHOUETTE
Bracelet

designer **MORGAN SHOOTER**

Templates (page 110)

Basic shrink kit (page 12)

1 sheet of white shrink plastic

1/4-inch (6 mm) hole punch

Craft knife

6-mm jump rings

Toggle clasp set

Simple aviary cutouts make a graphic statement in this striking bracelet.

❶ Use the template or a ruler to divide the shrink plastic into six 2 x 1¹/₂-inch (5.1 x 3.8 cm) rectangles. Trace one bird silhouette from the templates onto the center of each rectangle.

❷ Cut each bird out very carefully, using a craft knife and small curved manicure scissors. Then cut out each rectangle. Use the hole punch to punch a hole in each corner of each rectangle.

❸ Preheat your oven, following the shrink plastic manufacturer's instructions.

❹ Place the pieces between two sheets of parchment paper on a baking sheet. Follow the shrink plastic manufacturer's instructions to bake and shrink the pieces. Meanwhile, have something flat and smooth, such as a hardcover book, ready nearby to use as a flattener.

❺ When the rectangles are shrunk and flat, carefully remove the entire baking sheet from the oven, and carefully press down on the parchment-covered pieces with your flattener.

❻ If the pieces are a bit wonky after they cool, simply even them out by sanding the edges smooth.

❼ Use 10 jump rings to attach the rectangles together in a horizontal row. Then make a chain for each end of the bracelet using seven to 10 jump rings, depending on your wrist size (see the detail photos). Attach the toggle clasp with two more jump rings and you're finished!

STAMPED
Brooch

designer **CYNTHIA SHAFFER**

Basic shrink kit (page 12)

White shrink plastic

Portrait and ampersand
rubber stamps

Black permanent-ink stamp pad

Cotton swabs

Artist chalks

$1/8$-inch (3 mm) hole punch

Black permanent marker

Silver wire, 24 gauge, 12 inches
(30.5 cm) in length

3 green square beads

3 white pearls

Jewelry adhesive

Pin back

Stamps, artist chalks, and beads all come together in this striking brooch.

❶ Lightly sand one side of the shrink plastic. Remove any sanding residue.

❷ Use the portrait rubber stamp and black permanent ink to stamp the portrait in the center of the sanded side of the shrink plastic. Let the ink dry completely.

❸ Use the ampersand rubber stamp and black permanent ink to stamp the ampersand on the cheek of the already-stamped portrait image. Let the ink dry completely.

❹ Use the cotton swabs to lightly apply the chalk to the image, blending colors.

❺ Follow the shrink plastic manufacturer's directions to preheat the oven.

❻ Carefully cut out the stamped image. Then use the hole-punch to punch three evenly spaced holes in the bottom edge of the cut piece.

❼ Place the piece between two sheets of parchment paper on a baking sheet. Follow the shrink plastic manufacturer's instructions to bake and shrink the piece. (Cynthia baked the piece shown for 2 to 3 minutes.) Meanwhile, have something flat and smooth, such as a hardcover book, ready nearby to use as a flattener.

❽ Once the piece is shrunk and flat, carefully remove it from the oven, and press it with your flattener. Allow it to cool completely.

Continued...

STAMPED

Brooch

9 Sand the edges of the brooch if needed. Then run one side of the permanent black marker tip along the edge of the brooch to create a black outer edge.

10 Cut the wire into three 4-inch (10.2 cm) lengths. Curl up one end of one length of wire (see the photo). Slip one bead and then one pearl onto the wire. Insert the other end of the wire into one of the holes at the bottom of the brooch, and then wrap the wire around itself. (See page 24 for wrapping wire using pliers, but you can also just do this wrapping by hand, because the slightly funky wrap is part of the charm of the piece.) Trim off any excess wire and then use jewelry pliers to pinch the cut end into the wrapped wire to hide it. Repeat with the other two lengths of wire.

11 Lightly sand a spot in the center back of the brooch and remove any sanding residue. Use the jewelry adhesive to adhere the pin back to the back of the brooch.

LAUREL NECKLACE

designer **JESSICA POUNDSTONE**

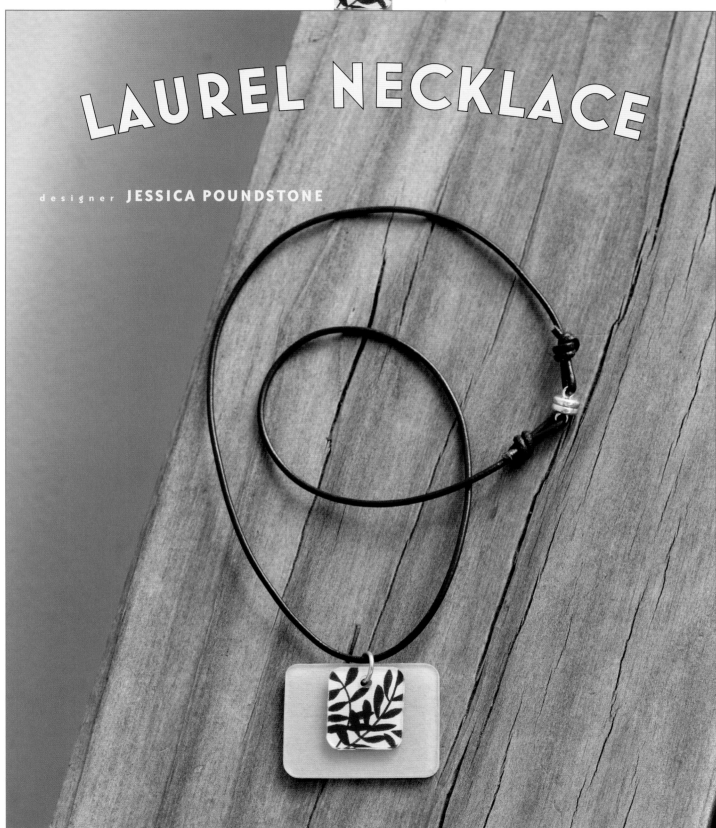

LAUREL
Necklace

You make the shrink plastic pieces for this necklace by adding color and imagery to the back (rough) side of the plastic. Then, you arrange the pieces so they're viewed through the smooth glossy front of each piece.

Templates (page 113)

Basic shrink kit (page 12)

Pre-roughened shrink plastic

1/4-inch (6 mm) hole punch

Brown colored pencil

Craft knife or razor blade

Small, flat paintbrush

White acrylic paint

Light teal acrylic paint

Acrylic varnish

7-mm jump ring

Leather cord, 23 inches (58.4 cm) in length

Magnetic clasp with loops

1 Trace only the templates for the two outline shapes onto the pre-roughened shrink plastic, and then cut out the shapes with scissors.

2 Place the small rectangle on top of the large rectangle, rough sides together. Center a short side of the small rectangle at the top of the top long side of the large rectangle (use the photo below for reference). Then punch a hole at the top center of both pieces simultaneously

with the hole punch. The top of the hole should be approximately 1/4 inch (6 mm) below the top edges of the pieces. (Punching both holes at the same time will ensure that the holes for your jump ring will line up after you shrink the pieces.)

3 Place the small rectangle rough side up on top of the laurel leaf template. Trace the design using the brown colored pencil (make sure it's sharp). For best results, use medium to hard pressure so that your design is opaque. Hold the piece up to a light when you're finished, and color in any small gaps that you missed.

4 Remove flecks of colored pencil (even small specks will look big once a piece has shrunk). Tap the piece on its edge, blow on it, and use the tip of your craft knife or razor blade to gently flick any flecks away.

5 Preheat your oven, following the shrink plastic manufacturer's instructions.

6 Place both pieces rough side up between two sheets of parchment paper on a baking sheet—making sure they aren't touching—and bake according to the shrink plastic manufacturer's instructions.

7 Once the pieces are shrunk and flat, carefully remove the entire baking sheet from the oven, and press down on the parchment-covered pieces with your flattener. Allow the pieces to cool completely.

8 Once more, flick off flecks and blow on the surface to remove any colored pencil dust so that the flecks don't smear when you paint the plastic. (If your laurel leaf piece still has a lot of colored pencil flecks or dust after shrinking, you may not have baked the plastic long enough.)

9 Paint a coat of white acrylic paint on the rough side of the small rectangle, directly over the laurel leaf design. You want the layer of paint to be about as thick as a coat of nail polish for best results. (Don't worry about getting paint on the edges or front of the earrings—you'll scrape that off later.) Paint a coat of light teal blue acrylic paint on the rough side of the large rectangle. Let both pieces dry thoroughly.

10 Paint a coat of acrylic varnish over the paint on both pieces. Let them dry thoroughly.

11 Carefully scrape away any paint or varnish around the edges of each rectangle, using a razor blade or craft knife held perpendicular to the edge. If any paint or varnish is on the front (shiny) side of the plastic, scrape it off with a fingernail so that you don't scratch the shiny surface.

12 Open the jump ring, and thread it through the hole in both pieces so that the shiny sides of each rectangle face the same way and the laurel leaf rectangle is on top of the light teal rectangle.

13 Each end of the magnetic clasp is attached with an overhand loop knot: Thread one end of the leather cord through the ring on the clasp. Slide the clasp to about 3 inches (7.6 cm) from one end of the cord. Bend the cord at this spot and fold the end of the tail back against the length of the cord, keeping the clasp near the bend in the cord. Make a loop with this doubled section of the cord and tie a knot by pulling the clasp through the center of the loop. Use flat-nosed pliers to pull both the tail and the rest of the cord tight to secure the knot. Trim the tail. Slide your pendant onto the cord. Tie the other end of the magnetic clasp onto the other end of the cord in the same manner.

CASCADING WORDS
Necklace & Bracelet

designer **ANNA BOKSENBAUM**

Favorite poem, song lyric, etc.

Basic shrink kit (page 12)

1 sheet of inkjet or pre-roughened shrink plastic (see the Tip)

Computer

Inkjet printer

Sealer (Anna uses matte spray finish.)

FOR THE NECKLACE

2 x 3.6-mm brass chain, 34 inches (86.4 cm) in length

4-mm jump rings (1 for each charm and 2 more)

Lobster clasp

6-mm jump ring

FOR THE BRACELET

4.5 x 2.5-mm brass chain, 7 inches (17.8 cm) in length

4-mm jump rings (2 for each charm)

Lobster clasp

6-mm jump ring

magine wearing a poem, song lyric, or favorite piece of literature around your neck. This necklace, featuring lines from the Amy Lowell poem "In Excelsis," may look complicated, but it uses the most basic jewelry-making techniques. The bracelet is the perfect complement.

FOR THE NECKLACE

❶ Choose a poem, song lyric, or piece of literature you love (you need 60 to 70 words to replicate the look of the necklace featured).

❷ Using a text document on your computer, set the line spacing to double space, the font to Book Antiqua, and the size to 18. Type or copy and paste your text into the document. (Anna added the poet's name and turned it into a charm she attached to one end of the necklace.)

❸ Use the space bar to divide the words into an odd number of blocks of texts with between two and four words in each one. Leave 1 inch (2.5 cm) of space between each block of text in your document. Determine which text charm will be the center of the necklace, and make that one the longest.

❹ Insert your shrink plastic sheet into your printer, making sure you will print on the rough or inkjet side of the sheet (see page 22 for more on printing on shrink plastic). Print the document onto the shrink plastic and allow it to dry. Allow at least half an hour for drying if you aren't using inkjet shrink plastic.

❺ Cut your sheet of text into horizontal strips. Then, use a hole punch to punch a hole at the start of each text block, keeping the spacing of the holes consistent.

❻ Use small, sharp scissors to cut each charm from the strips. Trim each charm into a pleasing rectangle with nice straight lines.

Continued...

 TIP *To achieve the look of the necklace shown, Anna uses pre-roughened ("rough and ready") shrink plastic in her inkjet printer without any problems. If you're worried about possibly damaging your inkjet printer, use inkjet shrink plastic instead.*

CASCADING WORDS
Necklace & Bracelet

fill the cup

are you who

Like white water

and open.

I am empty

hands and feet.

As a new jar

My mouth is open,

whiteness of your

I drink your lips, I eat the

among red apples.

striped wasps buzzing

7 Preheat the oven according to the shrink plastic manufacturer's instructions, and line a baking sheet with parchment paper. Arrange the charms on the sheet at least 1/2 inch (1.3 cm) apart. Have a heavy book handy nearby (Anna swears by *Joy of Cooking*), ready to use as a flattener.

8 Bake the charms according to the manufacturer's directions. (Anna bakes hers for about 3 minutes.) Remove the charms from the oven and immediately cover them with the heavy book to flatten them. Remove the book and allow the charms to cool.

9 Seal the charms with the finish of your choice. The charms in the project were sealed with two coats of matte spray finish. Allow the charms to dry completely.

10 Get out your pliers, jump rings, clasp, and chain, and rearrange your poem if the pieces have become scrambled. Cut two segments of chain: one 18 inches (45.7 cm) in length and one 16 inches (40.6 cm) in length. Set aside the 16-inch (40.6 cm) piece of chain. Lay out the 18-inch (45.7 cm) chain, and find its center link. Use one 4-mm jump ring to attach the longest (center) charm to the center link. Work backward from the center link on either side of it, attaching the next poem piece to every other link of the chain with a 4-mm jump ring. Make sure the chain isn't twisting as you work and all the charms are facing the same direction.

11 When all the charms are attached, hold up the cascade (pretty, no?). Now attach the last link of each side of the charm chain to the last link of each side of the plain 16-inch (40.6 cm) chain using the flat-nose pliers and a 4-mm jump ring.

12 Attach the lobster clasp to one side of your necklace and a 6-mm jump ring to other side.

~Amy Lowell

FOR THE BRACELET

1 Pick two to four words that you would like on your bracelet. Using a text document on your computer, set the font to Book Antiqua and the size to 20. Type your phrase, leaving $1^{1}/_{2}$ inches (3.8 cm) of space between each word.

2 Insert your shrink plastic sheet into your printer, making sure you print on the rough or inkjet side of the sheet (see page 22 for more on printing on shrink plastic). Print the words onto the shrink plastic and allow the ink to dry for at least half an hour so that it doesn't smudge.

3 Cut the text into horizontal strips. Use the hole punch to punch one hole on each side of every word. Use small, sharp scissors to cut each charm out in an oval shape, leaving plenty of room around the holes you punched.

4 Follow steps 7 through 9 on the previous page to bake and seal your charms.

5 Determine the length you want your finished bracelet to be. Seven inches (17.8 cm) is the standard length for a bracelet. Determine the length of chain you need between each word, and the length of chain you need on either side of the words, remembering to include the word charms and the lobster clasp in your calculations. Attach the word charms to the pieces of chain using the 4-mm jump rings. Keep track of the direction you're working in, and make sure that the chain isn't twisting as you work and that the charms are all facing the same way. Attach the last pieces of chain to either side of the assemblage.

6 Attach the lobster clasp to one side of your bracelet and a 6-mm jump ring to the other side.

SPOT-OF-TEA
Brooches

designer **JODIE ANNA**

Templates (page 121)

Basic shrink kit (page 12)

White inkjet shrink plastic

Computer

Inkjet printer

1/4-inch (6 mm) hole punch

Sealer (Jodie Anna uses acrylic spray sealer.)

2 inches (5 cm) of silver chain

2 jump rings

Jewelry adhesive

2 brooch backs

There's something so cozy and relaxing about a spot of tea. This brooch was designed by a British jeweler remembering Sunday afternoons at her grandmother's house.

① Scan the templates into a document on your computer. Print the images onto the shrink plastic, using both the slowest and the highest-quality settings possible. (See page 22 for more on printing on inkjet shrink plastic.) The ink will be slightly tacky and can easily smear, so set the freshly printed plastic aside to air dry in a safe place for at least 5 minutes, preferably longer.

② Once the ink is dry, cut out the teapot, teacup, and drop of tea, leaving white outlines around the images. Then use the hole punch to punch one hole in the spout of the teapot and another hole at the top of the drop of tea.

③ Preheat your oven, following the shrink plastic manufacturer's instructions. (Jodie Anna bakes her pieces at 250°F [120°C].)

④ Place all three pieces between two sheets of parchment paper on a baking sheet. Follow the shrink plastic manufacturer's instructions to bake the pieces. Keep a close eye on the oven: Over-baking some brands of white inkjet shrink plastic can cause discoloration. Meanwhile, have something flat and smooth, such as a hardcover book, ready nearby to use as a flattener.

⑤ When the pieces are shrunk and flat, carefully remove the entire baking sheet from the oven, and press down on the parchment-covered pieces with your flattener. Allow the pieces to cool completely.

⑥ Sand the edges if needed, and then apply the sealer to the pieces. If you use acrylic spray sealer, apply two or three coats, remembering to allow adequate drying time between each coat.

⑦ Use one jump ring to attach the chain to the spout of the teapot. Use the other jump ring to attach the drop of tea to the end of the chain, taking care not to twist the chain.

⑧ Use sandpaper to roughen the back of each brooch back slightly—this will create tiny grooves that will help the jewelry adhesive do its work. Wipe off any sanding residue, apply the glue to the brooch backs, and attach one brooch back to the back of the teapot and the other brooch back to the back of the teacup. Let your brooches sit undisturbed for at least 24 hours as the glue sets.

CAT AND MILK
Brooch

designer **KATHY SHELDON**

Template (page 112)

Basic shrink kit (page 12)

#6 plastic container*

Black, red, blue, and gray ultra-fine-point permanent markers

White acrylic paint

Sealer (optional, see step 6)

Pin back

Jewelry adhesive

* This piece was made using the bottom section of a large #6 clamshell takeout container from the deli section of a grocery store. See page 23 for more on using #6 plastic.

This brooch is made from a takeout container plucked from the recycling bin. This kind of plastic shrinks extra thick, an asset when making brooches.

❶ Cut a rectangle slightly larger than the template from the bottom of the plastic container.

❷ Place the plastic over the template and trace the black outlines (and the details for the cat) with the black ultra-fine-point permanent marker. Allow the marker ink to dry completely. Use the red marker to trace the bottle's lid and logo, the blue marker to color in the bowl, and the gray marker to lightly color in the cat.

❸ Preheat the oven to 325°F (163°C). Cut the design from the plastic, leaving an outline of clear plastic around all sides.

❹ Place the piece between two sheets of parchment paper on a baking sheet, and bake in the preheated oven for about 3 minutes or until it is shrunk and flat. Meanwhile, have something flat and smooth, such as book, ready nearby to use as a flattener.

❺ When the piece is shrunk and flat, carefully remove it, baking sheet and all, from the oven and press down on the parchment-covered piece with your flattener. Allow the piece to cool completely.

❻ Turn the plastic over and paint the milk in the bottle and the areas behind the lid and the cat and bowl with one or two coats of the white acrylic paint. Allow the paint to dry completely. I left this brooch unsealed, but you can use any sealer of your choice—just test it first to make sure it won't cause the design to run.

❼ Use the jewelry adhesive to adhere the pin back to the back of the brooch. Allow the glue to set for 24 hours before wearing.

SWEETHEART
Necklace

designer **KATHY SHELDON**

Digital photo or scan of a photo

Basic shrink kit (page 12)

White inkjet shrink plastic

Computer

Inkjet printer

#2 pencil

Circle or oval template (50 to
60 percent larger than the size you
want your final piece to be)

1/4-inch (6 mm) hole punch

Artist chalks (if hand-tinting a
black-and-white photo)

Cotton swabs

Sealer (I use matte acrylic
spray sealer.)

Metallic gold marker

Three 6-mm gold jump rings

Gold chain, 18 inches (45.7 cm)
in length

Gold barrel clasp

Make a pendant of a loved one by printing a photo on inkjet shrink plastic. Color a black-and-white image with artist chalks for a hand-tinted look.

① Scan your photo (if not digital) into a document on your computer. Adjust the size of your photo so that it prints about 50 to 60 percent larger and 50 percent lighter than your desired final piece. If using a black-and-white photo, remember that gray areas will shrink to black unless significantly lightened. (See page 22 for more on printing on inkjet shrink plastic.) Use the inkjet printer to print the image onto the shrink plastic. Allow the ink to dry completely.

② Preheat the oven according to the shrink plastic manufacturer's instructions. (I baked this piece at 275°F [135°C].)

③ Use the pencil and a circle or oval shape to trace your desired pendant shape around the image on the shrink plastic. Carefully cut the image out just inside the penciled outline.

④ Use the 1/4-inch (6 mm) hole punch to make a hole at the center top of the pendant.

⑤ To hand-tint a black-and-white photograph, color the selected areas very lightly with the artist chalks and cotton swabs.

Continued...

TIP *For the project shown, I scanned a color photograph into my computer and changed the scan to black and white so I could give it an old-fashioned hand-tinted look.*

SWEETHEART
Necklace

6. Place the pendant between two sheets of parchment paper on a baking sheet. Follow the shrink plastic manufacturer's instructions to bake and shrink the piece. (I baked the pendant shown for about 2 1/2 minutes.) Keep a close eye on the oven, because over-baking some brands of white inkjet shrink plastic can cause discoloration. Meanwhile, have something flat and smooth, such as book, ready nearby to use as a flattener.

7. When the pendant is shrunk and flat, carefully remove it, parchment and all, from the oven, and press down on the parchment-covered piece with your flattener. Allow the pendant to cool completely.

8. Seal the front of the pendant. (I sprayed the pendant shown with one light coat of matte acrylic spray sealer.) Let dry.

9. Sand or file the pendant's edges smooth. Remove any sanding residue, and then run the tip of the metallic gold marker around the edge of the pendant. Let dry completely.

10. Use one jump ring to attach the pendant to the chain. Use another jump ring to attach one end of the barrel clasp to one end of the chain. Then use the final jump ring to attach the other end of the barrel clasp to the other end of the chain, and you're finished.

PAPER PLANE RIDE
Necklace

designer ANASTASIA BURRINGTON

PAPER PLANE RIDE

Necklace

A little careful cutting is all you really need to do to create this origami-inspired pendant. Let your imagination take flight!

Template (page 120)

Basic shrink kit (page 12)

White or clear inkjet shrink plastic

Computer

Inkjet printer

Craft knife

1/8-inch (3 mm) hole punch

Sealer (Stasia uses clear nail polish.)

Four 3-mm silver jump rings

Silver chain, 18 inches (45.7 cm) in length

Silver lobster clasp

❶ Scan the paper airplane template into a document on your computer. Print the image onto the inkjet shrink plastic at both the slowest and highest quality settings. (See page 22 for more on printing on inkjet shrink plastic.)

❷ The ink will be slightly tacky and can easily smear, so set the freshly printed plastic aside to air dry in a safe place for at least 5 minutes, preferably longer.

❸ Preheat your oven, following the shrink plastic manufacturer's instructions. (Stasia bakes her earrings at 300°F [150°C].)

❹ It's easiest to cut out the areas around the ribbons before cutting the entire image from the shrink plastic. Use a craft knife with a sharp blade for these, take it slowly, and you'll do just fine. Then cut out the rest of the image using scissors.

❺ Use the hole punch to punch a hole at the dot near the front of the paper plane.

❻ Place the piece between two sheets of parchment paper on a baking sheet. Bake according to the shrink plastic manufacturer's instructions. (Stasia baked the piece shown for 3 minutes.) If the piece starts to curl, don't worry—read Oh, No! It's Curling! on page 20. As soon as the piece comes out of the oven, while it's still warm and a little soft, press it with something flat and smooth, such as a hardcover book. Let it cool completely.

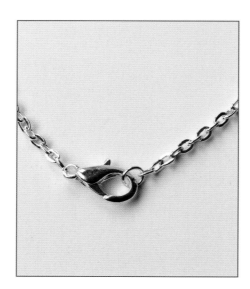

7 Carefully sand the edges if needed, and then apply the sealer to the front of the piece. (You may want to test any sealer first to make sure it won't make the printed ink run.)

8 Cut the silver chain into two 9-inch (22.9 cm) lengths.

9 Use one jump ring to attach one length of chain to the hole in the baked pendant. Use another jump ring to attach the second length of chain to the space between the ribbons (use the photo for reference).

10 Attach a jump ring to the end of one length of chain. Use the final jump ring to attach the lobster clasp to the end of the other length of chain.

BIRDS-ON-A-WIRE
Necklace & Earrings

designer **HEATHER DAVIDSON**

Templates (page 111)

Basic shrink kit (page 12)

1 sheet of pre-roughened shrink plastic

#2 pencil with eraser

1/4-inch (6 mm) hole punch

Blue and purple colored pencils

1/8-inch (3 mm) hole punch

Oven-safe baking dish (with a smooth surface)

Sealer (optional, see step 7)

Chain

Jump rings

Clasp

2 ear wires

The inspiration for this set came from a neighborhood walk at sunset. You make these pieces by baking twice: once to shrink the pieces and a second time at a higher temperature to fuse the pieces together.

FOR THE NECKLACE

❶ Use the #2 pencil and a straightedge or ruler to trace the template shapes for the front and back of the necklace onto the rough side of the sheet of shrink plastic. Don't trace the bird design yet. Carefully cut out the shapes just inside your pencil lines.

❷ Use the 1/4-inch (6 mm) hole punch to punch the hole in the back piece as indicated on the template. Erase any remaining pencil marks and be sure to remove all eraser residue.

❸ Color the front piece evenly but not too heavily with the blue colored pencil— you should still be able to see the bird design through the blue if you lay the piece back over the template. Using the photos for reference, apply the purple colored pencil very lightly over the blue to add the shading. Remember that the colors will intensify when the piece shrinks down.

❹ Use the #2 pencil to trace the design onto the front piece.

❺ Place both pieces rough-side up on a baking sheet lined with parchment paper. Make sure the pieces aren't touching or too close together.

❻ Bake the pieces following the shrink plastic manufacturer's instructions. (Heather baked the pieces shown at 325°F [163°C] for 3 minutes.) As soon as the pieces come out of the oven, while they're still warm and a little soft, press them with something flat and smooth, such as a hardcover book. Let them cool.

Continued...

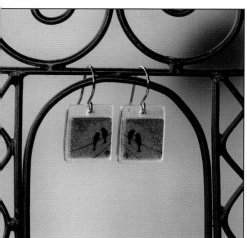

Note: **The next step, fusing, requires good ventilation. It can be done with a toaster oven or a conventional oven, but because you are heating the plastic at a high temperature, you must use adequate ventilation. Turn on ventilation fans and open nearby windows. (You can also do this step outdoors with a toaster oven and an outdoor extension cord in dry weather.) See page 23 for more on fusing.**

7 Place the back piece rough side up in the oven-safe baking dish, then layer the front piece rough side up on top. Make sure the front piece is centered and the hole isn't covered up. (You can stack both pieces rough side down to seal the design between the two pieces of plastic, avoiding the need to seal the finished piece, but the image will be reversed and the appearance of the finished piece will differ from the project shown. Whichever you choose, just make sure both pieces are either rough side up or rough side down.

8 Bake the layered pieces at 450°F (233°C) for 10 to 15 minutes. Every oven is different, so take a quick look at 10 minutes (or even a little earlier, in case your oven cooks hot). It's done when the roughness of the plastic smooths out and the edges have rounded but the holes have not yet closed up.

9 Once the plastic is smooth, very carefully remove the dish from the oven and let it cool down. *The shrink plastic will be much too hot to touch or remove from the pan!* As it cools and separates from the glass, it will make a cute pinging noise.

10 When the piece is completely cool, sand any rough edges. If you fused the pieces rough side up, seal the piece with the sealer of your choice (see page 21). Let any sealer dry completely.

11 Add a jump ring to the pendant and attach it to a purchased necklace chain or to a length of chain with a clasp and jump ring added.

FOR THE EARRINGS

1 Follow steps 1 through 10 for the necklace, but use the earring templates to trace the shapes and the design onto the shrink plastic, and use the 1/8-inch (3 mm) hole punch to punch the hole in each earring back piece. After the fused pieces are cool and any sealer is completely dry, simply hang them on the ear wires and your set is complete!

SHAPED FLOWER
Earrings

designer **CATHE HOLDEN**

Make these sweet little earrings by shaping fresh-from-the-oven shrink plastic. Changing the color is as easy as picking a different colored marker.

Template (page 112, to see punch shapes needed)

Basic shrink kit (page 12)

Pre-roughened shrink plastic

Pink and green permanent markers (or colors of your choice)

1-inch (2.5 cm) flower punch*

1-inch (2.5 cm) scalloped-circle punch*

1/8-inch (3 mm) hole punch

Thin gloves (optional, see step 4)

Wooden thread spool

Small paintbrush with a rounded handle (or other tool with a small pointed end)

2 light pink glass seed beads

2 silver head pins

2 silver spacer beads

2 silver jump rings

2 silver leverback ear wires with open drop loops

*
The templates on page 112 show the shapes and sizes of the punches Cathe uses.

❶ Use the flower punch to punch at least two flower shapes from the shrink plastic. (You may want to bake more than two and then use the two that come out the best.) Color the rough side of the punched flower shapes with the pink

permanent marker, keeping in mind that the color will be more vivid once the plastic shrinks.

❷ To make the leaves, use the scalloped-circle punch to punch one scalloped circle. Use the scalloped-circle punch again to cut the circle in half and create two scalloped leaf shapes. Color the rough side of the punched leaf shapes with the green permanent maker.

❸ Use the 1/8-inch (3 mm) hole punch to make a hole in the center of each flower shape and the end of each leaf shape.

❹ Follow the shrink plastic manufacturer's instructions to bake each flower shape individually. The next step is hot, so you might want to wear thin gloves. Once the flower has shrunk, immediately place the hot flower onto the hole in the top of the wooden thread spool. Press the center hole of the flower into the hole of the spool using the rounded

end of the paintbrush handle to create a bowl effect. You can press either glossy side out or glossy side in—each creates a different look in the final flower. For the earrings shown, the flowers were formed glossy side out.

⑤ Bake both leaves, following the shrink plastic manufacturer's directions. Because they are small, they may take less time than usual, so watch carefully as they shrink. Flatten the leaves if necessary when you remove them from the oven.

⑥ Thread one light pink seed bead onto a head pin, poke the head pin up through the inside of a pink flower, add one spacer bead, and make a simple loop. Repeat for the second flower.

⑦ Add a jump ring to each flower's simple loop, slide on one leaf, and then attach the jump ring to an ear wire.

BLOOMING FLOWERS
Bracelet

designer **CATHE HOLDEN**

Basic shrink kit (page 12)

Pre-roughened shrink plastic

Blue, yellow, and green permanent markers
(or colors of your choice)

2-inch (5.1 cm) daisy punch (see Note)

1-inch (2.5 cm) flower punch (see Note)

1-inch (2.5 cm) scalloped circle punch (see Note)

1/8-inch (3 mm) hole punch

Thin gloves (optional, see step 5)

Wooden thread spool

Small paintbrush with a rounded handle
(or other tool with a small pointed end)

21 yellow glass seed beads

21 gold head pins

14 gold eye pins

14 gold spacer beads

Gold-plated jump rings

Gold-plated chain, 7 inches (17.8 cm) in length

Gold-plated clasp set

O h, this one is so much fun! With just a bit of magic (okay, heat), shrink plastic goes from flat to flower.

Note: I know, it stinks when you want to make a project, but you can't find the exact same punch. The templates on page 112 show the shapes and sizes of the punches Cathe uses. You can use other flower-shaped punches—the end result will just look a bit different.

❶ To make the blue flowers, color the rough side of the shrink plastic with the blue permanent marker, keeping in mind that the color will be more vivid once the plastic shrinks. Let dry completely. Use the 2-inch (5.1 cm) daisy punch to punch at least seven daisy shapes from the colored plastic (you may want to punch extras in case some don't form well).

❷ To make the yellow flowers, color the rough side of the shrink plastic with the yellow permanent marker, keeping in mind that the color will be more vivid once the plastic shrinks. Let dry completely. Use the 1-inch (2.5 cm) flower punch to punch at least seven flower shapes from the colored shrink plastic.

❸ To make the leaves, color the rough side of the shrink plastic with the green permanent marker. Let dry completely. Use the scalloped circle punch to punch at least 15 scalloped circles. Then use the scalloped circle punch to cut each circle into two leaf shapes.

❹ Use the 1/8-inch (3 mm) hole punch to make a hole in the center of each flower shape and the end of each leaf shape.

Continued...

BLOOMING FLOWERS

Bracelet

⑤ Follow the shrink plastic manufacturer's instructions to bake each flower shape individually. You may want to wear thin gloves for this next step. Once the flower has shrunk, immediately place the hot flower onto the hole in the top of the wooden thread spool. Press the center hole of the flower into the hole of the spool using the rounded end of the paintbrush handle to create a bowl effect. You may press glossy side in or glossy side out—each creates a different look in the final flower. On the bracelet shown, the blue flowers were shaped glossy side in and the yellow flowers were shaped glossy side out.

⑥ Bake all the leaves, following the shrink plastic manufacturer's directions. Because they are small, they may take less time than usual, so watch carefully as they shrink. Flatten the leaves if necessary when you remove them from the oven.

⑦ For each blue flower, thread a yellow seed bead onto one head pin, leave about $3/4$ inch (1.9 cm) of wire, and make a simple loop (see Making a Simple Loop, page 24). Repeat this with another bead and head pin, but this time leave a little shorter length of wire before making the simple loop. Open the end of one eye pin, attach one long and one short head-pin-and-yellow-bead assemblage, then close the eye pin (see the top photo for reference). Poke the end of the eye pin up through the inside of one blue flower. Thread on one spacer bead, and make a simple loop. Make seven of these total.

⑧ For each yellow flower, thread a yellow seed bead onto a head pin, poke the head pin up through the inside of a yellow flower, add one spacer bead, and make a simple loop. Make seven of these total.

⑨ Spread the chain out horizontally in front of you, and arrange the flowers in an alternating pattern. Use the jump rings to attach the flowers to the chains, adding some leaves to the jump rings with the flowers and some leaves on their own jump rings in between the flowers.

⑩ Attach the clasp set to the chain.

RAINY DAY
Necklace & Ear Threads

designer **KATHY SHELDON**

Necklace & Ear Threads

L et it rain! The ear threads these raindrops hang from are comfortable to wear; adjust them so your drops "fall" above the umbrella necklace at whatever length you desire.

Templates (page 119)

Basic shrink kit (page 12)

Matte shrink plastic

Dark green, bright green, and gray ultra-fine-point permanent markers

Sky blue and light green colored pencils

Cotton swab

1/8-inch (3 mm) hole punch

Silver-plated jump ring

Large, long needle

Butane lighter (or other soot-free source of flame)

Sealer (I use liquid dimensional sealer.)

Silver-plated snake chain with clasp, 18 inches (45.7 cm) in length

2 sterling silver ear threads, 4 inches (10.2 cm) in length, with open jump rings

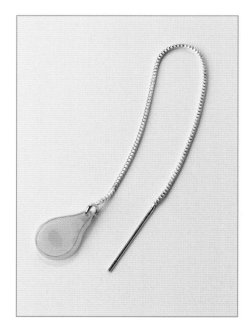

1 Use the templates and the dark green and bright green ultra-fine-point permanent markers to trace the umbrella, keeping in mind that the colors will be more vivid once the pieces are shrunk. The white polka dots on the umbrella are left uncolored: I found it easiest to trace the circle of each polka dot in bright green and then color in the rest of the umbrella.

2 Use the template and the gray ultra-fine-point permanent marker to trace the outline only of the raindrop onto the shrink plastic twice.

3 Use the sky blue and light green colored pencils to color in the raindrops. Because the shrink plastic is unsanded, the colors will go on very light, which is what you want. Use the cotton swab to both blend the blue and green a bit and to remove any colored pencil flecks from the raindrops.

4 Cut the umbrella and both raindrops from the plastic, taking care to leave just a slight border of plastic around each image.

5 Preheat the oven according to the shrink plastic manufacturer's directions. (I bake my pieces at 300°F [150°C].)

6 Use the 1/8-inch (3 mm) hole punch to make a hole at the top of each raindrop. (You'll make the hole for hanging the umbrella by using the large needle after that piece is baked.)

7 Place the pieces between two sheets of parchment paper on a baking sheet. Follow the shrink plastic manufacturer's instructions to bake and shrink them. (I baked the pieces shown for about 3 minutes.) Meanwhile, have something flat and smooth, such as a hardcover book, ready nearby to use as a flattener.

8. When the pieces are shrunk and flat, carefully remove the baking sheet from the oven, and press down on the parchment-covered pieces with your flattener. Let the pieces cool completely.

9. To make a hole in the tip of the umbrella, very carefully heat the large, long needle using the butane lighter, and poke the needle through the plastic to create the hole.

10. Sand the edges if needed, and then seal the pieces. (I used liquid dimensional gloss to seal the pieces shown.)

11. Use the jump ring to attach the umbrella to the necklace chain. Use the open jump rings at the end of the ear threads to attach the raindrops. Now wait eagerly for the next rainy day!

CALLA LILY
Earrings

designer **KATHY SHELDON**

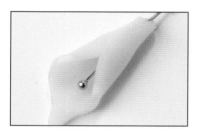

Template (page 113)

Basic shrink kit (page 12)

Matte shrink plastic

#2 pencil

Soft white eraser

Light green and yellow
colored pencils

Cotton swab

Thin gloves

2 gold-plated crimp tubes, 2 x 2 mm

2 gold-plated ball head pins

Crimping pliers (optional,
see the Tip, page 100)

2 gold-plated ear wires

T hese elegant earrings are made by shaping the shrink plastic as soon as you remove it from the oven.

Note: **This piece isn't complicated, but getting the hot shrink plastic to form just the way you want it to is tricky. Cut extra shapes because it may take a few attempts before you get your technique down and have two well-shaped calla lilies to turn into earrings.**

1. Use the #2 pencil to trace the template shape onto the shrink plastic at least twice.

2. Cut the shapes out, cutting just inside the outline. Use the soft white eraser to remove any pencil marks remaining.

3. Preheat your oven according to the shrink plastic manufacturer's directions. (I baked the earrings shown at 300°F [150°C].)

4. In the center of each piece, color a very faint oval with the light green pencil. Go over the green lightly with the yellow colored pencil. Use the cotton swab to blend the colors and remove any colored pencil flecks.

5. Bake and shape the pieces one at a time. To do so, place one shape between two sheets of parchment paper on a baking sheet. Follow the shrink plastic manufacturer's instructions to bake the shape until it is shrunk and flat. (I baked the earrings shown for about 3 minutes.)

6. Now, prepare to move quickly. With the gloves on, very carefully take the piece directly from the oven (don't bother removing the baking sheet), and place it on a flat surface. Quickly fold the top of the piece, right side over left, to form the calla lily. Use enough pressure to form the cone-shaped top, but not so much that you squish the whole thing or flatten it. If you don't like the result, pop the piece back into the oven for another 3 to 4 minutes until it flattens

Continued...

back out, and repeat the step. You usually get to reheat a piece once before it gets too stiff to shape again. Repeat steps 5 and 6 to make a second calla lily.

7 Slide a crimp tube onto one ball head pin. Position the crimp tube 1/2 inch (1.3 cm) from the ball head and crimp it (see the Tip). Slip the plain end of the ball head pin up through the opening at the top of the lily until it catches on the crimp tube.

8 Make a wrapped loop with the head pin wire (see Making a Wrapped Loop, page 24), starting about 1/2 inch (1.3 cm) up from the calla lily. Repeat steps 7 and 8 with the second head pin and calla lily. Then slip the loops onto the ear wires, the earrings into your ear lobes, and go look in the mirror.

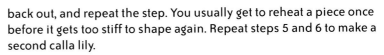

TIP *To crimp your crimp tube once it's in place on the head pin, first squeeze it in the crimping pliers' U-shaped notch (the notch farthest from the tip). Then turn the crimp tube so that it's at a 90° angle to the pliers, and place it into the notch closest to the tip. Gently squeeze the crimp tube so that it collapses in on itself into a nice round tube. Because this crimp tube isn't going to show, you can also just use flat-nose or chain-nose pliers to squeeze it tight onto the head pin.*

ORLA EARRINGS

designer **DONNA MALLARD**

S imple well-placed lines and shapes can have a big impact, as they do in these delicate earrings. Made with inkjet shrink plastic that can be printed on both sides, they make a bold statement as you're coming and going.

Templates (page 116)

Basic shrink kit (page 12)

Clear inkjet shrink plastic (the kind that prints on both sides of the plastic)

Computer

Inkjet printer

1/8-inch (3 mm) hole punch

Sealer (Donna uses matte acrylic spray sealer.)

Four 6-mm jump rings

2 marquis ear wires

❶ Scan the earring templates into a document on your computer. Print the images onto one side of the shrink plastic, using both the slowest and the highest-quality settings. (See page 22 for more on printing on inkjet shrink plastic.)

❷ The ink will be slightly tacky and can easily smear, so set the freshly printed plastic aside to air dry in a safe place for at least 5 minutes, preferably longer.

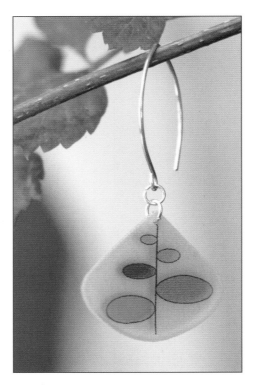

❸ Once the first side is dry, load the same sheet into your printer, and print the same images in the exact same places on the other side of the sheet. (See the Tip on the next page.) Follow the instructions in the previous step to let the ink dry completely.

❹ Preheat your oven, following the shrink plastic manufacturer's instructions. (Donna bakes her earrings at 325°F [163°C].)

❺ Once the second side of the printed plastic is completely dry, cut out the earring shapes with a slow, continuous motion, using the parts of the blades nearest to the base of the scissors. Remember to turn the plastic instead of the scissors.

❻ Hold the two earring shapes together. Punch a hole in both pieces simultaneously with the 1/8-inch (3 mm) hole punch about 1/4-inch (6 mm) from the tops of the earrings and centered.

❼ Place both pieces between two sheets of parchment paper on a baking sheet. Follow the shrink plastic manufacturer's

TIP *Many printers shake a little while printing the shrink plastic sheets, so the two printed sides may not end up perfectly aligned. If the designs don't quite match up, the shrinking process should take care of slight variations. If your printer can't seem to make the two sides match, just make one-sided earrings—they'll still look great.*

instructions to bake and shrink the earrings. (Donna bakes her earrings for 2 to 3 minutes; if your shapes still appear a bit warped after that time, give them another 15 to 30 seconds.) Meanwhile, have something flat and smooth, such as a hardcover book, ready nearby to use as a flattener.

⑧ Once the pieces are shrunk and flat, carefully remove the entire baking sheet from the oven, and press down on the parchment-covered pieces with your flattener. Mind that hot sheet!

⑨ Once the pieces are cool, sand the edges if needed, and then apply the sealer to both sides of the plastic.

⑩ Attach a jump ring to each earring. Then add another jump ring to the first jump ring for each. (These second jump rings keep the designs facing forward.) Attach each assemblage to an ear wire.

WRAP-AROUND UNICORN *Ring*

designer **TONIA MO**

Template (page 120)

Basic shrink kit (page 12)

Matte shrink plastic

Black fine-tip permanent marker

Thin gloves

Ring mandrel or lip balm tube, glue stick, or other thin cylindrical object (test the object for the proper ring size by slipping one of your rings on it)

Sealer (optional, see step 5)

TIP *Tonia recommends placing a silicon baking mat or a heavy sheet of cardboard over the unicorn so that it doesn't curl up and stick together while baking.*

Did you know unicorns like to chase their tails? Make this ring by shaping the shrink plastic as soon as you take it from the oven.

Note: The technique here is simple yet can be frustrating the first few times you try it. Grabbing a hot piece of plastic with gloved hands and then wrapping it quickly takes some practice—so cut out some simple ring-size strips to bake, and practice shaping them before trying the unicorn.

1 Use the fine-tip permanent marker to trace the unicorn template onto the shrink plastic, making sure to adjust the middle section so that the finished ring will shrink down to the right size for you. If you don't know your ring size, wrap a string around your finger to find its circumference, and then make your un-shrunk unicorn about one and one-half times that measurement.

2 Carefully cut out the unicorn, leaving a thin border of plastic around all sides.

3 Preheat your oven according to the shrink plastic manufacturer's directions. (Tonia bakes her rings at 300°F [150°C].)

4 Place the unicorn between two sheets of parchment paper on a baking sheet. Follow the shrink plastic manufacturer's instructions to bake and shrink the unicorn until it is shrunk and flat. (Tonia bakes her rings for 4 to 5 minutes.)

5 Here comes the tricky part! With your gloves on, take the unicorn directly from the oven (don't bother taking the baking sheet out), quickly wrap it around your cylindrical object to form the ring shape, and hold it in place for a few seconds. If the plastic hardens or cools down before you have it nicely shaped, just pop it back into the oven for another 3 to 5 minutes and repeat the step. You usually get to reheat a piece once before it gets too hard to work with.

6 You can leave your ring as is, or add sealer for extra protection (see Sealing Your Projects, page 21).

POLKA DOTS
Earrings & Bracelet

designer **STACEY RAWLINGS**

This project uses two types of paint markers on shrink plastic: one with a flat matte appearance and one with a shiny, raised finish that pops against the matte colors.

Templates (page 118)

Basic shrink kit (page 12)

2 sheets of white shrink plastic

Black fine-point permanent marker

Pink and brown matte permanent paint markers

White, pink, and light brown glossy permanent paint markers

1/4-inch (6 mm) hole punch

Small file (optional, see step 5)

Sealer (Stacey uses several light coats of acrylic spray sealer.)

Sixteen 10-mm silver-plated jump rings

2 silver-plated 4-mm ball stud earrings with loop

2 light topaz 4-mm Swarovski crystal bicones

1 light rose 4-mm Swarovski crystal bicone

2 silver-plated head pins

1 large (approximately 14-mm) silver-plated spring ring clasp

Two 9-mm silver-plated jump rings (more if needed to add length to the bracelet)

One 12-mm silver-plated jump ring

Silver-plated wire, 2 inches (5.1 cm) in length

Two 2-mm silver-plated smooth round beads

TO MAKE THE PLASTIC RINGS

1 Use the black fine-point permanent marker to trace the ring templates onto the shrink plastic. You'll need three large rings, six medium rings, and six small rings.

2 Color the large rings with the pink matte paint marker and the small rings with the brown matte paint marker, taking care not to smudge the black permanent marker lines with your fingers or the paint markers. Leave the medium rings plain white. Let the rings dry completely.

3 Use the white glossy paint marker to draw polka dots on the pink rings, the light brown glossy paint marker to draw polka dots on the white rings, and the pink glossy paint marker to draw polka dots on the brown rings. Vary the size and placement of the dots, and draw very lightly so that you don't accidentally drag and mix colors. Let the rings dry completely.

4 Preheat your oven, following the shrink plastic manufacturer's instructions. (Stacey bakes her pieces at 325°F [163°C].)

5 Cut out the rings, getting as close to the outline of the rings as possible

TIP *Stacey suggests making a couple of extra rings in each size in case some warp during baking.*

Continued...

POLKA DOTS

Earrings & Bracelet

TIP *If a baked ring comes out slightly warped, you can reshape it quickly while it's still hot—just be sure to wear gloves because both the plastic and the baking sheet will be hot.*

without cutting away any of the black. To cut out the center of a ring, punch a couple of holes inside the ring as close to the black outline as possible using the $1/4$-inch (6 mm) hole punch. Then use small curved scissors to very carefully cut out the inside circle. If a little plastic is left after cutting, use a small file or sandpaper, either before or after shrinking, to remove it.

6 Place the pieces between two sheets of parchment paper on a baking sheet. Follow the shrink plastic manufacturer's instructions to bake and shrink the earrings. (Stacey bakes the rings for $2 1/2$ to 3 minutes.) Meanwhile, have something flat and smooth, such as a hardcover book, ready nearby to use as a flattener.

7 After the pieces are shrunk and flat, carefully remove the entire baking sheet from the oven, and press down on the parchment-covered pieces with your flattener.

8 When the pieces are cool, sand the edges if needed, and then apply the sealer to both sides of the plastic.

TO ASSEMBLE THE EARRINGS

1 Use the 10-mm jump rings to attach one small, one medium, and one large ring together in a graduated chain. Use another 10-mm jump ring to attach the small ring to the loop of the ball stud earring. Repeat for the second earring, but, this time, attach the large ring to the ball stud earring.

2 Slide one light topaz crystal onto one head pin. Cut the head pin to approximately $1/2$ inch (1.3 cm). Make a simple loop (see Making a Simple Loop, page 24) that is large enough to fit around the plastic ring. Use needle-nose pliers to open the loop and attach it to the pink plastic ring at the end of one earring. Repeat this step to attach the light rose crystal to the brown ring on the second earring.

TO ASSEMBLE THE BRACELET

❶ Lay out the plastic rings horizontally with the large pink one in the center and then a white, brown, white, brown ring on each side. Use a 10-mm jump ring to attach each ring to the next one, and add a 10-mm jump ring to each final brown ring on the bracelet.

❷ Attach the clasp to a chain of two 9-mm jump rings, and then attach this assemblage to one end of the bracelet. Attach a 12-mm jump ring to the other end of the bracelet to function as the ring for the clasp.

❸ Use the 2-inch (5.1 cm) length of silver-plated wire to make the beaded centerpiece in the pink ring. Start by making a small simple loop. Add one silver-plated round bead, one light topaz crystal, and then the second silver plated round bead. Before cutting the extra wire and

looping the other end, place the piece in the center of the pink ring to make sure the beaded piece will fit in the center of the pink ring when attached to the two jump rings. Cut the remaining wire to approximately $1/4$ inch (6 mm) in length. Make a second small simple loop. Open the loops just enough to attach each to the jump ring on either side of the pink ring, attach them, and close the loops.

SHRINK PLASTIC TEMPLATES

Trace or scan all templates at 100 percent. Because shrinkage varies with different shrink plastics, you may need to adjust the size. See Making a Shrink Plastic Ruler on page 17.

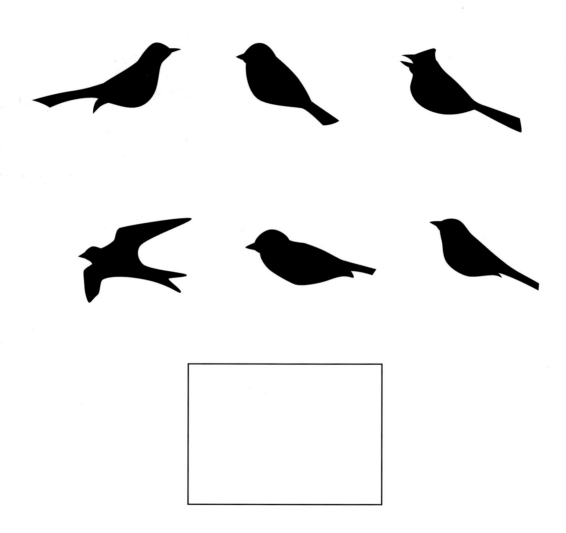

BIRD SILHOUETTE BRACELET

page 64

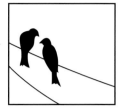

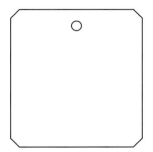

Earring Back

BIRDS-ON-A-WIRE EARRINGS
page 86

Necklace Back

BIRDS-ON-A-WIRE NECKLACE
page 86

SHRINK PLASTIC TEMPLATES

Daisy Punch Size & Shape

Scalloped Circle
Punch Size & Shape

Flower Punch Size & Shape

SHAPED FLOWER EARRINGS
page 89
&
BLOOMING FLOWERS BRACELET
page 92

CAT AND MILK BROOCH
page 78

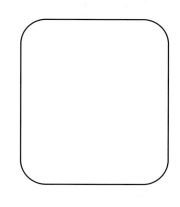

LAUREL NECKLACE
page 69

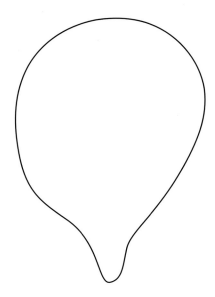

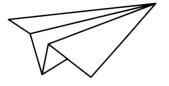

CALLA LILY EARRINGS
page 98

ORIGAMI PLANE EARRINGS
page 50

SHRINK PLASTIC TEMPLATES

FLOWER POWER NECKLACE & RING
page 29

Ring

Necklace

MEXICAN OILCLOTH NECKLACE
page 48

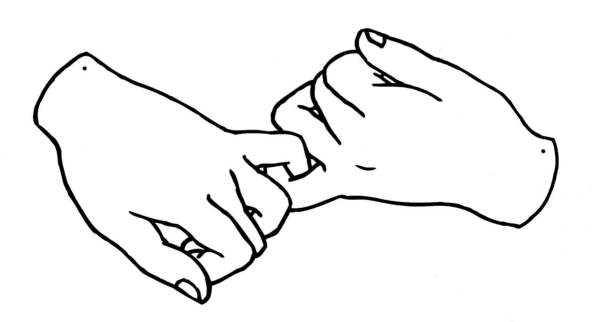

PINKIE SWEAR NECKLACE
page 60

SHRINK PLASTIC TEMPLATES

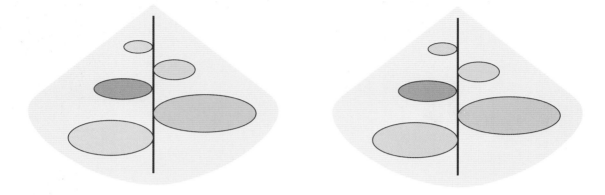

ORLA EARRINGS
page 101

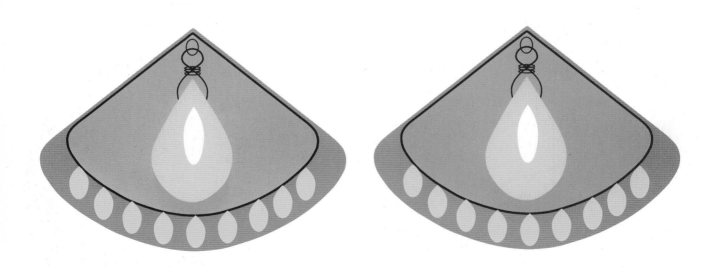

BOLLYWOOD EARRINGS
page 54

NOT-YOUR-GRANDMOTHER'S CAMEOS
page 57

SHRINK PLASTIC TEMPLATES

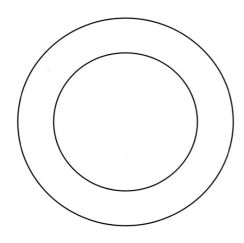

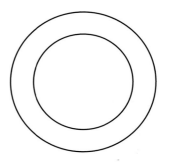

SIMPLE CIRCLE NECKLACE
page 52

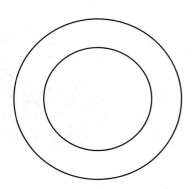

POLKA DOTS EARRINGS & BRACELET
page 106

SEVEN TREASURES EARRINGS
page 36

SPRINGTIME FRANCIE EARRINGS
page 32

TIGER LILY EARRINGS
page 26

RAINY DAY NECKLACE & EAR THREADS
page 95

SHRINK PLASTIC TEMPLATES

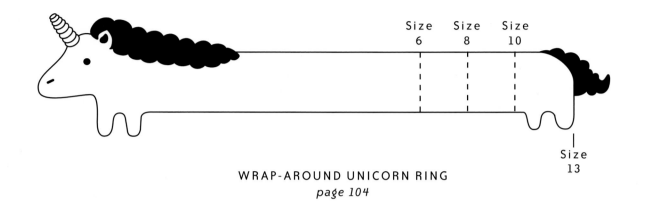

Size 6   Size 8   Size 10

Size 13

WRAP-AROUND UNICORN RING
page 104

PAPER PLANE RIDE NECKLACE
page 83

SPOT-OF-TEA BROOCHES
page 76

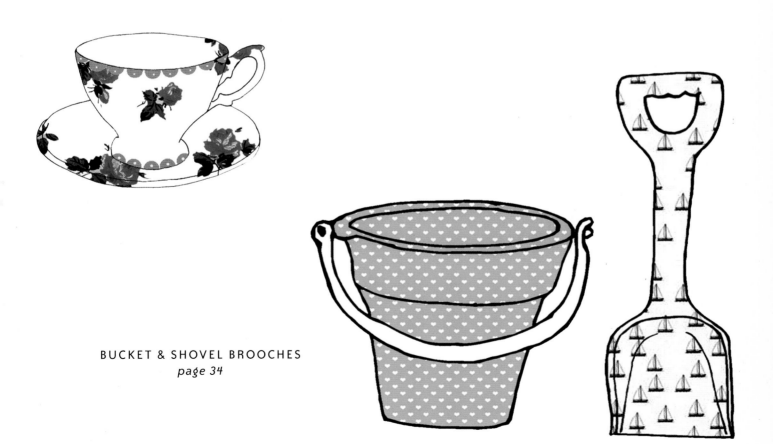

BUCKET & SHOVEL BROOCHES
page 34

SHRINK PLASTIC TEMPLATES

HIGH TEA CHARM BRACELET
page 62

LIGHTHOUSE NECKLACE
page 42

RUSSIAN DOLL SET
page 39

BONUS WOODLAND CREATURES GRAPHICS

Special thanks to sparrowgraphics.etsy.com for the Woodland Creatures and Russian Doll graphics.

ABOUT *the* DESIGNERS

JODIE ANNA of West Yorkshire, England, is captivated by the idea of how an object or image can trigger memories and a sense of nostalgia. She creates illustrations that narrate some of her happiest childhood memories and then develops those illustrations digitally, adding lovely vintage patterns to each item to create a crisp, finished image. To see more of her work, go to notonthehighstreet.com/jodieanna or jodieanna.blogspot.com.

ELIZABETH BADDELEY is a freelance illustrator living in New York City. She is currently pursuing an MFA in illustration from the School of Visual Arts. Elizabeth loves to draw and paint a variety of subject matter but finds herself continually turning to nature for inspiration. View her work at ebaddeley.com or misplacedmeadowlark.etsy.com.

ANNA BOKSENBAUM, a juvenile defender living in Brooklyn, New York, grew up in her mother's bead store. Today, she uses shrink plastic to make pieces that combine her love of text and jewelry. Both her made-to-wear and custom jewelry designs can be seen at brassisaac.etsy.com.

TAMARA BERG is a designer, food geek, craft maniac, celebration enthusiast, and all-around funsational gal. Often featured on the DIY Network and HGTV, she is the host and creator of *The Tamara Twist*, a lifestyle show with segments on food, travel, crafting, and home. Visit her website, tamaracentral.com.

STASIA BURRINGTON of Bellevue, Washington, is an internationally recognized freelance illustrator, as well as a sequential and fine artist. She attended the Cornish College of the Arts in Seattle, Washington, and holds a BFA from the University of Idaho. She spends a lot of time working on her Etsy shop, stasiab.etsy.com, and keeps a blog at stasiab.wordpress.com to document her process.

HEATHER DAVIDSON has studied figure drawing, ceramics, sculpture, and oil painting, but pencil is the medium she returns to most frequently. All of her designs are original, and she draws each piece of jewelry by hand. Heather lives in Seattle, Washington. To see more of her work, visit heatherdavidson.etsy.com.

ABOUT *the* DESIGNERS

JALENE HERNÁNDEZ is the owner of La Sirena Design. Originally from the Pacific Northwest, she has recently made Brooklyn, New York, her home base. When not pushing pixels, Jalene finds time to make cute (and sometime evil) things with her hands. Her creations can be found online at lasirenadesign.com and at lasirenadesign.etsy.com.

CATHE HOLDEN is a graphic-designer-turned-professional-crafter who shares unique craft projects on her blog, justsomethingimade.com. A Contributing Craft Editor for *Country Living* magazine and the author of an upcoming craft book from Chronicle Books, Cathe lives in beautiful Petaluma, California, with her husband, Jeff, and their three children.

DANA HOLSCHER'S line of one-of-a-kind earrings incorporates her background as an art and design graduate with her lifelong passion for fashion and crafting. Whether drawing, painting, sewing, or making jewelry, Dana, who lives in Fargo, North Dakota, is always immersed in a project of some kind. She draws each pair of her earrings by hand using her original designs, which are often inspired by vintage textiles. You can find more of her earrings at botny.etsy.com, as well as in many stores and galleries in the United States. Keep up with Dana's latest promotions and new listings at facebook.com/botny.

ERIN INGLIS resides in Vermont's beautiful Northeast Kingdom, where she spends most of her time adding bright colors to anything she can get her hands on. You can see her artwork, jewelry, and more at erininglis.com or brokenfingersart.etsy.com.

DONNA MALLARD trained early in life as an artist but later branched out and earned a degree in English from the University of California at Berkeley. Returning to her earlier passion, Donna is now a freelance graphic designer and crafter living in San Francisco. To view more of her work, visit duckndam.etsy.com or visit her blog at duckndam.blogspot.com.

TONIA MO is a student in Sydney, Australia. She sews and crafts using polymer clay, felt, and paper, but shrink plastic is her favorite medium. Check out her shop at greenmot.etsy.com.

JESSICA POUNDSTONE is a writer and jewelry designer who lives in Portland, Oregon, with her husband and two kids. She has been making jewelry for more than seven years and never gets tired of exploring the combinations of colors, patterns, and techniques that are possible with shrink plastic. Find Jessica's jewelry online at jewelrybyjessica.com and jessicapoundstone.etsy.com.

STACEY RAWLINGS is married and has three boys who keep her young or ancient, depending on the day's number of fights and injuries and the volume of noise emitted from each. Stacey has been creating things since birth and is never happier than when she has a pen, pencil, or paintbrush in her hand and is covered in a variety of mediums. You can find her handmade creations at beadedfrog.etsy.com.

CYNTHIA SHAFFER shot the photos in this book. Her art, photography, and craft projects have been featured in numerous books and magazines. She's the author of *Stash Happy Patchwork* (Lark, 2011) and *Stash Happy Appliqué* (Lark, 2012). For more information, visit her online at cynthiashaffer.com or cynthiashaffer.typepad.com.

MORGAN SHOOTER spends her days working in a small library and her nights feverishly crafting. She has combined her somewhat unhealthy obsessions with birds, kittens, and all things cute with her love of jewelry making. Morgan has been selling her work to the public since 2007. Check out her shop at missbluebirdandoscar.etsy.com.

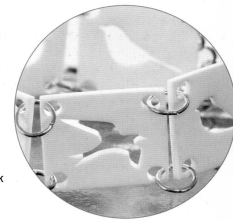

ACKNOWLEDGMENTS

This book would not have been possible without the talented and generous designers whose projects grace its pages. I can't thank them enough, and I can't encourage you enough to visit their shops and blogs (see page 125) to see more of their terrific shrink plastic jewelry.

Thank you, Aimee Ray, for providing your adorable doodles. Visit dreamfollow.com for all things Aimee.

Special thanks to Sparrow Graphics for allowing us to use the images for the Russian Doll set and the bonus Woodland Creatures. Check out their other wonderful images to use on shrink plastic at sparrowgraphic.etsy.com. The owners also sell jewelry findings at ladyjazz.etsy.com.

Big thanks to Cynthia Shaffer for shooting the gorgeous photos in the book and indulging me as we worked very closely from either side of the continent.

Thanks, once again, to Susan Wasinger, for pulling together my scatterbrained ideas and turning them into a beautiful book. And thanks to Kay Holmes Stafford for once again making sure the beautiful book was ready to go out into the world.

Thanks to Victoria Thulman and Chris Rich for sharp eyes and moral support.

ABOUT *the* AUTHOR

Kathy Sheldon is the author of and development editor for numerous gardening, outdoor living, and craft books, including *Craft Hope*, *Fa la la la Felt!* and *Heart-Felt Holidays*. She is a jewelry editor at Lark Crafts in Asheville, North Carolina. Visit her website shrinkshrankshrunk.com for more shrink plastic jewelry projects, graphics, and techniques.

INDEX

STAGING AN INTERACTIVE MYSTERY PLAY

A six-week program for developing theatre skills

Justine Jones and Mary Ann Kelley

MERIWETHER PUBLISHING LTD.
Colorado Springs, Colorado

Meriwether Publishing Ltd., Publisher
PO Box 7710
Colorado Springs, CO 80933-7710

Editor: Theodore O. Zapel
Assistant Editor: Nicole Rutledge
Interior and Cover Design: Jan Melvin

Library of Congress Cataloging-in-Publication Data

Jones, Justine, 1949-
   Staging an interactive mystery play : a six-week program for developing
theatre skills / By Justine Jones and Mary Ann Kelley. -- First edition.
      pages cm
   ISBN 978-1-56608-189-4
   1. Children's theater. 2. Playwriting--Study and teaching (Elementary)
   3. Theater--Production and direction--Study and teaching (Elementary)
   4. Improvisation (Acting)--Study and teaching (Elementary) 5. Participatory
   theater. I. Kelley, Mary Ann, 1948- II. Title.
   PN3157.J66 2012
   792.02'26--dc23
                                        2012039322

          1   2   3   12   13   14

To all my students at Los Alamos Middle School who shared so much of themselves!
And, as always, to Nick and Darryl.
— Justine Jones

To all of the young people who are growing because of drama in their lives;
To all of the teachers who use drama as a tool for life as well as a grade;
To all of the kids who were in my drama classes and have become such wonderful adults;
To my steadfast friends who have always been with me, giving me excitement, and peace, and courage;
To my own favorite child: this book's for you, with all my love and gratitude,
— MAK

Table of Contents

Foreword

This hands-on guide takes you step-by-step through the process of developing, writing, and producing an interactive murder mystery with middle or high school students. Starting with the benefits of students writing their own scripts, it proceeds to how playwriting can be a group process of collective creation and shows the educator/director exactly how to get the creative juices going. It takes you through brainstorming, character creation, plot development, planting clues, and writing dialogue. It then moves into the actual production itself, providing useful checklists for the director and stressing how to achieve maximum audience participation. Much emphasis is put on the improvisational skills needed to be a successful suspect! Also provided are lists of characters, locations, and plots. Synopses of five actual plays including cast lists and comments are included for use.

Preteens and teens have voices that need to be heard! They don't have to write lovesick poetry, either. Humorous endeavors can be equally as empowering. As teachers of drama/theatre, this is what we do. We are agents of empowerment! There are many ways we can give our students the tools they need to express themselves: music, art, photography, poetry. But what better way than to involve them in a group creative process: the writing and producing of a play? This is the goal of this book. Perhaps after participating in this kind of activity, some of the students will write their own plays and explore their own voices. As the poet Jayne Cortez says, "Find your own voice and use it!" We like to think of this as step one in a process of lifelong discovery.

Ten Years of Interactive Murder Mysteries Distilled for You!
√ benefits of students writing their own scripts
√ how playwriting can be collective creation
√ how to get the creative juices going
√ brainstorming
√ character creation
√ plot development
√ planting clues
√ writing dialogue
√ the production
√ useful checklists for the director
√ how to achieve maximum audience participation
√ improvisational skills needed to be a successful suspect
√ lists of characters
√ lists of locations
√ lists of plots
√ synopses of five plays
√ cast lists
√ comments

Introduction

How This Project Came to Be

A Note from Justine Jones

Back in the eighties at the high school where I taught, we were always looking for fundraising ideas. Selling candy and assembling pizzas got old, so we moved to creating cookbooks and telling fortunes at crafts fairs. But still, the search for a way to make money through theatre activities continued. We tried an improv-a-thon but it was too difficult.

At that time, dinner theatres were starting to have mystery dinners where the actors mingled with the guests until a "crime" was committed and they became suspects. There were also parties where each guest came as a certain type of character, and a mystery was enacted. It became possible to purchase kits with detailed dossiers of "crime scene" artifacts. Everyone could be a detective!

It occurred to me that if everyone could try to solve the crime then the entire class might be able to create it, as well. I had always been interested in facilitating young people's writing, be it poetry, oral history, or playwriting. Combining creative writing with original plays, making it a game, soon a fundraiser was a natural for my high schoolers.

Initially the project was not an entire class one. A small group of volunteers met after school to brainstorm ideas. Since the *Rocky Horror Picture Show* was big and interactive at the time, our first murder mystery was *The Rocky Horror Murder*. Audience members were guests at a performance of the play and one of the "actors" was murdered. This first effort was quite short and concentrated mainly on creative costuming and staging of some dance numbers from the musical. Truthfully, it was more karaoke than mystery.

Our second attempt moved closer to having a real plot as we staged *A Reunion with Death* where the cast relocated to the high school for their ten-year reunion dinner. The students loved projecting themselves into the future. Everyone volunteered to be killed! As I recall, it was death by Jell-O-smothering or something equally silly. But, of course, these were simply fun and entertaining fundraisers, not "real" plays.

When I moved and found myself at the middle school level, I encountered even more difficult problems. In addition to having no stage, no lights, no storage, and no budget, I had a total of one hundred and thirty twelve-year-olds in five different classes! I wasn't used to this age group and tried desperately to find appropriate material. Most of the plays I read were too adult, too childish, or too out-of-tune with the lives of 1990s pre-teens and teens. It was obvious to me that writing our own material was the way to go.

I tried some personal writing, which was too threatening for this age group. I tried spoofs of fairy tales, current events, or films. These were fun but short projects. We often strung together class improvs into shows of short vignettes. But always the students wanted to do a full-length play. Enter the return of the interactive murder mystery!

The wonderful thing about middle schoolers is that they are highly creative and imaginative and most are not yet jaded enough to censor the majority of their ideas! Hence, classroom brainstorming was broad and extravagant. There was never a shortage of ideas even if many of these were wild and impractical. And that's the important part of brainstorming: every idea is initially exciting and acceptable. That way, we never ran out of ideas. Guaranteed!

● ● ● ● ● ● ● ●

Question?
What to do with:
No Stage
No Lights
No Storage
No Budget
130 Twelve-Year-Olds
Five Classes

Answer
An Interactive
Murder Mystery!

● ● ● ● ● ● ● ●

Our first brainstorms and even plays ran along traditional lines. The word mystery seemed to connote big old houses, servants, and contested wills, the mainstays of traditional mysteries, a concept with which the kids seemed, for some reason, most familiar. Snowstorms, locked rooms, and disappearances also were popular. So we took these elements and combined them into our first original mid-school mystery, *A Willful Murder.*

What Is an Interactive Murder Mystery?

Perhaps the question should be: Why an interactive murder mystery? Why not just have fun doing *Ten Little Indians* or *The Mousetrap,* or for that matter, anything by Tim Kelly? Why even do a mystery?

Middle-school-age students love puzzles! Notice the shows they watch and the books they read. They love to see people their age triumphing over "bad guys" and feeling superior to the often bumbling adults who, at this age, seem to have all the power. For this reason I find that mysteries, especially ones which have a bit of humor in them, are quite successful.

But then, why interactive? I define interactive in two ways. The first is the interaction of the entire class in the process of creating the script. The second is the involvement of the audience in the process of choosing the murderer.

To be honest, involving the audience in a guessing game was initially a gimmick. I wanted the audience to pay attention to the clues the students had put into the script. As we performed these more often, I found that the audience usually looked forward to participating in the process by going so far as to take notes, throughout the performance. And when it came down to interviewing the suspects, their "inner detective" cut loose! It was such a pleasure to watch how intensely they interrogated the "suspects." They chortled with glee when they thought they'd caught the suspects in a lie! Afterwards, the suspects talked about "really being grilled" or "being raked over the coals." But they always smiled at the memory.

A Note on Violence

Perhaps the idea of murder concerns you. After all, we are educating young people. Is it acceptable to choose a murder mystery as a topic when there must be so many others? I have often considered this and am not quite sure what to answer. Why do I, for example, relax with a good old-fashioned crime mystery novel? Why not choose something more soothing?

Ever since playing *Clue* as a child, I have been intrigued by the who, what, and with what weapon of the murder mystery. Was it Mr. Green in the lounge with the revolver? Or Miss Scarlet in the conservatory with the knife? And why, oh why use a candlestick? I think it plays to our sense of curiosity and creativity. Certainly there is violence, but more than anything, solving it is a game of wits. Often, even, a bit of humor. Paying attention to the details, adding up the clues and throwing out the red herrings, finding the means, motive, and opportunity — what could be more fun than that? In a perverse way, the crime itself doesn't really matter, the solving of it does.

This leads me to the staging of the murder itself. (Many schools refuse to allow any kind of weapons on stage. This includes even wooden swords in my school!) Blood and gore is often abhorrent to many, and alienating members of the audience is certainly not what a director wants to do. For this reason, we have had to be very creative in the staging of our murders. Some have taken place Off-stage, the body brought on by the investigator. Most have taken place in a rather convenient blackout, the body discovered as the lights return. And others have included highly dramatic deaths scenes that barely fall short of being high camp. It all depends on the tone you have chosen to set with your script.

Because of this we have had to be highly creative in the methods of the murder. Poison had been our first choice simply because it contains no blood whatsoever and no weapons need be used. In *Willy Wonka* we used a very long string of licorice and in *Camp Minehaha* we used an arrow from the camp's archery range. Was it an accident?

Being creative is always such fun. Use your imagination. Did the cook really poison the soup or did someone slip something in it as they passed by? Was the sidewalk really that icy? Why was there an open grave with a spike at the bottom? Use your imagination and have fun with it. Remember — your goal is to create a puzzle, not horror or even suspense. It may sound odd, but murder can and, in this case, should be fun. (And often funny!)

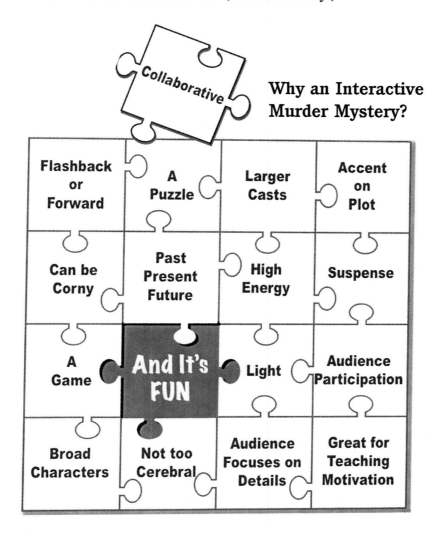

Why an Interactive Murder Mystery?

Collaborative

Flashback or Forward — A Puzzle — Larger Casts — Accent on Plot — Can be Corny — Past Present Future — High Energy — Suspense — A Game — And It's FUN — Light — Audience Participation — Broad Characters — Not too Cerebral — Audience Focuses on Details — Great for Teaching Motivation

Forty Ways to Die

Poison in:

food	drink	water bottle	medication
inhaler	flower/corsage	snuff box	perfume
air freshener	hairspray	eye drops	contact lens solution
lipstick	deodorant	ink	swimming pool
bath	Kool-Aid		

Strangled by:

rope	tie or bolo	plants	one's hair
licorice	branches of tree	curtain pull	

Accidents ... Or Not?

tile falls from roof	dart from dart game
arrow from archery set	slip on ice
fall in a hole	trip on a rock/uneven pavement
fall down stairs	awning dropped on head
backed over by car	drowned in pool/hot tub
scared to death	locked in an old freezer/trunk
trapped in a burning building	locked out in the cold
locked in a sauna/tanning bed	

Simple Suggestions for Interactive Mysteries

1. You need a large cast with many well-developed characters.
2. Characters should be "types" to which young people can relate.
3. Dialogue must be real life and up-to-date.
4. Sets must not be too complex.
5. There should not be too many scene changes.
6. Scene changes should not have lots of props.
7. Transitions between scenes must be quick, smooth, and entertaining.
8. Use humor.
9. The tone should be light, not sinister.
10. There should never be cruelty.
11. The puzzle should not be too complicated.
12. Everyone should have clear motives.
13. All characters should have strong feelings about all the others.
14. Violence should be Off-stage and perhaps only suggested.

15. Contemporary themes work best.

16. Conflicts between adults and young people should be appropriate.

17. Clichés and social groups work.

18. Eccentric characters (Grandpa living in the closet, the popcorn boy) make things interesting.

Before You Start, Ask Yourself:

- How much time do we have?
- Are we doing this primarily as a fundraiser?
- What are our resources?
- What is our rehearsal and performance space?
- What is our budget for props, costumes, and set?
- How simple or elaborate do we want to make this?
- What are my students' attention spans for rehearsals?
- How perfect does this need to be?

Week One
Getting Started

So, you've decided that you want to try this project with one or more of your classes. Now what? First of all, you need to set aside a period of time for the process. Coming up with the preliminaries, the theme, the characters, and the basic synopsis usually takes about a week of class time. Now might be a good time to hand out the Week One Expectations and Audience Expectations on pages 52 and 53.

Motivation — 2 Class Periods

Start with a Mystery

I usually start by showing the 1985 film, *Clue*, rated PG. This is a silly pastiche based on the popular board game and even includes many of the game's characters. In it, a group of strangers is summoned to an isolated old mansion during a storm. They are only told that it concerns a matter beneficial to them. Upon arrival, they meet a mysterious butler who tells them that the same person, his employer, Mr. Body, is blackmailing them all. Suffice it to say that murder and mayhem ensue, much to the delight of this age group. But the best part is that the film includes three alternative endings, all completely "logical" given the clues provided. This is a great lesson for the students because it shows that it is quite unnecessary to structure a puzzle that can only have one conclusion, thus giving them much more freedom in their script writing.

More Starters

Other pre-playwriting projects may include playing the board game *Clue*, playing the *Clue* game video, reading short mystery stories and trying to solve them, or even going through some of the available kits for murder mystery parties.

Let's Go to the Movies!

Clue 1985 — PG — 96 minutes

If you don't already own this gem, run out and buy it now! The plot twists, turns, and writhes. Everyone has a secret. Appearances deceive. The cast is perfect: Eileen Brennan, Tim Curry, Madeline Kahn, Christopher Lloyd, Michael McKean, Martin Mull, Lesley Ann Warren. Director: Jonathan Lynn.

(and to inspire the director)

Murder by Death 1976 — PG — 94 minutes

Think of your favorite literary detective. Now think of your favorite actors. Now put them together in a script by Neil Simon. That's *Murder by Death* directed by Robert Moore. Cast: Eileen Brennan, Truman Capote, James Coco, Peter Falk, Alec Guinness, Elsa Lanchester, David Niven, Peter Sellers, Maggie Smith, Estelle Winwood, James Cromwell.

Generating Ideas and Theme — 1 Class Period

Brainstorm

After the students are excited and motivated, it's time to brainstorm. It is vitally important at first to accept all ideas. Ask the class: What might be an interesting theme for our murder mystery? If *Clue* might be called *The Old Mansion Murder Mystery*, what might ours be called? How would it incorporate a location to make it interesting?

Times of Year

To get things started, suggest interesting times of the year. Holidays, for example. What might happen if the murder were set at Halloween? Would it take place at a costume party? Trick-or-treating? At a scary movie? At a fortune teller? Maybe even at a Halloween supply store or costume rental shop?

If it were set on the Fourth of July, it would be easy to incorporate picnics, fireworks, firecrackers, and family reunions. Or what about the seedy carnival that used to set up shop at the local park around this holiday? You get the picture.

Sometimes it's fun to set your play close to the time you actually present the play. What holidays and events can you take advantage of?

New Year's Eve — *Invitation to Murder*
Valentine's Day — *Arsenic and Valentine's Lace*
St. Patrick's Day — *Green with Envy*
April Fool's Day — *Murder! (No Fooling)*
Graduation — *Commencing to Murder*
Fourth of July — *Firecrackers, Sparklers, and Mayhem*
Labor Day — *Murder Is No Picnic*

Special Events

Think about special events. Graduation. Sweet sixteen parties. Family vacations. Moving to a new house. Someone new moving to the neighborhood. Awards ceremonies. Talent shows.

Spoofs

Kids love spoofs, and they watch a lot of television. What are their favorite shows? These change rapidly, of course, but as I write this, reality TV is big. What about *American Idol? Big Brother? Fear Factor? The Real World? Survivor?* These are ripe for spoofing. Plus the kids can have a chance to play some of their favorite celebrities. And which are the hit series, old or new? *24? The X Files? Friends?* What about cartoons? SpongeBob, South Park, The Simpsons, Scooby Doo — these are all part of the popular culture that surrounds this age group.

Celebrity News

Tabloids can provide celebrity scandals and that may be appropriate. Of course, teachers will have to monitor them closely, but what about a murder set at the awards ceremony for the sexiest man of the year? What about feuds between celebrities?

Organizations, Pets

What are some of the unusual organizations that might be holding conventions? Once we tried to write a script about a reunion of retired television advertisements with icons such as Mr. Clean and the Keebler Elves. Or what about a meeting for people who claim to have been abducted by aliens? Or people who have pit bulls? Or have pet iguanas? Of course, it is very important not to offend anyone, so avoid Scientology or people who come to your door on Saturday mornings.

Once you've given them these prompts the ideas usually start to flow. In the first ten minutes, we usually get twenty-five to forty ideas and run out of space on the chalkboard.

More Ideas

Why not have a few lists on hand in case your class hits a dry spell. *Improv Ideas: A Book of Games and Lists* (Meriwether Publishing Ltd.) has sixty-seven lists including places, enclosed spaces, character traits, clubs, obsessions, occupations, murder weapons, crimes, and weather.

Fleshing Out the Ideas

After you've collected as many as possible, read the entire list aloud and ask for brief ideas of what might be done with them. Inevitably some ideas will elicit groans while others generate enthusiasm. This can be a problem, as the students who suggested titles that were less than enthusiastically received often feel rejected/embarrassed and don't want to support their ideas. Admittedly, some are not worthy of support, but some just need a little explanation to make them clearer. So what can be done?

For example, one of the most often suggested ideas is *The Disneyland Murders*. When asked for clarification, it becomes clear that recreating Disneyland and the characters may not be a possibility given our financial limitations. The same might go for an underwater theme. But maybe not … Only you know what your particular space and budget can provide.

Selecting the Topic and Presentations — 2 Class Periods

Speak Up

I usually ask anyone, not only the student who suggested the idea, to advocate for it. If no one champions the idea, and if I think it could be a good theme, I do a short presentation on what might be done with this idea. After all the ideas have been discussed, we come to the vote.

Hint:

Check out prom and party catalogs for lots of kid-friendly themes plus scenery ideas. (Just change "A Romantic Evening at Mardi Gras" to "Mardi Gras Madness" and you have your murder theme.)

Your school probably has these catalogs on hand, or use the list below for starters:

Anderson's — www.AndersonsProm.com

Prom Nite — www.promnite.com

ShindigZ — www.shindigz.com

Stumps — www.stumpsprom.com

Oriental Trading Company — www.OrientalTrading.com

Party Celebration — www.partycelebration.com

Party Supplies Hut — partysupplieshut.com

Vote and Count

Each student may vote for three scenarios. We then tally the top three.

Plan Presentations

After this, I assign the students into groups: one group for each title. Hand out the Small Group Presentation — Play Theme Worksheet on page 54. Their job is to prepare a brief presentation about why this is the best idea. It is particularly important that these assignments are random, as the students need to expand their imaginations beyond their own favorites. Considerations must include opportunities for interesting but do-able sets and costumes, possibilities for a variety of characters, appeal to the potential audiences, etc.

Presentations and Q & A

Presentations usually take five to ten minutes each. I usually leave time for a few questions or comments after each group.

Is it Do-Able?

Presentations Should Include:
Sets
Interesting but possible
Costumes
Creative but available
Variety of Characters
Lots of interesting things for actors to do and audience to watch
Audience Appeal

Final Vote

Now to the final vote! Each idea has been creatively and enthusiastically presented. Hopefully there has not been time for political rallying, but realistically this can happen. Take another vote: each student votes once. If all goes well, a clear winner will emerge, and there will not be too many hard feelings!

This process usually takes two class periods and is well worth it. By the time the students have made their final choice, a great many ideas for the plot, characters, and set have been discussed. Excitement has built. And the kids have had a chance to think of even more ideas. The time is ripe to ask, *"What will happen?"*

Your Theme — Your Posters

Once the theme and title have been chosen you may want to have students think about how to present it to the public. You can start working on posters now or wait for the first tech week. If you want to have posters drawn by students to advertise the show, starting soon is a good idea.

This might be the moment to introduce a poster contest. The contest, open to all the class, will be for the poster idea that best promotes the play. It will be due at the beginning of Week Three.

Remember all posters must contain:

Who: The name of your company or class.

What: The name (working title) of the play. (Include that it is an interactive mystery and that refreshments will be provided.)

When: Both dates and times.

Where: Your venue.

How Much: Ticket prices for all categories. (student, adult, retired, etc.)

See Advertising Notes in Week Three for details!

CHECK THIS OUT

The fictional *Maui Murders* (page 121) shows a sample production with possible schedule and forms.

Week Two
Decisions, Decisions

Refining the Theme and Creating a Scenario — 1 Class Period

Brainstorm

After choosing the theme, we brainstorm again. All ideas are accepted. In the example of, say, *Murder at the Prom*, what might happen? Well, the Prom Queen might disappear. Alcohol may be discovered in the punch. The Prom King may not be present at the Prom. The chaperones might get into a fight with each other. Two girls may fight over having the same dress. It goes on and on. Note that the ideas do not have to connect chronologically or even logically. But you will find that often a pattern emerges and many of the seemingly disconnected ideas will seem to fit together into some sort of play/plot. Now might be a good time to hand out the Week Two Expectations and Actor/Playwright Expectations on pages 56-58.

Scenarios in Small Groups

Gather as many plot ideas as you can. Then divide into small groups and ask each group to devise a possible scenario. Here are two possible examples for a prom plot:

Scenario One: The Prom Location

The high school prom has been a problem for many years. Many parents believe that it should no longer be held at a local hotel, but should return to the high school gym. Other parents think that the prom should be held at the hotel as usual. There has been talk about students boycotting the prom altogether. The idea is that they will sign up to attend and then just not show and convene at the hotel anyway. In fact, a group of parents have gone ahead and rented a ballroom for the purpose, unbeknownst to the school authorities. The student government planning committee gets wind of this plot at the last minute.

Scenario Two: The Prom Theme

The theme for this year's prom is "Shipwrecked on a Desert Island." Instead of formal clothes, students are to come dressed in island-inspired clothing. Many girls feel cheated by this plan, as they have been looking forward to wearing gowns. There is much dissent and the decision has been made that attendees can wear either island wear or traditional tuxes and gowns. Unfortunately many of the boys have opted for Hawaiian shirts and shorts while their dates want to wear long evening gowns. Obviously, this has created many conflicts even before the students arrive at the prom.

As you can see, getting a starting concept is what's important. The Writing Crew can take it from here. But that's yet to come. First, we need to look at characters.

Characters and Plot

Plot can be influenced by character and vice versa. We have a theme and the beginnings of a plot. Now, we consider the characters. Who might be in our prom scenario? Parents, teachers, students, band members, caterers, hotel officials, party planners? Define them well. There will be different sorts of students, won't there? Using Scenario One, we might have the students in student government on one side and the rebels on the other. In Scenario Two, we might have the students who choose island wear and those who opt to go formal. And these may all be refined even further.

Individual Characters

It is now up to the students. After deciding on character categories, ask the students to decide who they might want to be. Sitting is a circle and taking detailed notes, go from student to student. The results are not always balanced, but usually this clears itself up on its own as the students see their peers' choices.

Creating Characters — 1 or 2 Class Periods

Character Names

Once the students have chosen a character, it's time to write biographies to thoroughly create the characters. Start with a name. I like to discuss what names mean to people. Ask students if they like their own names. Often students feel that the name they've been given doesn't quite suit them. Either they prefer their nickname or would like another name altogether. Why? What does the name connote to them? Does it sound too formal? Too casual? Do they think that they might grow into their name? My mother once told me that she was deciding between the name Justine and the name Jodean. What if I had been Jodean Jones? Or Jody Jones? Might I have had a different self-image?

Be aware of regionalisms. Jodean might be normal in the U.S. South but quite unusual in, say, New York City.

What's in a name? When I was growing up, the name Marilyn was quite glamorous. Today, it might be Angelina or even Britney? And what do you think of when you hear the name Jennifer? Or Brad? I find that the choice of name for the character often helps the students to get excited with their writing.

Need Names? Search the Internet

Names for celebrities? Celebrities' children? They're there. Some websites offer names with their meanings (babynamesworld.parentsconnect.com), others offer names by popularity (www.babynames.com).

A pleasant surprise was the Social Security Administration's website (www.ssa.gov/OACT/babynames/) that gives names by popularity by year since 1880! And you can search the one thousand most popular names by gender.

Character Bios

So students have their characters' names. Where do they go from here? I like to give them a Character Information form on page 59 to fill out before they write their narrative. It asks for information about: name, age, gender, race, educational background, family background, vocation/projected vocation, hobbies, likes/dislikes, favorite quote.

Let's see how fictional student Chris Smith describes her character, Barbara Brown. Also, after we have a brief idea of Barbara, we need to place her in the scenario to create a potential conflict.

Name: *Chris Smith*

Character Information

Character Name: *Barbara Brown*

Age: *15*   Gender: *Female*   Race/Ethnicity: *White/Caucasian*

Educational Background: *H/S sophomore at George Lewis High School*

Family Background: *Third child of Mel and Alice Brown. Two older brothers, Chad and Mike. A younger sister, Laura.*

Vocation/Projected Vocation: *Wants to be a professional country singer*

Hobbies: *Listening to music. Writing poetry. Showing her sheep in 4-H*

Likes/Dislikes: *Is very close to her religious family. Disapproves of the drinking that goes on among her peers.*

Favorite Quote: *"When you get to the end of your rope, tie a knot and hang on."*

Public Image: *On the surface Barbara is a very conservative straight arrow young woman. She seems very conventional, not terribly imaginative, the typical "good girl". She is a B student in school, but doesn't participate in many activities with the exception of choir where she sings soprano. She is very active in her church youth group and the 4-H club. Since her parents are farmers, she lives quite a way from the school, and she doesn't have many friends there. She is quiet and keeps to herself. Not too many people notice her.*

Hidden Truth: *Barbara has met a record producer at the local CD shop. He has offered to help her record a single. In order to do this she will have to skip school and take a bus to the city one day. She has been saving her lunch money in order to afford the ticket. She practices her song for hours a day. She has told no one except Loretta, the girl who sits next to her in choir. Loretta pretends not to believe her, but has secretly told several of her friends.*

Personal Conflicts: *Barbara hates lying to anyone, particularly her family and personnel at school. But she is convinced that they wouldn't let her go if she asked. She is getting more and more stressed as the deadline to record approaches.*

We see that Barbara is about to take a big, potentially dangerous step about which she is very conflicted. Does anyone notice her stress? Do they try to find out what it's about? Is she, perhaps, referred to the school counselor by a concerned teacher? Does she confide her plan to them? Do they tell her parents? What does this do to Barbara's trust in others?

You get the picture. Depending on how the other characters are written, many more potential plot developments may emerge.

Let the students write their bios at home or in class, whichever gives them the most time for thought and fits your schedule.

Presentation of Characters

Take one class period for students to present the information from their Character Information Forms to the class. The excitement will be palpable as the students hear the characters their classmates have devised. Your job will be to hold class discussion down while all characters are being presented.

After this process, plot twists and turns are bound to emerge! Obviously, many biographical details will not fit with the final plot, but the process of writing them has not only helped the individual students but the class as a whole. A picture is beginning to form.

● ● ● ● ● ● ● ● ● ●

Haven't You Been Clever?
The students have "performed" twice for the class: once in a group when they presented their group's scenario idea and once alone when they presented their bios. They're already getting used to the idea of performing before an audience. And the fact that this audience is warm and receptive makes the experience one they will want to duplicate.

● ● ● ● ● ● ● ● ● ●

The Group Plots — 2 Class Periods

You are now at the point of crafting the script! Collect all biographies. Choose volunteers for the Writing Crew. In my experience, three is optimum, but it is possible to work with up to five depending on the maturity level of the students. Since the writers now know who is going to be in this mystery, they can use details of these characters in the plot. It is very important to remember that it is more personal to the students if their characters directly contribute to the plot. No one wants to be just a cardboard character with no uniqueness. Sometimes, we have to change or modify characters, but it is important to use as many of the individual contributions as possible. And remember, much of the detail can remain hidden and not emerge until the questioning of suspects. Or it may be used as a red herring.

For example, perhaps Barbara is a central character in the play. She wants to audition for the record producer more than anything in the world and becomes enraged when she finds out that Loretta, the girl in choir she had confided in, has told the school counselor about the plan. Barbara is so angry that she runs away. Then, Loretta is found dead. Barbara is missing and the obvious suspect. But there may be many other characters that have similar motivations to kill this girl, as well. Perhaps Loretta was a well-known gossip. Perhaps she spread malicious rumors about students and staff.

This brings us to another essential. As soon as the plot is fleshed out and a victim decided upon, each actor must invent reasons, hidden or obvious, why their character had a motivation to dislike the victim or victims. We know, for example, that Barbara was irate at the betrayed confidence. Maybe Loretta had a boyfriend she was cheating on. Maybe she betrayed other even more serious confidences. Maybe she stole something from someone. Not all these motivations have to be stated in the script, but some need to be at least hinted at in order to make the murder motivated. Use the Murder Motives Worksheet on page 60. They may also be used as red herrings, or false clues.

It's About Time!

The "when" of your mystery doesn't have to refer to just the time of day or the season. Think of a historical mystery set in the Wild West or American Revolution. Why not find out what your students are studying in Social Studies and even partner with their Social Studies teacher for a mystery with authentic historical details?

Or how about a mystery set in the future on a distant planet? Let all the science fiction buffs wrap their minds around a future mystery. (Haul out the bubble wrap and aluminum foil!)

You may choose to set your mystery entirely in a different time or travel to that time.

The future is yours.

Plotting Your Murder

We have a lot of help from crime and dramatic literature as we go about our mystery writing. Just read or watch a mystery and you realize that, despite unique plot elements, there are basic rules. How good a mystery is depends on how well it works within the rules — written and unwritten — of crime fiction.

Thanks to Wikipedia, we bring you the following written by Ronald Knox in 1929: "[a detective story] must have as its main interest the unraveling of a mystery; a mystery whose elements are clearly presented to the reader at an early stage in the proceedings, and whose nature is such as to arouse curiosity, a curiosity which is gratified at the end." Knox also wrote the "Ten Commandments" of written crime fiction, which outlined his views on how mysteries should be written.

"Ten Commandments" of Crime Fiction by Ronald Knox

1. The criminal must be mentioned in the early part of the story, but must not be anyone whose thoughts the reader has been allowed to know.
2. All supernatural or preternatural agencies are ruled out as a matter of course.
3. Not more than one secret room or passage is allowable.
4. No hitherto undiscovered poisons may be used, nor any appliance which will need a long scientific explanation at the end.
5. No Chinaman must figure in the story.
6. No accident must ever help the detective, nor must he ever have an unaccountable intuition which proves to be right.
7. The detective himself must not commit the crime.
8. The detective is bound to declare any clues which he may discover.
9. The stupid friend of the detective, the Watson, must not conceal from the reader any thoughts which pass through his mind: his intelligence must be slightly, but very slightly, below that of the average reader.
10. Twin brothers, and doubles generally, must not appear unless we have been duly prepared for them.

Of course, there are many popular novels, plays, and films that break one or more of Knox's rules to great effect. (Where would the mystery world be without Earl Derr Biggers' Charlie Chan?) We offer them as a guide to get you thinking, not anything hard and fast, and must admit that we regularly ignore a commandment or two with every show.

Your mystery will need plotting. Let's take a brief look at plot elements for a play and how your mystery will use them:

Characters and Types

Crimes and Offenses

Means (weapons)

Motives

Red Herrings

Crime Scenes and Location of the Action

Atmosphere

As our plot begins with characterization, let's start there.

Characters and Types

Here's a list of characters and types that kids love to play. If they get stuck, encourage them to think about some of these.

Stereotypes at School
the academic
the airhead
the athlete
the bully
the cheerleader
the chess-clubber
the class clown
the debater
the foreign exchange student
the gangster from the hood
the goth
the hippie
the musician
the nerd
the new kid
the skater
the snob
the student government official
the theatre type
the tree hugger

Infamous People
Dr. Frankenstein/the Monster
Jack the Ripper
Jeffrey Dahmer
Son of Sam (David Berkowitz)

Pop Icons
50 Cent
Christina Aguilera
Contestants and Judges from "American Idol"
Kurt Cobain
Tom Cruise
Matt Damon
Johnny Depp
Characters from the TV Show "Friends"
Mel Gibson
Steve Irwin
Michael Jackson
Mick Jagger
Elton John
Angelina Jolie
Keira Knightley
Oprah Winfrey
Brad Pitt
Elvis Presley
Andy Roddick
Maria Sharapova
Britney Spears
Jerry Springer
Justin Timberlake
Prince William
Robin Williams
Tiger Woods

Stereotypes

the agoraphobe
the animal rights campaigner
the annoying little brother
the annoying little kid
the antique dealer
the artist
the aspiring novelist
the bag lady
the barrister
the boss/bossy one
the bum/hobo/beggar
the cable guy
the card reader
the cleaning woman
the computer tech
the construction worker
the country bumpkin
the country/city cousin
the cowboy
the crazed veteran
the crotchety old man
the cult member
the dentist
the ditzy blonde
the dog catcher
the earnest college student
the escaped convict
the escaped mental patient
the factory worker
the farmer
the FBI/CIA agent
the fitness trainer
the fix-it man
the flirt
the foreigner
the frantic parents
the gardener
the Girl Scout/Boy Scout
the good Samaritan
the goth
the gravedigger
the gypsy fortune teller
the hairdresser/manicurist

the head of the local community
   theatrical society
the henpecked husband
the high school guidance counselor
the hillbilly
the homeless guy on the corner
the hunting enthusiast
the juvenile delinquent
the kid-hating neighbor
the lifeguard at the pool
the local butcher
the local vet
the loved one
the mad doctor
the mad scientist
the maid/butler
the mailman
the man who only leaves his house
   at night
the military type
the minister
the museum curator
the musician
the mysterious new neighbor
the newspaper boy
the newspaper stand man
the night receptionist at the hotel
the nosy neighbor
the old lady who has dozens of cats
the old lady who likes cookies
the optometrist with the thick
   glasses
the pharmacist
the photographer for the local paper
the poet
the political activist
the pool shark
the president of the local
   political party
the president of the women's club
the priest/parson
the psychiatrist
the punk

the pushy stage manager
the recluse
the redneck
the redneck with a gun
the rich old lady with the big
   house up the hill
the school custodian
the shopkeeper
the ski bum
the soccer mom
the socialite
the spinster
the sports star
the state senator/representative
the stingy old man
the street busker
the surfer dude
the suspected witness protection
   program family
the sweet old lady
the tourists who don't speak English
the tram driver
the undertaker
the video game player
the vigilante
the visiting film producer
the waiter/waitress at the
   coffee shop
the witchy old lady
the woman who hears voices
the woman who wears too
   much makeup

About Stereotypes

Usually we encourage actors to create as unique and personalized characters as possible. Not so with mysteries. Mysteries abound with stereotypes — the more identifiable the better. You'll find some old friends on this page.

Crimes and Offenses

Often murder isn't the first crime committed in a mystery. Some mysteries don't even have murders, though including one is enticing. Why not have the "king of crimes" to solve? Here is a list of crimes that might get your group thinking. (Crimes or perceived crimes can often be a motive for another crime such as murder.)

Abduction
Arson
Assault
Bail jumping (failure to appear)
Bank robbery
Battery
Blackmail
Bomb threats
Bribery
Burglary
Carrying a concealed weapon
Credit card fraud
Defacing public property (graffiti)
Disappearance
Dognapping
Drive-by shooting
Driving while intoxicated
Drug abuse
Drug growing
Embezzlement
Extortion
Fencing (dealing in stolen goods)
Forgery
Fraud
Grand theft auto

Hit and run
Identity theft
Inhalant abuse
Intellectual property piracy
Kidnapping
Larceny
Money laundering
Mugging
Negligent use of firearms
Perjury
Plagiarism
Poaching
Possession of explosives
Receiving stolen property
Robbery
Running away
Shoplifting
Slander
Software piracy
Theft
Threatening phone calls
Vandalism
Violating curfew
Violation of probation
Writing bad checks

Means (Weapons)

What's a murder without a weapon? While finding a weapon is not essential to solving a murder, having a weapon (or more broadly, a means for committing the murder) is. This list of weapons might help get your plotters plotting.

Abandoned refrigerator
Acid
Anthrax or other biological poison
Arrow
Bandanna
Black widow or other poisonous spider
Blowtorch
Bomb
Brick
Carbon monoxide
Crowbar
Curare
Curtain cord
Electrical cord
Exploding staircase
Explosives
Fireworks
Fishing knife
Flashlight
Frozen mackerel
Frying pan
Glass shard
Gold paint
Hair dryer or radio in bathtub
Jump rope

Knitting needle
Laser pointer
Lawnmower
Leg of lamb
Machete
Man-eating plant
Microwave oven
Nail file
Piranha
Plastic explosives
Poison gas
Poisoned food
Poisoned medication
Poisoned projectile (dart, thorn)
Poisonous snake
Rope
Samurai sword
Saturday Night special
Scorpion
Shark
Statue
Swimming pool
Switchblade
Telephone cord
Wild animal

Something to Think About
    It's probably not a good idea to use a particularly gruesome murder technique or weapon. And using a weapon that has recently been used in an actual murder that has been in the news recently or a weapon similar to one in a current film or TV show just wouldn't be interesting.

Motives

The "why" of a crime is always important. Why would a person do that? All of your suspects should have good motives for the featured crime. Below is a list of motives to get you started:

Jealousy over:

boyfriends/girlfriends

clothes

college admission

contests/positions won (student government, Homecoming queen, etc.)

friends/social crowd

grades

looks

money

opportunities (getting a record contract, winning a part in the school play, etc.)

possessions

publicity/fame

social status

Revenge for:

an old murder/crime

getting invited somewhere another person didn't

gossip/negative publicity

reputation bashing

Stealing:

someone's heart

someone's test results

the test questions

Cheating:

at a beauty pageant

at a talent show

in a contest

on a friend

on a job interview

on a spouse/boyfriend/girlfriend

on a test

on the job

on your taxes

Lying about:

age

qualifications

feelings

abilities

preferences

name

social status

who you are

Other Motives:

a disagreement

being annoyed

being ignored

being in the wrong place at the wrong time

being taunted

blackmail

bullying

cutting in line (queue jumping)

divorce

honoring a promise

loitering

losing a contest

missed opportunities

not being left in the will

not getting hired

past cruelties/slights

plagiarism

protecting family

protecting reputation

protecting self

righting a wrong

seeing a crime being committed

suspicious behavior

Red Herrings

Literarily speaking, a red herring is a false clue designed to throw the reader off the track and to make it trickier to solve the mystery. Practically, it's lots of fun to devise these in order to make your mystery more convoluted and entertaining!

"Red herring" sounds fishy. Why do we call it that? Supposedly from a practice noted as early as the 15th century. Red herrings (cured by salting and smoking) were used to train scent hounds. The strong fish odor was easy for young dogs to follow. Later, as the dog's training got more sophisticated and they followed more subtle scents, the trainer would drag a red herring across the trail the dogs were supposed to be following. This often diverted inexperienced dogs. The wiser dogs learned to follow the original scent, even though a more obvious and easy to follow one was available.

Add a Twist!

Let the clues be so obvious that everyone assumes they're red herrings ... but they're not!

Now you see how it fits together. In mystery fiction, a red herring occurs when the actions of a particular character are highlighted in a way that throws suspicion on the character. Even though that character is innocent, the red herring draws attention away from the true culprit. (An event can also be a red herring.)

One thing to always remember about red herrings is that they always occur in context, so we cannot provide you with a handy list of specific red herrings. What we can do, though, is to give you a few examples.

You know how it is always the butler whodunit? Why's that? Well, he looks and acts suspiciously just by the nature of his position. He wears those funny uniforms and speaks in such an uppity accent, doesn't he? In order to make him even more suspicious why not add some significant pauses and rapid covering up of ... what?

Or how about adding some odd noises when least expected? Emphasize plot and character situations that seem really suspicious in order to distract from the real suspect. For example, if everyone has a motive for wanting the victim dead then there will be a fair bit of confusion.

Conversely, emphasize the real culprit so strongly that the audience is convinced that nothing could be *that* obvious! Tricked you!

Example:

A student sneaks into the classroom, furtively takes something small from the teacher's desk, carefully pockets it and sneaks back out.

What it looks like: A sneaky theft.

What it really is: The student has been regularly bullied in class. The teacher has seen the student at lunch and told him that his mother has called the school to remind him of a counseling appointment later that day. The appointment is to address his being bullied. The date and time are on the teacher's desk and the teacher OK'd the student going into the classroom to get the information. The student is very tentative about having to see a counselor and hopes that the class bully doesn't see him get the appointment info from the teacher's desk.

How it fits into the plot: The teacher's discipline report that was on her desk is missing. The bully has been killed. Everyone knows the bully has been tormenting the student. Someone saw the student's mysterious visit to the teacher's desk.

The Crime Scene and Location of the Action

Crime scenes and mystery locations come in two varieties: the classic spooky, mysterious, evocative place where something just has to happen, and the ordinary everyday locale where crime intrudes its ugly face. In either case, the scene is important and must work with your mystery. Let these get your group thinking:

airplane	faculty lounge	railway station
amusement park	fast food joint	recreation room
artist's studio	funeral parlor	reservoir
beauty parlor	grocery store	restaurant
cabin of a boat	gym	riding stable
cafeteria	hotel lobby	school classroom
candy shop	hotel room	set of a film shoot
coffee shop	ice cream shop	ski lift
concert hall	Internet café	soccer field
counselor's office waiting room	kitchen	subway car
deck of a boat	laundromat	swimming pool
dentist's office	lawyer's office	tennis court
deserted old house	moon	theatre auditorium
dining room	movie theatre	train
doctor's office	museum	video store
dog pound	park	
dorm room	pool hall	
drawing room	practice room	
dry cleaners	principal's office	

At the risk of sounding self-serving, you really should get a copy of *Improv Ideas* by Justine Jones and Mary Ann Kelley, published by Meriwether Publishing Ltd. In it, you'll find three pages of locations (including fantasy locations!) plus another full page of rooms in a house, a densely-packed page of crimes — real and imaginary, a page of murder weapons, and a page of motivations. And should your crime involve a secret, *Improv Ideas* even has a page of secrets.

Atmosphere

The location of your play is not the only thing to consider when working on setting. What time of day is it? What is the weather like? What would noir be without atmosphere?

afternoon	full moon	night
balmy	gale force winds	noon
blizzard	hail	overcast
breezy	hazy	partly cloudy
bright	heatwave	pea soup fog
brisk	high noon	pitch black
chilly	humid	rain
clear	hurricane	scattered showers
cloudless	ice storm	sleet
cloudy	late	small craft warnings
comet	lightly falling snow	squall
crisp	lightning	stormy
dark	lunar eclipse	sunny
dawn	meteor shower	sunrise
downpour	midnight	sunset
drizzle	misty	sweltering
drought	monsoon	thunder
dry	moonrise	tornado
dust storm	morning	total eclipse of the sun
early	muggy	tropical storm
flood	murky	windy
foggy	new moon	witching hour, the

What would "a dark and stormy night" be without "dark," "stormy," and "night?" What would *Little Shop of Horrors* be without a "total eclipse of the sun?"

Decide if you actually need to see the atmosphere you have chosen, or will mentioning or discussing it be enough? (Some directors and designers suggest if you show it, you don't have to talk about it, if you talk about it, you don't have to show it.) Don't let this keep you from buying a fog machine if you were already planning to, though — the kids love them.

Developing the Plot

There are two ways to develop the plot. The crime could have already been committed, and your script is recreating this crime through flashbacks. This is what most mystery parties do. Or you can create a structure in which a crime will be committed, and everyone involved in the play is a potential victim or murderer. I have always done the latter. This way you can keep the audience guessing until the last moment. Try to stay away from the obvious. Surprise them.

Choosing the Victim

Play with ideas that could lead to the murder of certain characters. For example, perhaps Loretta doesn't die, even though she seems an obvious victim. Maybe Barbara is found murdered. Why? What would anyone have against Barbara? Try several different characters as potential murder victims until one or two obvious choices emerge. Remember also that if you are doing the play more than once you will need to have a different victim and murderer each performance. Hence, the many motivations for the characters.

How It All Fits Together

Ask the class how they see their character fitting into the play. They've already given motives for killing three of the characters, now find out how they see themselves fitting into the play. Use the How I Fit In Worksheet on page 61. The class fills it out and the adult director can pass it on to the Writing Crew.

Choosing the Murderer

Now that the victim has been decided, who will be the murderer? They all have motivations to dislike each other especially the victim. This will sound strange, but *it really doesn't matter.* Yes, that's what I said and mean. As I said before, in the movie *Clue*, the clues led to three very different conclusions. They can do the same here and still be logical. Since the process of creating the play is the focus here, the murderer really is incidental.

Plot Development

Will you:

Start with the murder already done and spend the play in flashbacks and discovery?

Or:

Let the play build up to the murder allowing the audience to see relationships and motives build?

The choice is yours!

I never, ever, tell the cast who it is. The reason for this is that in the past, cast members have cheated and told audience members the identity of both victim and murderer. Since we like to make a game of this (complete with prizes), knowing the murderer has been counterproductive and led to much resentment. I usually whisper to the murderer right before the play starts. Of course, the chosen one has to have logical motivations for the crime, but these may emerge when the suspect is being interviewed.

Weeks Three and Four
Writing, Acting, and Technical

Writing

The adult director chooses the Writing Crew based on student interest, creativity during the previous weeks, theatrical aptitude, demonstrated work ethic, and ability to work with others (plus a certain gut instinct that we all develop).

The Writing Crew writes the script based on previous class work. See handouts and possible schedule on pages 70-72.

Job Description: Create the script for the play.
- Take no more than two weeks.
- Use all actors with the basic characters they have created.
- Use the basic plot devised by the class.
- Writers should not plan to perform in major roles in the final production.

Writing Goals for Week Three:
1. Work as a group to create a scenario for the entire play in one week, defining each scene with place, characters, and basic action that furthers the plot. Dialogue will come next week, but writers should note interesting phrases and conversations as they occur.
2. Meet with technical crews to coordinate crew activities with the needs of the play.
3. Present scenario to class on last day of week.

Need More Time?
You may expand all timelines as you need to. Just create a schedule and stick to it so everything gets done.

It's probably not a good idea to abbreviate your schedule for your first mystery.

Start with the following from the class
- Character bios with possible motives
- Basic theme
- Location
- Basic plot

Optional from the class
- Crime
- Title
- Weapon(s)
- Atmosphere

CHECK THIS OUT

Find scenarios for five actual middle school plays on pages 146-156.

Plot

Beginning

- Introduce situation: time, place(s) — offer ideas for the set and shift crews to make scenery and scene changes smooth and fast, weather/atmosphere — offer ideas for the sound effects crew.

- Introduce characters and their personalities and conflicts. Consider introducing characters in groups. (Families, friends, organizations that unify groups, etc.)

- Inciting Incident — Introduce problem(s)/conflict(s).

Middle

- Develop characters.

- Develop conflicts — Give enough conflicts for about one-fourth to one-third of the cast to be the victim. Give enough conflicts for about one-fourth to one-third of the cast to be the perpetrator.

- Develop clues, hints, and red herrings — For the purpose of this play, clues, hints, and red herrings are interchangeable as it will only become obvious whether they are real clues or red herrings when the murderer is found out. At least one clue per perpetrator is appropriate at this point.

- Crisis — Present the murder.

- Show reactions to the murder — All characters should be aware of the murder and have a reaction to it. Some of the reactions may serve as clues.

Ending That the Writers Are Responsible For:

- The detective (character representing the law) summarizes the situation and introduces the suspects.

The Real Ending of the Show:

- The audience interviews the suspects in rotation.

- The detective announces the perpetrator.

● ● ● ● ● ● ● ● ●

Important

The script will continue to change and grow in the rehearsal period. The Writing Crew *does not* have to turn in a "final product." It *should* produce a script that gives enough material to lead to a final product in the next few weeks.

● ● ● ● ● ● ● ●

Writing Goals for Week Four:

1. Create dialogue for the play.

2. Meet with technical crews to coordinate crew activities with the needs of the play.

3. Present scenario to the class on the last day of the week.

The Writing Crew usually takes two to three weeks of class time to finish a script. During this time, the rest of the class plays improv games to strengthen acting, character, and spontaneity skills, acquires prizes, plans and builds the set and props, finds costumes, selects music, etc. Let's start with acting.

Acting

The adult director works with all students on acting skills using improv games.

Improvisation games are important to the development and rehearsal of the play. In our books *Improv Ideas: A Book of Games and Lists* and *Drama Games and Improvs for the Classroom and Beyond,* we detail over 150 activities that can be used for the development of many different skills. For our purposes here, however, we have divided a few ideas for improv activities into three categories: games for developing the plot, games for developing the characters, and games for thinking quickly on your feet.

Naturally, we hope that your cast is familiar with basic improvisational skills, but here we include a few suggestions in each category that you may find helpful while writing, developing, and rehearsing your play.

Games for Developing Plot

Headline Prompts

- Collect quirky headlines from tabloids such as the *Enquirer* and the *Weekly World News.*

- Have small groups draw a headline and then improvise short three-to-five minute scenes based around this headline.

- Alternatively, you can use titles of urban legends such as "The Babysitter," "A Walk in the Graveyard," or "The Mexican Pet." It does not matter if the groups are at all familiar with the "real" story. The object is to develop a plot with a beginning, middle, and end. Hopefully, there will be some hint of a mystery and some suspense. For another Headline Game, see page 65.

Suspense

Ghost stories and urban legends are classic for developing suspense. In a way, they are similar to jokes in that they build up to a sort of punch line. In order to focus on including this essential component into your scripts, we suggest you gather together plots of some of the more well known urban legends. You can find urban legends and ghost stories in Jan Harold Brunvand's *Encyclopedia of Urban Legends* or Judy Dockrey Young's *The Scary Story Reader.* You will note that there are many similarities: vulnerable characters (children, teenagers, or the elderly) in peril in an isolated location (a country road or an abandoned old house). The threat is usually vague (strange noises, weird phone calls) and the suspense comes in trying to remain safe from these potential threats.

After the class has heard and examined a few of these, divide them into groups of four and have them develop original plot ideas that comprise some or all of these elements. These can then be presented to the class as stories or simply presented as plots.

Alternatively, you may want to present as improvised radio dramas (see *Drama Games and Improvs: Games for the Classroom and Beyond* pages 187-191).

31

CSI: Your Home Town

We detailed this in *Improv Ideas* (pages 134-137), but you may simply make your own lists of rooms, murder weapons, and imaginary crimes committed. Divide students into groups of four to six and have each group choose a weapon, room, and type of crime. An example might be a kidnapping in the pool with a rubber ducky. After these decisions are made, each group develops a scene about their crime. These scenes may show the crime being committed, the aftermath of the crime, or even the solving of the crime complete with detective!

Frozen Pictures

A good activity to follow "CSI" is the telling of the complete story of the crime in a series of five to ten frozen pictures. The emphasis here should be on the development of the plot through the beginning, middle, and end. It may be a good idea to discuss classic plot development here (setting, rising action, climax, and denouement); although, there are different structures that may also be used. Be creative! An example of a CSI plot might be as follows:

- Picture One: Children and parents are playing in and lounging by the pool.
- Picture Two: Someone jumps into the pool with a large inflatable rubber ducky.
- Picture Three: All the children gather around to see it.
- Picture Four: Play resumes.
- Picture Five: Children leave the pool, including the one with the inflatable ducky.
- Picture Six: The remaining children look around for a lost friend.
- Picture Seven: Alarmed, children get out of the pool, looking for the friend.
- Picture Eight: A policeman arrives and interviews people.
- Picture Nine: Someone points to the abandoned rubber ducky.
- Picture Ten: The lost child is found unconscious underneath the rubber ducky.

Games for Developing Characters

If I Were (Metaphor) Game

Have each cast member make a profile about their character using the following prompts: (see the worksheet on page 64)

What car would he/she be? Which model and year?

What color?

What drink?

What TV program?

What type of weather?

What kind of animal?

What historical time period?

What type of music/song?

For fun, read a few of these aloud to the class and have them try to guess which of the characters these might be (assuming they are familiar with the character and his/her role in the play).

Motivations

Make a list of common motivations a character might have. Some of the familiar ones might be to get approval, to discourage, to assert independence, etc. It is always good to try to make these specific to individual characters in the play. Stress that each character will have a couple (one or two) major motivators and several less overwhelming ones.

Write these on individual index cards. Have two students come forward and draw one motivation each. Give them a location or a situation or both, and then start a scene in which they play their motivations. Have the audience raise their hands when they think they have guessed the motivations *or* run the scene for one or two minutes and then have the group guess.

There's a list of motivations in *Improv Ideas* on page 131 and a ready to print and cut apart version of the list on the accompanying CD-ROM of that book.

Happy Hands

As a class, make lists of emotions (see the famous *How do you Feel Today?* chart, if you have it!) and parts of the body that can be used to express these emotions (hands, feet, head, etc., *not* heart, liver, or kidneys!) As in "Motivations," have two cast members draw one from each list and improvise a scene in which they each play the expression of their primary emotion.

You can find the *How Do You Feel Today?* chart at poster shops or educational supply houses. Or you can buy the posters online at How do you Feel Today? Productions http://www.howdoyoufeeltoday.com/.

Talk Show

Choose a host and three guests for a talk show based on a timely topic such as why punishment for crime should be tighter, why the drinking age should be lowered to sixteen, or another topic that might touch on the theme of the play. Each guest plays his or her character in the play and answers the host's questions and responds to other guests the way he or she thinks his or her character would. This should include not only attitudes towards the topic but also physical and vocal mannerisms.

Games for Thinking on Your Feet

Park Bench

- Place a bench in front of the room. Actor One sits on the far left side, not knowing his/her identity.
- Actor Two enters and establishes his/her identity and his/her relationship to Actor One. Examples include a famous singer and a star-struck fan, a runaway teen and the policeperson who finds them, or an angry customer and the owner of a store.
- As soon as the Actor One discovers who he/she is, they play a short scene.
- When the scene is over Actor One finds a motivation for exiting (the singer wants to avoid the fan, the teen decides to go home, and the store owner goes to get the refund!).
- The game restarts with Actor Two sitting on the bench and Actor Three entering.

Murder in the Dark

- The entire cast spreads out around the room, closing their eyes and moving slowly through the space.
- The director circulates and taps one person on the shoulder. This person will be the murderer.
- The murderer opens his/her eyes and circulates, eventually tapping a victim lightly on the head.
- The victim continues to move while counting to five. Then he/she screams and falls to the ground dead.
- The group gets three chances to guess the murderer's identity.

Tell Me About the Time You (TMATTY)

- The director makes a list of unusual situations such as "the time you broke your leg," "the time you met Brad Pitt," or "the time you were stranded in an airport during a tornado."
- One at a time cast members come to the front of the room and are given one minute to tell us about these harrowing and/or exciting moments. Each one-minute story has a beginning, middle, and a logical ending.
- Check out *Improv Ideas* (page 159) for fifty ideas for TMATTY.

Word Tennis

- Two cast members face off in a competition to see who can name the most items in a certain category quickly and accurately.

- If a player stumbles or answers incorrectly he must immediately sit down, and someone else takes his place. This may be played with two teams or as an entire cast. Categories might include colors, types of dogs, girls' names, countries in Europe, etc.

- Of course, *Improv Ideas* has a list of topics! See page 173 for over 100 topics.

Suspect Interview Questions

In addition to playing improv games to enhance characterization and quick thinking, the cast might also want to practice answering questions about the crime while in their characters. Below are some sample suspect interview questions they might want to answer, both as an innocent person and as the perpetrator. For a handout of these questions, see page 73.

1. How well did you know the victim?
2. In what capacity? For how long?
3. Who do you think had a reason to hate him/her?
4. Who do you think might have killed him/her?
5. Why?
6. Where were you when the murder happened?
7. What did you think of the victim?
8. Were you surprised when he/she was killed?
9. What purpose could this murder have served?
10. Did he/she deserve it? Why or why not?
11. How do you feel about the murder?
12. Why should we believe you?
13. Have you ever been violent?
14. Do you have a temper?
15. How do you feel conflicts should be resolved?
16. Have you ever been the victim of an injustice? What was it?
17. Is violence/murder ever justified?
18. Will you miss the victim?
19. What do you think should have been done to resolve the conflict?
20. Why do you think anyone would do such a thing?
21. How should the murderer be punished if he/she is caught? Why?
22. How do you think he/she can be identified?
23. Did you ever know there was a problem?

24. Do you have any reason to hate the victim?

25. Why do you suppose you might have been chosen as a suspect?

26. Have you ever been in legal trouble before?

27. How do you feel about being a suspect?

28. Tell us why you couldn't have done the murder.

29. Tell us why you would have no reason to hate the victim.

30. Tell us why you are here.

31. How do you usually respond in this kind of situation?

32. Are you impulsive?

33. Do you believe in "an eye for an eye?"

35. How do you feel about revenge?

35. Did the victim deserve what he/she got?

36. Are you a reasonable person?

37. Have you ever had a mental or emotional illness?

38. Do you take any medications?

39. How do you feel right now?

40. What do you value the most?

41. What really makes you angry?

42. What do you think of the other suspects?

43. How do you think _____ would describe you?

44. How would you describe yourself?

45. Is murder ever justified?

46. How could this conflict have been resolved nonviolently?

Technical

Who Does What in the Murder Mystery?

Week Three sees the class divided into the groups that will take care of all of the jobs that must be done to actually present the mystery. Except for the writers, class members are actors focusing on their "day jobs" as well as their creative jobs. This is the week when most of the show's technical work gets done. Students focus on acquiring prizes and organizing refreshments as well as helping with costumes, props, scenery, and electrics.

Your mantra for the next two weeks must be "Keep It Simple." (Or, if you want a memorable acronym, try KISS — Keep It Simple and Sensible.)

All of the thorny problems and convolutions should be in the plot, not the technical side.

Some students may be on more than one crew, as all groups will not meet at the same time. (Example: the Costume Crew will start meeting as soon as the characters have been written into the plot. They will meet with the writers and then work with the actors on acquiring costumes. As soon as all costumes are decided upon and arranged for, the people on the Costume Crew are freed to work on another crew such as Prize or Hospitality.)

Other students will work on the same project from the beginning of crew work until the close of the show. (The Electrics Crew will be focused on acquiring and recording sound effects from the very beginning and checking regularly with the writers to make sure they are all thinking along the same lines. Later, the same crew may create the lighting cues and acquire any lighting instruments they can for the show. Very likely, this small but active crew will run all lighting and sound cues and most will not be able to perform.)

Crew Selection — A Suggested List of Crews

- Writers/Assistant Directors
- Prize
- Publicity
- Ticket
- Program
- Scenery
- Electrics: Lighting, Sound, and Special Effects
- Prop
- Hospitality

Discuss Crews

Discuss what each crew is responsible for, their working time frame, due dates, and whether they will also be able to perform. You'll find a list of crew duties and possible timelines for all of the crews here. Handouts for crews are in the Resources section. Distribute after class makes crew choices.

Prize Crew

(see handouts and possible schedule on pages 74-79)

Job Description: Acquire the prizes to be awarded to the audience members who correctly deduce/guess the perpetrator.

- Decide (with the director's guidance) how many prizes will be awarded.
- List potential donors for those prizes.
- Take no more than three weeks to line up all prizes.
- Give everyone in the class at least one prize acquisition assignment and follow up with the students.
- Conduct role-playing exercises with the class until everyone is comfortable.
- Record prize commitments as they come in.

● ● ● ● ● ● ● ●

Prize Crew

The people who bring that extra fun and excitement to the show!

● ● ● ● ● ● ● ●

Choosing the Prize Crew

It's probably a good idea for the director to organize the core Prize Crew. They are the ones responsible for organizing the prize search and assigning the class members to their solicitations. They need to brainstorm potential prize sources and how to tactfully approach those sources. Prize Crew members should be friendly, outgoing, and articulate. They should be aware of the businesses in the area and, preferably, personally and favorably known to the merchants they will approach for donations.

The Prize Crew should also be aware of potential prize sources represented by the families and acquaintances in the class.

Training and role-playing go into preparing to ask for donations, how to graciously accept donations, and how to gracefully accept rejection.

Acquiring Prizes

Your budget allowing, small prizes may be purchased from your local dollar store or companies such as Geddes, Smiles, and Oriental Trading Company, thus assuring that each person who deduces the correct perpetrator gets something. However, this is not necessary for the event to be fun. Don't lose track of the purpose of this project, either: it's a fundraiser!

Everyone should make at least one prize request. See the Sample Prize Interview (on page 74) that can help students role-play before they actually approach potential donors. Everyone in the class should participate. Look on this as a very practical experience in speech as well as a way to enhance your show with prizes.

Prize Ideas

(We had all of these from our community of 18,000) —

Banks: savings bond

Book shop: book or DVD

CD shop: gift certificate

Cinema: free ticket to a film

Comic shops: comics, action hero toy

Department store: cosmetics, socks

Doughnut shop: a dozen doughnuts

Flower shop: flower arrangement or vase

Gym: free one week membership

Ice cream shop: one ice cream scoop

Local artists: scarves, caps, pots, painting, ceramics

Parents: baked goodies

Pizza parlor: large pizza

Restaurants: two-for-one meal

Salon: makeover or manicure

Sports shop: soccer ball

Supermarket: gift certificate

Toy shop: teddy bears or other toys

The idea is to be bold and ask — a trait some of us have in greater measure than others. While we're on a roll, why not try your local:

Auto parts store: accessory such as first aid kit or steering wheel cover (fuzzy dice, anyone?)

Cable TV outlet: free month of cable

Candy store: candy

Convenience store/service station: snacks, drinks, or gas

Dance studio: free session/short course

Deli: item, lunch

Dentist: free toothbrush

Dollar store: item

Garage: oil change

Theatre (community or professional): ticket

Don't forget BOGOs — the ever popular buy-one-get-one. Often donors are delighted to arrange a BOGO when an outright donation might be less attractive.

You'll find a Self Evaluation for Prize Solicitation Form on page 78 should you want to keep track of the assignment.

Publicity Crew

(see handouts and possible schedule on pages 80-82)

Job Description: Plan, design, and write all publicity. Print and distribute posters and flyers. Arrange for print, broadcast, and online publicity.

- Design graphics for the show. (*Optional:* hold a class-wide contest for the best graphics.) If you started a poster contest when you selected your theme, now is the time to announce the winner. (Student vote? Director's choice?)
- Plan publicity campaign to appeal to target audience but include the public at large.
- Create posters and flyers that contain all pertinent information about the play.
- Write school announcements, press releases, and radio announcements as appropriate.
- Distribute posters and flyers.

Publicity Includes:

Who: The Name of Your Group

What: Title of Show — An Interactive Mystery

When: Days, Dates, and Times

Where: Your Venue

Ticket Information: How Much, Where to Purchase

Publicity Hint:

In addition to posters and flyers posted in assigned places, give a flyer to each participant as a souvenir. Also, give posters to all parents who work outside the home to post in their workplaces.

Ticket Crew

(see handouts and possible schedule on pages 84-87)

Job Description: Plan, design, print, and sell tickets for the show. Manage all checked out tickets and incoming monies.

- Design and print (or order) tickets for the show.
- Number tickets if they are not already numbered. This helps keep track of ticket sales.
- Check tickets out to class to sell. Keep track of tickets checked out.
- Count, report, and deposit money for tickets with director/adult in charge.
- Manage any ticket sales contests the class decides on.
- Be available to sell any tickets at the door that have not been pre-sold.

Think about adult help. Keeping track of money might be a way to use parent volunteers. Students should get into the habit of turning in money and ticket stubs at the beginning of each class period.

Program Crew

(see handouts and possible schedule on pages 88-89)

Job Description: Plan, design, and print the programs for the show.

- Use show graphics as a basis for the program.
- Work with directors and crew heads to create complete cast and crew lists with correct spelling and identification.
- Recognize all prize donors.
- Provide a sample program for everyone to proofread one week before program goes to printing.
- Print and fold programs and have them ready to hand out to patrons.

Programs can be simple or complex. See page 144 for a sample one-sheet program for *The Maui Murders.*

Scenery Crew

(see handouts and possible schedule on pages 94-98)

Job Description: Design, build, paint, and move the scenery for the play.

- Work with the writers to design/plan scenery that serves and enhances the plot.
- Use scene breakdown to plan scenery for each scene.
- Acquire and build scenery.
- Paint scenery.
- Move the scenery as needed during the play.
- Strike (remove) scenery from performance area at end of show.
- Take scenery apart, discard, salvage, and store appropriately.

Costume Crew

(see handouts and possible schedule on pages 99-102)

Job Description: Coordinate, acquire, and manage costumes for the play.

Important: Actors should use their own clothing or acquire their own costumes whenever possible.

- Work with the actors to determine what their characters would wear.
- With actor's help, create a costume sheet for each character.
- Create a master costume plot for the production.
- Provide storage and costume racks for all costumes and accessories for rehearsal and performances.

Costume Hints

1. Chairs make excellent costume "racks" during the show. A chair backstage for each actor is quite a practical solution to costume management.

2. Discourage actors from bringing in any costume pieces that are valuable or cannot be replaced.

Electrics Crew: Lighting

(Note: Handouts and possible schedule for all parts of the Electrics Crew are available on pages 103-107)

Job Description: Coordinate, design, and operate the lighting cues and effects for the play.

- Work with the writers to design/plan lighting that serves and enhances the plot.
- Assure appropriate lighting for audience safety.
- Use the Scene Breakdown to plan lighting for each scene.
- Acquire, connect, and control all lighting elements.
- Using the script, create a master lighting plot for the production.
- Run the lighting for the play.
- Strike (remove) lighting from performance area at end of show.
- Store equipment appropriately.

Lighting can be as simple as room lights on, room lights off. Don't let things get so complicated you lose track of the purpose of the show.

Electrics Crew: Sound

Job Description: Coordinate, acquire, record, and play back sound effects and background music for the play.

- Work with the writers to choose sound that enhances the production.
- Provide appropriate music for before the show, intermission, and after the show.
- Using the script, create a master sound plot for the production.
- Instruct MCs in the use of microphones.
- Run the sound for the play.
- Strike (remove) sound equipment from performance area at end of show.
- Store equipment appropriately.

Sound Ideas

It's no secret that sound design is a growing theatrical industry. Digital sound makes a lot of things possible. You can get sound effects on CD or online. And it can take as much time as you want to give it. Know your priorities and stick with them. A brief musical cue with which to open scenes with is often enough.

Don't forget the possibility of *live sound!* Crew members can create sound effects in real time. Watch *Prairie Home Companion* or *Radioland Murders* for inspiration.

Electrics Crew: Special Effects (FX)

Job Description: Coordinate, acquire, and operate any special effects for the show.

- Work with the writers to choose effects that enhance the production.
- Using the script, create a master effects plot for the production.
- Assure that any desired effects are legal and operated safely.
- Run the effects for the play.
- Strike (remove) effects equipment from performance area at end of show.
- Store equipment appropriately.

Special effects are so much fun, and it's easy to get carried away. Remember: **KISS.** The show is about plot and acting.

Prop Crew

(see handouts and possible schedule on pages 90-93)

Job Description: Coordinate, acquire, and manage props for the play.

- Using the script, create a master prop plot for the production.
- Involve the class in acquiring the props. Label props with owner names.
- Build props that are not in stock or cannot be borrowed.
- Provide secure storage of props when they are not in use.
- Require all actors to be responsible for setting up and storing their own props.
- Create prop tables at each entrance. On butcher paper covering the table, mark space for each prop that should be there and the actor responsible.
- Work with actors to strike (remove) props from performance area at end of show.
- Return props to owners immediately after final performance.

Hospitality Crew

(see handouts and possible schedule on pages 110-114)

Job Description: Coordinate all personnel, equipment, supplies, and refreshments needed for a positive audience experience.

- Post sign-ups for refreshments.
- Follow up to ensure refreshments will be at the performance space when needed.
- Acquire refreshment supplies including plates, napkins, flatware, cups, and tablecloths.
- Arrange for ice, coffee pots, hot plates, Crock-Pots, platters, and serving pieces for the performances.
- Acquire pencils and pads of paper for the audience members to record their clues and questions.

- Ensure cleanliness and appropriate temperatures of performance space.
- Provide change and a cash box if any tickets will be sold at the door.
- Provide ticket sellers if tickets will be sold at the door.
- Provide ushers to take tickets, hand out programs, and seat audience members.
- Provide staff to serve refreshments.
- Provide a clean-up crew for performance space for both before and after performances.

Don't Forget Parents!

Enthusiasm for the murder mystery in the classroom often communicates to participants' families. Parents and even siblings often volunteer for jobs. It's a good idea to have a little list of things that need to be done with a note on how complicated or responsible those jobs are. The super-mom who could effortlessly organize the physical shift of the school to the next block can be counted on to organize all your desserts. (She probably knows most of the other mothers, too.) The handy dad who has a garage full of tools might be just the person to hinge together those flats you need for a background. *Don't be proud — Ask for and accept help.*

Weeks Five and Six
Reading and Rehearsal in Ten Days

Goal:

1. The Writing Crew presents its work on the script. Everyone understands that the script is a work in progress.

2. The actors read the script completely as written in the characters they have chosen or been assigned.

3. Actors make notes during the reading.

4. The class discusses the script.

5. With the leadership of the adult director, the group entertains appropriate script change ideas and adopts the ones that benefit the show.

6. Rehearsals. In the first week of rehearsals, the script is still a living document with reasonable changes possible.

7. Actors not working on a rehearsed scene memorize lines or work quietly with their crews.

8. The script is set before the last week of rehearsal begins. The cast will rehearse the script as finalized at this point. This gives everyone an opportunity to learn the show.

9. Dress rehearsals take place with all available costumes, props, lighting, and scenery. Technical changes may occur during this time if they can be seamlessly integrated into the rehearsals.

10. During the final three days, the entire cast interviews all characters as potential suspects.

11. The class chooses final suspects and rehearses the play with those suspects in mind.

12. The class moves all elements of the show to the final performance space and sets up all scenery, props, sound, quick change booths, etc.

| | Week Five | | | | | Week Six | | | | |
Goal	Day 1	Day 2	Day 3	Day 4	Day 5	Day 1	Day 2	Day 3	Day 4	Day 5
1	▓									
2	▓	▓								
3	▓	▓								
4		▓	▓							
5		▓	▓							
6		▓	▓	▓	▓					
7			▓	▓	▓	▓	▓			
8					▓	▓				
9						▓	▓	▓	▓	▓
10								▓	▓	▓
11									▓	▓
12										▓

The Day of the Event Checklist

1. Collect desserts supplied by students or parents
2. Set tables
   a. cover with paper
   b. plates
   c. napkins
   d. flatware
   e. pencils/writing utensils
   f. paper
   g. programs
   h. cups
3. Set up technical
   a. scenery
   b. backstage
4. Bring in and place props and costumes
5. Set up dessert table
6. Set up sound system
7. Set up lights
8. Rehearse
9. Choose suspects/rehearse
10. Choose murderer/inform

Final Rehearsals and Performances

(Note: Find detailed schedules for Weeks Five and Six and the day of the show on pages 116, 118, and 119)

Interviewing the Suspects

Now we get to a very important component of the experience: the interviewing of suspects. I always choose as many suspects as I have audience member tables. This is why I need to sell tickets in advance and have a fairly reliable head count. So, during the final scene of the play, the agent or detective "chooses" the suspects from the cast. These, of course, have been predetermined so that these cast members are familiar with the backup stories for the questioning.

As the suspects are revealed, they form a line of seemingly-bewildered characters. They are then told to go to tables where they will be interviewed. Audience members have been prepped by the detective/cop/agent to ask specific questions, not ones like: "Did you do it?" or "How old are you?"

Sample questions might be:

Did you have any reason to dislike the victim?

How long had you known him? In what context?

What did you think of her?

Who do you think might have had a reason to kill him? Why?

Where were you when the body was discovered?

You never know what questions will pop up, and this is why the suspects need to be experienced at fielding these questions. They need to appear to be answering honestly and thoroughly. They need to have a complete backup story. Basically, all of them should play equally innocent and guilty. The use of improvisational rehearsals can make suspects convincing.

Remember that each suspect knows if he/she is the guilty one, *but no one else does!* Also remember that, in this case, the fun is in the interviewing and the guesswork. Getting it "right" is really not that important (unless you're overly eager to win a prize) as any one of the suspects could just as easily be guilty.

After the Interviews, the Moment of Truth, Prizes, and More Food

1. After all the suspects have been interviewed at all the tables, the audience guesses the perpetrator by voting on the ballots provided. They write their deductions (guesses) and their own names on the paper provided.

2. The cast goes through the audience collecting the guesses in hats and delivers them backstage to the sorting crew.

3. The director discloses the perpetrator's name to the Prize Crew.

4. While the crew checks the guesses, the audience members may help themselves to refreshments. The count usually takes no more than five minutes as the backstage crew rapidly puts the correct guesses into a hat.

5. The Prize Crew puts the correct guesses into a hat for the prize drawing.

6. The moment of truth arrives. All suspects are lined up and the detective reveals *whodunit!* After the perpetrator is subdued, he/she is asked why he/she did it. The actor should have a convincing statement which they present to all before being removed in handcuffs. Some actors like to make this very dramatic by not going easily. They scream out: *"He deserved it!"* or *"I'll get my revenge on you all!"* or *"I will return!"* as he/she is being led away. It's a great tension reliever!

7. Draw names. The names of those who guessed correctly and whose names have been drawn (you arrange to draw the number of names corresponding to the number of prizes you have) are read and prizes awarded. They may be anything from a plate of cookies to donated gift certificates from local businesses.

8. After all is done, the murder victim, perpetrator, and the rest of the cast take a bow.

9. Sometimes cast and crew prepare a final dance number just for fun.

Logistics

An audience member, school principal, or other impartial guest is chosen to draw from winning names (if there are more winners than prizes) from the hat. The MC (the detective?) announces the prize winner(s) until all prizes are given away.

The person who announces the prize may be a cast member, the detective, the MC, the director, or even the person who obtained the prize or the donor. That person announces the prize for the selected winner.

If there are more prizes than winners, there is a general drawing until all prizes are given away. This is important, as the donors deserve to have their prizes announced at the performance for which they donated!

Final Notes

The entire process can take from one to two hours. I prefer the large more developed scripts, but it depends on how much time you have for rehearsal. Since it is very difficult for me to get rehearsals after school, we rehearse everything in class. This, of course, places time restrictions on scripts. Basically, it's all up to you!

The Follow-Up Thank You Notes

The person who arranged for the borrowed item, service, or prize should be the one to write the formal thank you note after the show. Remind students that the best thank you notes do not start with "thank you." Notepaper with the show logo is a nice touch.

Everyone who did anything for the show should be formally thanked with a nicely written note as well as given program credit.

Note recipients include:

Adult helpers	Prize donors
Prop donors	Costume donors
Scenery donors and helpers	Sound donors and helpers
Lighting donors and helpers	Printing helpers
School office staff	Ticket outlets

Resources

This section contains the practical help you'll need
to create your own mystery. You'll find:

√ Ideas and assessment for each week

√ Rubrics to hand out or post

√ All the handouts promised/mentioned earlier

Week One Materials

Ideas and Assessment for Week One

Room Configuration

Class seating in a large "U" will facilitate watching the film and discussing activities. Small groups may go to the open end of the "U" for their presentations to the group.

Atmosphere

The atmosphere should be one of respect of others' ideas and a sense of adventure. Before each lesson discuss the day's activities and expectations.

Equipment and Materials

_____ Large screen TV or projection capabilities

_____ Videotape or DVD player

_____ Videotape or DVD of *Clue*

_____ Chalkboard and chalk or whiteboard and markers (An alternative would be an overhead projector, film, and markers.)

_____ Roll sheet for assessment

_____ Writing materials for director to take notes

_____ Handouts: Small Group Presentation — Play Theme

_____ Pencils provided by students

Assessment

(For more structured evaluations use: *Audience Expectations* and *Week One Expectations* guidelines.)

Evaluations should be casual enough to encourage students to go out of their comfort zone and participate in class activities. Use a copy of your roll sheet and the plus, check, minus (+ √ –) notation to evaluate students this week.

Watching Film:

• Actively watching film without distracting others

• Participating in class discussion of film

Brainstorming Themes:

• Volunteering own ideas

• Accepting others' ideas

Selecting Play Topic:

• Articulately discussing pros and cons of ideas before the group

• Graciously accepting group decisions on possible topics

• Contributing to small group's presentation ideas (handout)

51

Week One Expectations

Activity	Goal	Mastering	Contributing	Learning	Is not yet engaged
Brainstorm Class Mystery	Brainstorms basic ideas about own mystery play: character, motives, means, plot, timing, red herrings, clues, title, etc.	Offers ideas for more than one theme, either generating ideas or enhancing others'.	Offers a plot idea or enhances someone else's idea.	Enhances at least one plot idea by someone else.	Does not contribute.
	Accepts ideas from others without judgment or discussion.	Accepts all ideas.	Accepts most ideas.	Accepts some ideas. Wants to discuss ideas.	Does not accept ideas of others without judgment or discussion.
Speak Up	Presents a mystery theme to class.	Presents a basic mystery idea to the class.	Listens to all presentations with attention and courtesy.	Listens to all presentations.	Does not present any ideas or listen to ideas of others.
Group Presentations	Contributes ideas to group effort and adds to the ideas of others.	Contributes ideas to group effort *or* adds to the ideas of others.	Contributes an idea to group theme.	Contributes minimally to group presentation.	Does not present or add to ideas.
	Works in a group to flesh out brainstormed ideas with possible setting, characters, events, etc. These are both original offerings and embellishments on earlier ideas.	Works in a group to flesh out brainstormed ideas with possible setting, characters, events, etc. These are only embellishments on earlier ideas.	Works with the group in examining most of the ideas for plot.	May urge own idea being given preference.	Does not participate in group process. Does not contribute or only interested in own idea.
	Presents group's plot ideas to class (singly or in small group).	Presents ideas in an enthusiastic and organized manner.	Helps group devise an organized and enthusiastic presentation.	Contributes minimally to group presentation.	Does not participate in presentation.
Vote	Votes for favorite idea.				Does not vote.

Audience Expectations for Week One

A Good Audience Member	Level					
	Mastering	**Contributing**	**Learning**	**Not Yet Engaged**	**Unfocused**	**Detriment**
Receives Participates in the performances of others by watching with empathetic and appropriate behavior.	Obviously engaged with the performance.	Is focused on the performance.	Watches quietly.	Does not watch and/or is not quiet.	Distracts others during the performance or critique.	Intentionally distracts others during the performance or critique.
Understands Shows a willing suspension of disbelief, understands and accepts the work as performed.	Actively understands, accepts, and responds to the premise of the work and the individual and group performances.	Accepts and responds to the premise of the work and the group performance.	Passively accepts the premise of the performance.	Does not seem to understand what the performance is about and rejects suspending disbelief.		
Responds Responds appropriately to individual and group performances and technical efforts throughout the presentation.	Responds appropriately to all parts of the performance.	Responds and applauds appropriately to various performance elements.	Applauds appropriately at the end of the performance.	Responds inappropriately or not at all to the performance.		
Critiques Evaluates performances knowledgeably, compassionately communicates that evaluation.	Bases critique on the perceived intent of the performance, theatrical standards, and similar performances. Communicates critique with sensitivity.	Bases critique on the accepted theatrical standards and similar performances. Communicates critique appropriately.	Bases critique on own opinions. Communicates critique appropriately.	If critiques, bases critique on undefined standards.	If critiques, does not consider the feelings of the performers.	Critique intentionally hurts the feelings of the performers.

Small Group Presentation — Play Theme

The people in our group are: _____
_____
_____

Theme: _____

Working Title: _____

This idea should be considered because (please include your group's thoughts on uniqueness of plot, actor appeal, and audience appeal): _____
_____
_____
_____
_____
_____
_____
_____
_____

Technical Considerations

Location/Set (include ideas for scenery and effort of construction and shifting): _____
_____
_____
_____
_____

Sound and Lighting Requirements: _____
_____
_____

Costumes: _____
_____
_____

Week Two Materials

Ideas and Assessment for Week Two

Room Configuration

Keep the classroom set up in the "U" shape of Week One. It will facilitate the group sessions and chairs can be moved easily for the small group work.

Atmosphere

Now things are happening! Excitement and enthusiasm may cause some to interrupt others or in other ways appear rude. Emphasize listening to others when ideas are being shared. Before each lesson, discuss the day's activities and expectations.

Equipment and Materials

_____ Chalkboard and chalk or whiteboard and markers (An alternative would be an overhead projector, film, and markers.)

_____ Roll sheet for assessment

_____ Handouts: Character Information Forms and Murder Motive forms

_____ Pencils provided by students

Assessment

Continue casual evaluations with roll sheets. Use a roll sheet plus, check, minus (+ √ –) notation.

Stress listening skills and everyone's ideas should be heard and respected.

Character Name Discussion: Volunteer own ideas. Accept others' ideas.

Character Bio Form: Filled out completely and legibly. Extra credit for unique ideas on the second page.

Victim Discussion: Respectfully listen to others' ideas. Volunteer own ideas. Graciously accept group decisions on possible victims. Listening carefully will help students decide their own motivations to kill the victim (necessary for Murder Motive assignment).

Character Motivations: Offers at least three motivations for own character to be the murderer. Written legibly and articulately.

Week Two Expectations

Activity	Goal	Mastering	Contributing	Learning	Is not yet engaged
Brainstorm	Offer plot elements that enhances the class's theme. (Does not have to be used.)	Obviously engaged in discussion.	Engaged in discussion.	Mostly engaged in discussion.	Offers no plot elements or discussion.
	Accepts ideas from others without judgment or discussion.	Accepts all ideas.	Accepts most ideas.	Accepts some ideas. Wants to discuss ideas.	Does not accept ideas of others without judgment or discussion.
Small Group Scenario	Work in a group to create a scenario based on the class's theme. Develop setting, characters, events, etc.	Works within the group, offering several ideas that develop the scenario	Works within the group to offer an idea that develops the scenario.	May urge own idea being given preference.	Does not participate in group process. Does not contribute or only interested in own idea.
	Accepts ideas from others without judgment or discussion.	Accepts all ideas.	Accepts most ideas.	Accepts some ideas, wants to discuss ideas.	Does not accept ideas of others without judgment or discussion.
	Submitted on time.	Turned in on due date.	Turned in on due date.	Turned in late.	Not turned in.
	Presented to the class.	Projects enthusiasm for and understanding of scenario. Speaks loudly and distinctly. Voice is well modulated. Presentation is well paced.	Projects enthusiasm for and understanding of scenario. Speaks loudly and distinctly. Pace may be hesitant.	Projects enthusiasm for scenario. Speaks loudly and distinctly.	Makes presentation reluctantly. May not be audible to all listeners. Shows little understanding of scenario.
Character Biography Side 1	Chooses name for own character that allows for maximum engagement with scenario.	Thoughtfully chooses a name showing foresight as to how that character might fit into plot.	Deliberates before choosing a name for own character.	Chooses a character name that has potential for working in the scenario.	Chooses a name with no evident thought or foresight.
	Chooses background (educational and family) for own character that allows for maximum engagement with scenario.	Chooses a background showing foresight as to how that character might fit into plot.	Deliberates before choosing a background for own character.	Chooses a character background that has potential for working in the scenario.	Chooses a background with no evident thought or foresight.
	Chooses a present (vocation/projected vocation, hobbies, likes, and dislikes) for own character that allows for maximum engagement with scenario.	Chooses a realistic present showing foresight as to how that character might fit into plot.	Deliberates before choosing a realistic present for own character.	Chooses a character present that has potential for working in the scenario.	Chooses a present with no evident thought or foresight or that is unrealistic.
	Chooses a quote that distills facets of own character.	Chooses a quote for character, having looked at many possibilities.	Deliberates before choosing a quote for own character.	Chooses a quote that may reflect character.	Chooses a quote with no evident thought or foresight or that has nothing to do with the character.

Week Two Expectations, continued

Activity	Goal	Mastering	Contributing	Learning	Is not yet engaged
Character Biography Side 2	Thoughtfully creates a public image for character.	Has at least three public perceptions with complete illustrative narrative.	Has at least two public perceptions with narrative. Some narrative may be brief.	Has at least one public perception, narrative may be brief.	Has one public perception, narrative may be vague or incompletely presented.
	Presents a hidden truth for character that is interesting and believable.	Provides at least three details that make the truth compelling and interesting.	Provides at least two details that make the truth interesting.	Provides at least one detail that makes the truth interesting.	Has one detail that does not further the characterization.
	Chooses a personal conflict that reflects both the public image and the hidden truth.	Provides at least three details that lead to suspense and makes an early resolution desirable.	Provides at least two details that lead to suspense and make an early resolution desirable.	Provides at least one detail that makes an early resolution desirable.	Provides at least one detail.
Presents Character to Class	Uses recognized speaking skills for presentation.	Speaks loudly and distinctly. Presentation is well paced. Voice projects enthusiasm for and understanding of character.	Speaks loudly and distinctly. Presentation is well paced.	Speaks loudly and distinctly.	Makes presentation reluctantly. May not be audible to all listeners. Shows little understanding of character.
	Presentation follows organizational and time guidelines.	Is well organized and focused. Does not deviate more than 15 seconds from recommended time.	Is well organized and does not deviate more than 20 seconds from recommended time.	Deviates 30 seconds or more from recommended time.	Is incomplete and too short or rambling, unfocused, and too long.

Actor/Playwright Expectations for Week Two

A Good Actor/ Playwright	Level					
	Mastering	Contributing	Learning	Not Yet Engaged	Unfocused	Detriment
Contributes Makes informed contributions to plot and characters that enhance the play.	Offers varied, informed, and creative plot and character suggestions based on the prompt.	Offers creative plot and character suggestions based on the prompt.	Offers some ideas for character or plot. Ideas may be poorly developed or not completely relevant.	Does not offer suggestions	Suggestions off topic and show no understanding of activity.	Belittles the work of others.
Participates Actively works for the benefit of the play and the group.	Enthusiastically joins the group process. Bases performance on own ideas or those of others as best serves the work. Leads or follows others as appropriate.	Focused on the process. Evidently enjoys the experience.	Tacitly goes along with the group's wishes.	Must be continually prompted and encouraged or does not participate at all.	Is only concerned about own ideas and role in the play.	Intentionally makes group work difficult.
Evaluates Evaluates own groups' performances knowledgeably and communicates evaluation with sensitivity.	Bases critique on the perceived intent of the performance, theatrical standards, and similar performances. Communicates critique with sensitivity.	Bases critique on the accepted theatrical standards and similar performances. Communicates critique appropriately.	Bases critique on own opinions. Communicates critique appropriately.	Critiques — if at all — are based on undefined standards.	Critique does not consider the feelings of the performers.	Critique intentionally hurts the feelings of the performers.
Understands Shows a willing suspension of disbelief, understands the purpose of the work.	Actively understands, accepts, and responds to the premise of the work and the individual and group performances.	Accepts and responds to the premise of the work and the group performance.	Passively accepts the premise of the performance.	Shows no evidence of understanding what the performance is about.	Rejects suspending disbelief.	Belittles the exercise.

58

Name _____

Character Information

Character Name: _____

Age:_____ Gender:_____ Race/Ethnicity:_____

Educational Background: _____

_____

Family Background: _____

_____

Vocation/Projected Vocation: _____

_____

Hobbies:_____

_____

Likes/Dislikes: _____

_____

Favorite Quote: _____

_____

_____

Your Public Image: _____

_____

_____

The Hidden Truth:_____

_____

_____

Personal Conflicts: _____

_____

_____

Name _____

Murder Motives

My Character's Name: _____

    Using information from your own character biography and the character biographies of others, please list three characters your character could be motivated to murder. Include the reasons for your selections based on at least one of your own character's traits and at least one trait for the potential victim. You may use a situation of your own invention to precipitate the murder.

Motive 1: My character could kill _____ played by_____

because (about them) _____

_____

_____

_____

and (about me) _____

_____

_____

Motive 2: My character could kill_____ played by _____

because (about them) _____

_____

_____

_____

and (about me) _____

_____

_____

Motive 3: My character could kill _____ played by_____

because (about them) _____

_____

_____

_____

and (about me) _____

_____

_____

Name _____

How I Fit In

Character Name: _____

Costume

I can see my character wearing_____

_____

_____

_____

_____

_____

I can provide the following costuming for my character: _____

_____

_____

_____

_____

Crews
In addition to acting, I would like to be on the following crew(s): (List up to three in order of preference.)

_____

_____

_____

_____

_____

Weeks Three and Four Materials

Ideas and Assessment for Weeks Three and Four

Room Configuration

These weeks are for crew work and playing games. A central callboard will add a practical and professional touch. Each crew should have a "home base" where they can post their own jobs and schedules, too. Cubbies or mailboxes for each crew in a central area are a plus (that helps the directors and crews communicate among each other). If crew work takes place on the outside edges of the classroom, then by simply turning chairs around, a game/performance space magically appears. Toward the end of Week Four, a rehearsal space exactly like the performance space should be taped onto the floor.

Atmosphere

During the opening class business, outline what will happen on that day. The atmosphere should be one of energy and accomplishment. Weeks Three and Four are the weeks that writers and crews will get most of their preparation done. It's also a time of drama games, improvisation, and fun. Focus, cooperation, respect, and patience should be the bywords.

Equipment and Materials

_____ Overhead projector/screen and transparencies of crew duties and schedule (nice but not necessary)

_____ Roll sheet for assessment

_____ Handouts: Crew duties/schedules to those who have chosen that crew

_____ Writing implements and paper provided by students

_____ Phone (not absolutely necessary, but an asset)

_____ Technical equipment

_____ All front-of-house equipment and supplies

Assessment

The class schedules, rubrics, and crew job descriptions say it all. Jobs either get done or they don't. Actors either play the games or they don't. Are the jobs done and completed on time? Working cooperatively with other crew members and productively on ones own is essential.

Note: While all students are required to make at least one prize request, they are not required to actually obtain a prize. That they made the solicitation and completed the Self Evaluation for Prize Solicitation form should be sufficient.

Week Three Possible Schedule

NOTE: The director may choose to have the Writing Crew meet outside the regular classroom space (library, etc.), checking in at the beginning and end of each class. This will give them 35 minutes of class time a day to write, reducing the time they will have to meet outside class time.

Day	Class Business 5 min	Activity 1 10 minutes	Activity 2 15 minutes	Activity 3 10 minutes	Class Business Handouts & Homework 5 min
1		Game: Headlines Game	Director announces writing crew and sends them to work. Director defines and distributes responsibilities of each crew/committee.	Students divide into committees based on interest. Begin crew work. (Adult director regroups as necessary.)	Handout: Crew Responsibility Descriptions
			Writing crew meets. Sketches out scenes.		
2		Game: If I Were (Metaphor) Game	Crews meet among themselves. Organize presentations and handouts for next day. Adult director moves among crews.	Game: Park Bench	
			Writing Crew organizes characters by scene, making sure all actors/characters are included in the play.		
3		Game: Suspense	Costume, Props, and Sales Crews present to class 8 minutes each. Distribute forms to be filled out as homework.		Homework: Actor's Costume Form, Actor's Prop Form, Poster Place Brainstorm list.
		Writing Crew creates tentative scenic and electric requirements.	Writing Crew meets with Scenery and Electric Crews 25 min.		
		AFTER SCHOOL. Writing Crew meets to prepare scenario using all actors and incorporating necessary technical elements.			
4	Collect Forms. Collect everyone's prop and costume forms and poster brainstorm ideas. Forms go to crews.	Game: Motivations	Game: Murder in the Dark	Crews meet. Collate prop, costume, poster forms into master forms. Give master forms to Writing Crew.	Homework (if not finished in class): Master Costume Form, Master Prop Form, Poster Places.
		Writing Crew continues to organize scenario scene-by-scene with an emphasis on dramatic structure. Emphasis on clear exposition, interesting characters, conflict, and suspense.			
		AFTER SCHOOL. Writing Crew works scenario (no dialogue), addressing prop and costume issues as necessary. Any crew that needs more time may arrange with adult director/sponsor to meet after school.			
5	Post Master Forms. Costume and Prop committees post Master Forms. Publicity posts Place Brainstorm.	Game: CSI – Your Home Town	Writing Crew presents scenario. Class discussion of scenario. Suggestions from the class.		Homework: Writing Crew Only.
		OVER WEEKEND HOMEWORK. Writing Crew meets among itself to polish scenario (no dialogue), addressing prop scenic, electrical, and costume issues as necessary. Create a breakdown for each scene: where it is, who is in it, what happens.			

If I Were (Metaphor) Game

Character Name: _____

Please fill out the following *as your character*. (This is not what your character likes; it is what your character would be.)

If you were a car, what would you be (make, model, year)?

_____

_____

What color would you be?

_____

_____

What TV program would you be?

_____

_____

What type of weather would you be?

_____

_____

What kind of animal would you be?

_____

_____

What historical time period would you be?

_____

_____

What type of music/song would you be?

_____

_____

Headline Game

Quick-witted Astrologer Wins Lottery at Bake Sale

Dangerous Dogcatcher Steals Computer at Political Rally

Use the Headline Game to practice plot building. Here's how:

- Divide students into groups of three or four.
- Randomly choose one idea from each category.
- Allow five minutes to assemble the headline and brainstorm ideas. They may change number, change pronouns, and rearrange the order to make the headline work. (If your group is experienced with improv, let them start right away.)
- Students improvise a scene with a beginning, middle, and ending.
- Time limit for scene — three to five minutes.
- Discuss what made the scene interesting and what could make it better.

Adjectives

angry	wandering	star-struck
sad	dim-witted	lovelorn
enraged	nasty	lonely
sweet	fussy	helpful
curious	flirtatious	mysterious
confused	mean-spirited	murderous
bewildered	magical	suspicious
nutty	dotty	hysterical
posh	brilliant	thoughtful
smelly	absent-minded	overbearing
elegant	weak	lavishly dressed
lost	strong	spendthrift
miserly	politically incorrect	dangerous

Need more adjectives? Try *Improv Ideas'* list on page 13.

Characters

teacher

dog catcher

lover

movie star

novelist

poet

policeman

doctor

veterinarian

engineer

librarian

firefighter

waitress

barber

manicurist

tourist

pop star

Hindu priests

astrologer

warmongers

political pundits

newscasters

journalists

photographers

juvenile delinquents

pizza parlor owners

rock and roll band members

opera singers

little old ladies

computer gamers

hackers

escaped criminals

Elvis impersonators

show girls

Settings

in a cage in a zoo

on a park bench at closing time

in a deserted alleyway

in the crowd

in a crowded theatre

in a queue for a big event

at a political rally

at a book signing

in a swimming pool

at a rock concert

in a kitchen

at a posh restaurant

at your best friend's wedding

in a taxi cab in New York

on a boat going down
the Amazon

on a crowded airplane
in a storm

at a press conference

at an Internet café

in a library

in the back of a pickup truck

on the space shuttle

at the opera

on a sinking ship

at the scene of a crime

under a car

on the moon

in a racing locomotive

in a traffic jam

in the dark

at the back of a bus

in a submarine

in a dark alleyway

at a bake sale at a kid's school

Activities

steal a computer

dance a jig

win a race

tell the future

receive an award

find a dime

go to the races

have an accident

get violently sick

run for shelter

jump for joy

find a large pearl

win the lottery

make a film on an iPhone

receive some terrible news

get chosen to be on
a game show

get shot

wreck a car

lose a purse

visit a museum

marry

shoplift

break a leg

see a ghost

lose a fortune

lose a coat

discover a long-lost relative

witness a crime

watch a terrible film

listen to a boring lecture

get stuck in the rain

fall in love

You'll find more interesting characters in "Focus on Characters and Types" on pages 19-20.

"Focus on The Crime Scene and Location of the Action" on page 26 has more settings.

Want more of a challenge? Add atmosphere to your setting. The list in "Focus on Atmosphere" on page 27 can help.

Actors and Games for Week Three

Activity	Week	Who	Goal	Level			
				Mastering	**Contributing**	**Learning**	**Not Yet Engaged**
Plot Game: Headlines Game Plot Game: Suspense Plot Game: CSI: Your Home Town Plot Game: Frozen Pictures	3	Entire class	Uses game to demonstrate understanding of plot structure through the improvisation skills of imagination, enthusiasm, and risk taking.	•Understands game concept. •Demonstrates thorough understanding of plot structure. •Uses imagination to enhance plot. •Plays with enthusiasm. •Takes risks willingly.	•Shows effort to understand game concept. •Demonstrates good understanding of plot structure. •Uses imagination to enhance plot. •Participates in exercise. •Shows discomfort when taking risks.	•May not understand game concept. •Demonstrates some understanding of plot structure. •May not be able to use imagination to enhance plot. •Participates in exercise without enthusiasm. •Hesitant to take risks.	Does not participate in game.
Character Game: If I Were (Metaphor) Game Character Game: Motivations Character Game: Happy Hands Character Game: Talk Show	3	Entire class	Uses game to demonstrate understanding of character creation through the improvisation skills of imagination, enthusiasm, and risk taking.	•Understands game concept. •Demonstrates thorough understanding of character creation. •Uses imagination to enhance characterization. •Plays with enthusiasm. •Takes risks willingly.	•Shows effort to understand game concept. •Demonstrates good understanding of character creation. •Uses imagination to enhance characterization. •Participates in exercise. •Shows discomfort when taking risks.	•May not understand game concept. •Demonstrates some understanding of character creation. •May not be able to use imagination to enhance characterization. •Participates in exercise without enthusiasm. •Hesitant to take risks.	Does not participate in game.
Spontaneity Game: Park Bench Spontaneity Game: Murder in the Dark Spontaneity Game: TMATTY Spontaneity Game: Word Tennis	3	Entire class	Uses game to demonstrate understanding of spontaneity through the improvisation skills of imagination, enthusiasm, and risk taking.	•Understands game concept. •Demonstrates thorough understanding of spontaneity. •Uses imagination to enhance performance. •Plays with enthusiasm. •Takes risks willingly.	•Shows effort to understand game concept. •Demonstrates good understanding of spontaneity. •Uses imagination to enhance performance. •Participates in exercise. •Shows discomfort when taking risks.	•May not understand game concept. •Demonstrates some understanding of spontaneity. •May not be able to use imagination to enhance performance. •Participates in exercise without enthusiasm. •Hesitant to take risks.	Does not participate in game.

Actors – Weeks Three to Six

Activity	Week	Who	Goal	Level			
				Mastering	**Contributing**	**Learning**	**Not Yet Engaged**
Prize Requests	3, 4	Entire Class	Role-plays asking potential prize donor for prize in preparation for actually making the request of a community member.	Role-plays asking prize donor for prize, remembering to speak courteously, loudly, and articulately. Has necessary information ready and answers questions accurately on the first try.	Role-plays asking prize donor for prize. Usually remembers to speak courteously, loudly, and articulately. Has most necessary information ready and answers questions accurately. Uses another opportunity to role-play to show mastery.	Role-plays asking prize donor for prize. Remembers to speak courteously, loudly, and articulately more than half the time. Shows some uncertainty. Can provide necessary information and answer questions accurately after a pause. Uses another opportunity to demonstrate contributing or mastery skills (only higher score recorded).	Role-plays asking prize donor for prize. Rarely speaks courteously, loudly, or articulately. Shows uncertainty. Not able to provide necessary information or answer questions accurately. Uses additional opportunities to demonstrate contributing or mastery skills (only highest score recorded).
	3, 4	Individual	Requests prize from potential donor.	Requests at least one prize for the show. Turns in self-evaluation form complete and on time.		Requests at least one prize for the show. Turns in self-evaluation form either late or incomplete.	Requests prize but does not document the request or acquire a prize.
Ticket Sales	3, 4		Role-plays selling tickets in preparation for actually making the request of a community member.	Role-plays selling tickets, remembering to speak courteously, loudly, and articulately. Has necessary information ready and answers questions accurately on the first try.	Role-plays selling tickets. Usually remembers to speak courteously, loudly, and articulately. Has most necessary information ready and answers questions accurately. Uses another opportunity to role-play to show mastery.	Role-plays selling tickets. Remembers to speak courteously, loudly, and articulately more than half the time. Shows some uncertainty. Can provide necessary information and answer questions accurately after a pause. Uses another opportunity to demonstrate contributing or mastery skills (only higher score recorded).	Role-plays selling tickets. Rarely speaks courteously, loudly, or articulately. Shows uncertainty. Not able to provide necessary information or answer questions accurately. Uses additional opportunities to demonstrate contributing or mastery skills (only highest score recorded).
	3, 4	Individual	Makes list of potential ticket purchasers.	Makes list of at least twenty potential ticket purchasers.	Makes list of at least ten potential ticket purchasers.	Makes list of at least five potential ticket purchasers.	Either makes list and does not offer tickets or does not make list but sells tickets.
			Offers tickets to those on list.	Mastering: Offers tickets to those on list. May sell tickets to those not on the list.			
Costumes	3, 4	Individual	Chooses a costume from own wardrobe or finds one easily obtainable.	In first week of crew work, chooses costume that suits character.	Chooses a costume that is appropriate to the character before end of fourth week.	Has a costume other than the street clothes of the day.	No costume, uses street clothes.
	4		Creates and submits costume information to costume crew.	Mastering: Provides costume information to costume crew by due date.		Provides incomplete information or turns information in late.	No costume information.
	6		Makes necessary costume modifications.	Modifies costume as necessary to support the show.	Changes costume somewhat as directed.	Does not modify costume as directed.	Has no costume.

Actors – Weeks Three to Six

Activity	Week	Who	Goal	Level			
				Mastering	**Contributing**	**Learning**	**Not Yet Engaged**
Costumes	6	Individual	Cares for costume.	Maintains costume during rehearsals and performances, storing it in the designated place when not in use.	Usually has costume in designated place.	Frequently has costume out of designated place.	Has street clothes or costume elements out of designated place.
	6		Has costume when needed.	Has approved costume at rehearsal and performance space on due date.	Has costume at some rehearsals.	Has costume for performance.	Has no costume, uses street clothes.
	6		Strikes (removes) costumes after show.	Mastery: Takes costumes home/returns to owner immediately after show.		Leaves costume at performance or rehearsal site after show, removing it at a later date.	Has no costume, uses street clothes.
Props (as applicable)	3	Individual	Chooses props.	Mastery: Chooses props that suit own character and the show.		Chooses prop that is not appropriate for character or show.	Does not choose own props.
	3		Provides information to Prop Crew.	Mastery: Provides prop information to Prop Crew by due date.		Provides prop information to Prop Crew that is incomplete or late.	Does not provide prop information.
	3, 4		Acquires props.	Mastery: Acquires hand props appropriate for own character as approved by Prop Crew.		Acquires prop that is not appropriate for character or show.	Does not provide own props.
	3, 4		Labels props.	Labels props with owner's name.			Does not label props.
	3, 4, 5, 6		Modifies props.	Modifies own props as directed by Prop Crew to support the show.	Modifies props somewhat as directed.	Does not modify props as directed.	Does not provide own props.
	6		Maintains props.	Maintains props during rehearsals and performances, storing them in the designated place when not in use.	Usually has props in designated space. Always knows where props are.	May frequently have props in someplace other than designated place.	Does not keep props in designated place. May not be able to find props when needed.
	6		Has props for performance.	Mastery: Has approved props at performance space on due date.		Has incomplete props or provides props late.	Has no props to the detriment of the show.
	6		Strikes (removes) props.	Mastery: Strikes (removes) own hand props without prompting.		Strikes (removes) hand props with prompt.	Required someone else to strike (remove) props.

Writing Crew (Assistant Directors)

Job Description: Create the script for the play.

- Take no more than two weeks.

- Use all actors with the basic characters they have created.

- Use the basic plot devised by the class.

- Writers should not plan to perform in major roles in the final production.

Writing Ideas

Start with the following from the class:

- Character bios with possible motives
- Location
- Basic theme
- Basic plot

Optional from the class

- Crime
- Weapon(s)
- Title
- Atmosphere

Plot

Beginning

- Introduce situation: time, place(s) — offer ideas for the set and shift crews to make scenery and scene changes smooth and fast, weather/atmosphere — offer ideas for the sound effects crew.

- Introduce characters and their personalities and conflicts. Consider introducing characters in groups. (Families, friends, organizations that unify groups, etc.)

- Inciting Incident — Introduce problem(s)/conflict(s).

Middle

- Develop characters.

- Develop conflicts — Give enough conflicts for about one-fourth to one-third of the cast to be the victim. Give enough conflicts for about one-fourth to one-third of the cast to be the perpetrator.

- Develop clues, hints, and red herrings — For the purpose of this play, clues, hints, and red herrings are interchangeable as it will only become obvious whether they are real clues or red herrings when the murderer is found out. At least one clue per perpetrator is appropriate at this point.

- Crisis — Present the murder.

- Show reactions to the murder — All characters should be aware of the murder and have a reaction to it. Some of the reactions may serve as clues.

Ending that the writers are responsible for

- The detective (character representing the law) summarizes the situation and introduces the suspects.

The Real Ending of the Show

- The audience interviews the suspects in rotation.

- The detective announces the perpetrator.

Writing Crew Possible Schedule

NOTE: "Day" column indicates day of the week based on a five-day week and 35-minute work period. "Meeting" column indicates the work period and jobs to be accomplished.

Week	Day	Meeting	Activity	Done
3	1	1	Sketch out scenes using class' plot and character ideas from the first two weeks. Plan extracurricular writing work together and with director/sponsor.	
3	2	2	Organize characters by scene, making sure all actors/characters are included in the play.	
3	3	3	Prepare list of scenic, lighting, sound, and effects needs.	
3	3	4	Meet with Scenery and Electrics Crews about ideas for set, lighting, sound, and effects.	
3	3	5	Outside class time: Prepare scenario using all actors and incorporating necessary technical elements.	
3	4	6	Organize scenes emphasizing exposition, interesting characters, conflict, and suspense.	
3	4	7	Outside class time: Finish scenario, addressing prop and costume issues as necessary. Allow for at least three possible suspects with convincing motives.	
3	5	8	Present scenario to class.	
3	5	9	Over weekend: polish scenario (no dialogue), addressing prop scenic, electrical, and costume issues as necessary. Create a breakdown for each scene: where it is, who is in it, what happens.	
4	1	10	Meet with Scenery and Electrics Crews and adult director. Use scenic breakdown to coordinate crew activities with the needs of the play.	
4	1	11	Meet with Costume and Prop Crews and adult director. Use scenic breakdown to coordinate crew activities with the needs of the play.	
4	1	12	Make plan/schedule to create dialogue for entire play before Friday. Begin dialogue work.	
4	2	13	Dialogue for play.	
4	2	14	Outside class time: Dialogue for play.	
4	3	15	Dialogue for play.	
4	3	16	Dialogue for play.	
4	4	17	Dialogue for play, suspense, and characterization.	
4	4	18	Outside class time: Dialogue for play.	
4	5	19	Suspense and characterization.	
4	5	20	Outside class time: Meet with adult director for help with problems and to receive suggestions. Then amongst selves, finish the script. Arrange to copy the script before the next class meeting. Create tentative rehearsal schedule, deciding which writers will rehearse which scenes. Ideally, more than one scene can be rehearsed at a time.	

Writing Crew Possible Schedule, continued

Week	Day	Meeting	Activity	Done
5	1	21	Have script copied before class.	
5	1	22	Present script for class reading.	
5	2	23	Class reads script, discusses, and Writing Crew and adult director make appropriate changes.	
5	3	24	Class continues to read script and writers and adult director make appropriate changes. Rehearsals by scene begin.	
5	4	25	Rehearsal by scene. Script changes as appropriate.	
5	5	26	Rehearsal by scene. Script changes as appropriate. Last day of script changes by class.	
5	5	27	Outside class time: Meet with adult director for help with problems and to receive suggestions. Using class changes and adult director's input, make finishing touches to script. Word process script, leaving room for stage directions and notes. Arrange to copy final script before next class meeting.	
6	1	28	Full dress rehearsal by scene.	
6	2	29	Full dress rehearsal by scene. Rehearsal starts where last rehearsal left off.	
6	3	30	Full dress rehearsal for the first half of play. Take notes. Help backstage as needed. Make appropriate suggestions for improvement.	
6	3	31	Speed through of the first half of play.	
6	4	32	Full dress rehearsal for the second half of play. Take notes. Help backstage as needed. Make appropriate suggestions for improvement.	
6	4	33	Speed through of the second half of play.	
6	5	34	Assist adult director with full rehearsals. Take notes. Help backstage as needed. Make appropriate suggestions for improvement.	
6	5	35	Fill in where needed during performances.	

NOTE: Writers may also perform. Anticipated work outside of class time: 17 hours.

Sample Suspect Interview Questions

These are the type of questions your audience sleuths might ask. Are you prepared for them? What questions specific to your play could you add to the list?

1. How well did you know the victim?
2. In what capacity? For how long?
3. Who do you think had a reason to hate him/her?
4. Why do you think they might have killed him/her?
5. Why?
6. Where were you when the murder happened?
7. What did you think of the victim?
8. Were you surprised when he/she was killed?
9. What purpose could this murder have served?
10. Did he/she deserve it? Why or why not?
11. How do you feel about the murder?
12. Why should we believe you?
13. Have you ever been violent?
14. Do you have a temper?
15. How do you feel conflicts should be resolved?
16. Have you ever been the victim of an injustice? What was it?
17. Is violence/murder ever justified?
18. Will you miss the victim?
19. What do you think should have been done to resolve the conflict?
20. Why do you think anyone would do such a thing?
21. How should the murderer be punished if he/she is caught? Why?
22. How do you think he/she can be identified?
23. Did you ever know there was a problem?
24. Do you have any reason to hate the victim?
25. Why do you suppose you might have been chosen as a suspect?
26. Have you ever been in legal trouble before?
27. How do you feel about being a suspect?
28. Tell us why you couldn't have done the murder.
29. Tell us why you would have no reason to hate the victim.
30. Tell us why you are here.
31. How do you usually respond in this kind of situation?
32. Are you impulsive?
33. Do you believe in "an eye for an eye?"
35. How do you feel about revenge?
35. Did the victim deserve what he/she got?
36. Are you a reasonable person?
37. Have you ever had a mental or emotional illness?
38. Do you take any medications?
39. How do you feel right now?
40. What do you value the most?
41. What really makes you angry?
42. What do you think of the other suspects?
43. How do you think _____would describe you?
44. How would you describe yourself?
45. Is murder ever justified?
46. How could this conflict have been resolved nonviolently?

The Prize Crew

Job Description: Acquire the prizes to be awarded to the audience members who correctly deduce/guess the perpetrator.

- Decide (with the director's guidance) how many prizes will be awarded.
- List potential donors for those prizes.
- Take no more than three weeks to line up all prizes.
- Give everyone in the class at least one prize acquisition assignment and follow up with the students.
- Conduct role-playing exercises with the class until everyone is comfortable.
- Record prize commitments as they come in.

Choosing the Prize Crew

It's probably a good idea for the director to get the Prize Crew going. The crew needs to brainstorm potential prize sources and how to tactfully approach those sources. Prize Crew members should be friendly, outgoing, and articulate. They should be aware of the businesses in the area and, preferably, personally and favorably known to the merchants they will approach for donations.

The Prize Crew should also be aware of potential prize sources represented by the families and acquaintances in the class.

Training and role-playing should go into preparing to ask for donations, how to graciously accept donations, and how to gracefully accept rejection.

Below is a sample sales pitch that students can role-play before they actually approach potential donors. Stress that this is just a sample and that students should find what they are comfortable with.

Sample prize interview (in person)

Hello! My name is_____ and I am a student at _____. We are putting on a fundraising presentation of an original interactive murder mystery (you might want to explain a bit about the plot and format here). It will be performed on _____, and we will be giving out door prizes to those in the audience who correctly guess the murderer (or you may want to say 'whodunit!') We wonder if your business would be interested in donating a door prize to us for this enterprise. In return, your name will be printed prominently in the program as well as being announced when the prize is awarded.

We anticipate around _____ people will attend, many of them adults, and we feel that this will be good publicity for your business as well as supporting our school's drama department.

Your donation will be tax deductible since our school is a nonprofit organization.

If you want to donate I will give you a form to fill out: one copy for your records and one for the school. I can take the prize with me now, or you can call me to let me know when to pick it up.

Thank you so much for your time.

Prize Crew Possible Schedule

NOTE: "Day" column indicates day of the week based on a five-day week and 35-minute work period. "Meeting" column indicates the work period and jobs to be accomplished. If a plus (+) follows the day, then that activity begins on the day noted and continues until it is completed.

Week	Day	Meeting	Activity	Done
3	2	1	Meet with adult director to decide number of prizes.	
3	2	2	Provide crew list to Program Crew.	
3	2	3	Brainstorm list of potential prize donors and post for class to add to (homework).	
4	1	4	Provide updated and accurate crew list for program.	
4	1	5	Provide accurate and updated prize list for program and MC.	
4	1	6	Arrange for secure prize storage.	
4	2	7	Meet with class and assign (get volunteers for) prize requests.	
4	2	8	Make master list of class members and prize acquisition assignments (at least one per class member).	
4	3	9	Collaborate with (class/adult director/writers) on choice of MC for performances.	
4	5	10	Conduct role-playing of prize requests.	
5	1	11	Provide updated and accurate crew list for program.	
5	1	12	Provide accurate and updated prize list for program and MC.	
5	1	13	Provide thank you notes and sample thank you notes for cast members to acknowledge their prize donations.	
5	1+	14	Record prize commitments as they come in; post in a prominent place (class business).	
5	1+	15	Follow up prize acquisition assignments by class members.	
5	1+	16	Store prizes in secure area as they come in.	
6	1	17	Provide updated and accurate crew list for program.	
6	1	18	Provide accurate and updated prize list for program and MC.	
6	4	19	Arrange prize display for performances.	
6	4	20	Work with MC to acknowledge prize donors appropriately.	

Prize Source Brainstorm

Student	Possible Prize Donor	OK

Prize Solicitation

Each student soliciting door prizes should be ready with the following information:

Student name

School name

That your drama class is presenting an original interactive murder mystery

Performance date(s)

That there will be door prizes for those who correctly guess the murderer

That you hope the business will donate a door prize

That the business gets recognition in the program and when the prize is presented

Number of people anticipated to attend

Reiterate that it will be good publicity for business

That it is tax deductible as the school and program is not-for-profit

And each student should also:

Have donation receipt ready to fill out in duplicate

Have pen to fill out receipt. Clipboard is optional but nice

Be ready to make arrangements to get prize to school before the performance

Be ready to talk about the teacher, what the money from this show will be used for, and a little about the show (without giving anything away!)

● ● ● ● ● ● ● ●
Prize Receipt
See a sample prize
donation receipt from
The Maui Murders,
page 128.
● ● ● ● ● ● ● ●

The Follow-Up Thank You

The person who arranges for the prize should be the one to write the formal thank you after the show. The best thank you notes do not start with "thank you." Note paper with the show logo is a nice touch.

Name _____

Self Evaluation for Prize Solicitation

Date of solicitation: _____

Business/Individual from which prize solicited: _____

Name of contact person: _____

My solicitation   was ❑   was not ❑   successful.

Appointment

Date appointment made: _____

Date of appointment: _____

Time of appointment: _____

I was on time. Yes ❑   No ❑

I had all material I needed to make the solicitation. Yes ❑   No ❑

I wore: _____

_____

_____

I made the following grooming efforts: _____

_____

_____

Prize Master Check-In

Student	Prize and Prize Source	Prize Contact and Phone	Prize at Theatre	Prize in Program	Thank You

Publicity Crew

Job Description: Plan, design, and write all publicity. Print and distribute posters and flyers. Arrange for print, broadcast, and online publicity.

- Design graphics for the show. (*Optional:* hold a class-wide contest for the best graphics.) If you started a poster contest when you selected your theme, now is the time to announce the winner. (Student vote? Director's choice?)
- Plan publicity campaign to appeal to target audience but include the public at large.
- Create posters and flyers that contain all pertinent information about the play.
- Write school announcements, press releases, and radio announcements as appropriate.

Publicity Crew Possible Schedule

NOTE: "Day" column indicates day of the week based on a five-day week and 35-minute work period. "Meeting" column indicates the work period and jobs to be accomplished. If a plus (+) follows the day, then activity begins on the day noted and continues until it is completed.

Week	Day	Meeting	Activity	Done
3	2	1	Meet with director, writers, and program crew about ideas for publicity graphics and campaign (use ideas generated in second week if available).	
3	2	2	Plan poster location brainstorm session with class.	
3	2	3	Provide crew list to Program Crew.	
3	3	4	Brainstorm with class for poster locations.	
3	5	5	Plan publicity campaign including poster locations. Use poster brainstorm ideas from class.	
3	3+	6	Design graphics if needed. Work with Program Crew.	
3	3+	7	Create show flyers and posters.	
3	3+	8	Write school announcements, press releases, and radio announcements.	
4	1	9	Provide updated and accurate crew list for program.	
4	5	10	Conduct role-playing of placing posters and flyers.	
4	5	11	Distribute posters and flyers to class for posting.	
4	5	12	Post posters and flyers in places not on class list.	
4	5	13	Deliver press releases and announcements to appropriate places.	
5	1	14	Provide accurate and updated crew list for program.	
5	1+	15	Monitor publicity. Adjust as necessary.	
6	1	16	Provide accurate and updated crew list for program.	

Publicity Brainstorm

Publicity Idea	Yes	No	Cost	Crew Head	Crew Members	Start Date
Banner(s)						
Email network — school						
Email network — personal						
Flyers (8 1/2 x 11) black on color						
Flyers (8 1/2 x 11) black on white						
Flyers (8 1/2 x 11) color						
Magnets						
Media — press releases						
Media — print ads						
Media — radio spots						
Media — television						
Pizza box/food delivery mini-flyer						
Postcards						
Posters (11 x 17) black on white						
Posters (11 x 17) black on color						
Posters (11 x 17) color						
School announcements						
Social networks — Facebook, Twitter						
T-shirts						
Table tents						
Website, drama, school						

Poster/Flyer Distribution

Student	Possible Place	OK

The Adult Director Thinks about Tickets and Hospitality

Ticket Sales

How many tickets could you possibly sell? _____

Don't forget that you have to set up your stage and refreshment area as well as seat guests. Set up the performance site early and work it all out.

How many tickets do you usually sell? _____

How many tickets do you need to reserve as comps? _____

How many tickets do you think you can sell for this event? _____

Rolls of tickets with stubs work great for this kind of show. Make sure your students know how to sell with the stub, which part to keep, etc.

Venue

Where to have the mystery?

The school cafeteria is a great place as eating à la dinner theatre is a great selling point. Make sure the audience is able to see the stage/performance area easily from their seats. You may have to seat on only one side of the table.

Don't forget to provide wheelchair seating plus chairs for companions of your wheelchair patrons. Perhaps card tables would make your ADA seating easier.

Ticket Pre-Sales

As your prizes and refreshments rely on an accurate count of audience members, you have to sell tickets quickly and efficiently. Don't forget, you must have a precise count by mid-week of your production.

Start ticket sales early.

Plan for Walk-Ins

Your posters should say that seating is by pre-sales only. Have a policy in place for walk-ins that you can't seat because of a sell-out or tight planning. If unticketed patrons come to your first performance, you're in great shape. Sell them a ticket for the next show. If it happens for your final performance, have them wait until the show starts. There may be some unused tickets. If there are no seats, better luck to them next time.

Hospitality Supplies

Start socking away supplies *soon*.

Most drama teachers are hoarders. If we see something interesting we buy it with the idea of "I can use this later." Start thinking now about plates, napkins, and flatware for your mystery. If you find a good buy, pick them up.

If you have arranged with your money person to have an open purchase order to you, you can start soon.

Comps

Comps. Will you have complimentary tickets? If so, for whom? School staff. Business partners? Helpful parents? Senior citizens? Make a list of whom you wish to comp and then decide how many comp tickets you want to distribute. Subtract that amount from the total possible tickets sold.

A Comp Solution — A Preview: If you find yourselves wanting to issue a great number of complimentary tickets but find that they would seriously cut into your tickets sales (not to mention be a burden to your refreshment folks), why not invite all of them to a preview? The preview should be a no-stopping final dress rehearsal that gives your cast a chance to perform for an audience and you a chance to honor your supporters. You might even choose an interesting special victim and perpetrator.

Ticket Crew

Job Description: Plan, design, print, and sell tickets for the show. Manage all checked out tickets and incoming monies.

- Design and print (or order) tickets for the show.
- Number tickets if they are not already numbered. This helps keep track of ticket sales.
- Check tickets out to class to sell. Keep track of tickets checked out.
- Count, report, and deposit money for tickets with director/adult in charge.
- Manage any ticket sales contests the class decides on.

Ticket Crew Possible Schedule

NOTE: "Day" column indicates day of the week based on a five-day week and 35-minute work period. "Meeting" column indicates the work period and jobs to be accomplished. If a plus (+) follows the day, then activity begins on the day noted and continues until it is completed.

Week	Day	Meeting	Activity	Done
3	2	1	Plan ticket sales. Know how many seats are available for each performance.	
3	2	2	(Contest Optional) Plan ticket sales contest.	
3	2	3	Provide Ticket Crew names to Program Crew.	
3	2	4	Make sign-up sheet for ticket sellers. Encourage sign-ups.	
3	3	5	Start to acquire tickets for show.	
3	3	6	Ask class members for general ideas of how many tickets they want to sell.	
4	1	7	Turn in crew changes to Program Crew.	
4	1+	8	Number tickets if necessary.	
4	1+	9	Create packets of tickets (multiples of five or ten) for each seller. Record ticket numbers for each seller.	
4	3	10	Make master list of ticket sellers.	
4	3	11	Make ticket sales chart.	
4	5	12	Manage ticket sales contest (optional).	
4	5	13	Lead role-play in ticket sales demonstration.	
4	5	14	Check tickets out for class to sell. Keep track of quantity and ticket numbers of tickets checked out to each seller.	
4	2	15	Get adult box office help for each performance.	
4-5	all	16	DAILY: Collect ticket sales money.	
4-5	all	17	DAILY: Record ticket sales for each person.	
4-5	all	18	DAILY: Turn in ticket money to adult director or sponsor.	
4-5	all	19	DAILY: Keep chart of ticket sales in dollar amounts and ticket quantities.	
5	1	20	Provide accurate and updated crew list for program.	
6	1	21	Provide accurate and updated crew list for program.	
6	5	22	Provide change and a cash box if tickets will be sold at the door.	
6	5	23	Be available to sell tickets at the door.	
6	5	24	(Contest Optional) Announce ticket sales winners at performances. Award Prizes.	

Ticket Sign-Up Form

Student	Ticket Packets Needed (multiples of 5) Per Performance		For Crew Use Only Ticket Numbers		OK
	Perf. 1	Perf. 2			

Ticket Sales Master List

Seller		Mon		Tue		Wed		Thur		Fri		Total	
		Qty	Amt	Qty	Amt	Qty	Amt	Qty	Amt	Qty	Amt	Qty	Amt
	AD												
	CH												
	AD												
	CH												
	AD												
	CH												
	AD												
	CH												
	AD												
	CH												
	AD												
	CH												
	AD												
	CH												
	AD												
	CH												
	AD												
	CH												
	AD												
	CH												
	AD												
	CH												
	AD												
	CH												

Today's Advanced Ticket Sales

Date:_____

Money

Change

Pennies:_____ x $00.01 = _____

Nickels:_____ x $00.05 = _____

Dimes:_____ x $00.10 = _____

Quarters:_____ x $00.25 = _____

Halves:_____ x $00.50 = _____

Dollars:_____ x $01.00 = _____

Total in Change (a) $_____

Cash

Ones:_____ x $1.00 = _____

Fives:_____ x $5.00 = _____

Tens:_____ x $10.00 = _____

Twenties:_____ x $20.00 = _____

Fifties:_____ x $50.00 = _____

Hundreds:_____ x $100.00 = _____

Total in Bills (b) $_____

*Checks (Count then photocopy if required)*_____ = **Total Checks (c) $_____**

Total Change:	$_____	(a)
Total Bills:	$_____	(b)
Total Checks:	$_____	(c)
Total in Ticket Sales:	$_____	(d)

Tickets

Qty	*Type of Ticket*	*Price*	*Line Total*	
____	Advanced Sales Adult	x $5.00 = $	_____	(e)
____	Advanced Sales Student	x $3.00 = $	_____	(f)
____	Day's Total Advanced Sales	= $	_____	(g)

Box Office Staff

Adult/Sponsor: _____

Student: _____

Student: _____

Student: _____

The Math

(d) Total in Ticket Sales (Money) should equal (g) Day's Total Advanced Sales (Tickets)

Program Crew

Job Description: Plan, design, and print the programs for the show.

- Use show graphics as a basis for the program.
- Work with directors and crew heads to create complete cast and crew lists with correct spelling and identification.
- Recognize all prize donors.
- Provide a sample program for everyone to proofread one week before program goes to printing.
- Print and fold programs and have them ready to hand out to patrons.

Program Crew Possible Schedule

NOTE: "Day" column indicates day of the week based on a five-day week and 35-minute work period. "Meeting" column indicates the work period and jobs to be accomplished. If a plus (+) follows the day, then activity begins on the day noted and continues until it is completed.

Week	Day	Meeting	Activity	Done
3	2	1	Meet with director, writers, and Publicity Crew about ideas for graphics (use ideas generated in second week if available).	
3	2	2	Ask directors and crew heads for cast and crew names for program.	
3	2	3	Compile Program Crew list for program.	
3	4	4	Create master program information to be added to and corrected as needed. Save on designated computer and give electronic copy to the adult director.	
3	2+	5	Arrange to print programs.	
3	2+	6	Design graphics if needed. Work with Publicity Crew.	
4	1	7	Ask Prize Crew for prize donor names.	
4	1	8	Ask director for volunteer names.	
4	2+	9	Lay out program using show graphics, title, writers, date, directors, (designers), cast/role names, time and location, crew names, donor names, volunteer names, and other acknowledgements.	
4	2+	10	Plan extra-curricular program work with director/sponsor if necessary.	
4	2	11	Post sample program to cast and crew for proofing.	
5	1	12	Collect updated program information from directors and crews. Make corrections on master program.	
5	2	13	Post corrected program to cast and crew for proofing.	
6	1	14	Collect updated program information from directors and crews. Make corrections on master program.	
6	2	15	Post corrected program to cast and crew for final proofing.	
6	2+	16	Provide camera-ready program to printer. Print/copy programs.	
6	4+	17	Fold programs. Have programs ready for ushers.	

Possible Program Layout

Front Page

(School or Drama Program) presents

Title

Writer(s)

Graphics

Date

Page 2

Title

Date

Adult Director

Student Directors

Cast

Setting of the Play (Time and Location)

Page 3

Prize Donors

Acknowledgements

Volunteers

Back Page

Crews (acknowledge the crew heads first in the crew listing)

Scenery Construction and Painting

Stage Crew

Lighting

Costume

Props

Sound

Special Effects

Graphics

Publicity

Box Office and Ticket Sales

Hospitality and Ushers

Prop Crew

Job Description: Coordinate, acquire, and manage props for the play.

- Using the script, create a master prop plot for the production.
- Involve the class in acquiring the props. Label props with the owner's name.
- Build props that are not in stock or cannot be borrowed.
- Provide secure storage for props when they are not in use.
- Require all actors to be responsible for setting up and storing their own hand props.
- Create a prop table at each entrance. On butcher paper covering the table, mark spaces for each prop that should be there and the actor responsible.
- Work with actors to strike (remove) props from performance area at end of show.
- Return props to owners immediately after final performance.

Prop Crew Possible Schedule

NOTE: "Day" column indicates day of the week based on a five-day week and 35-minute work period. "Meeting" column indicates the work period and jobs to be accomplished. If a plus (+) follows the day, then activity begins on the day noted and continues until it is completed.

Week	Day	Meeting	Activity	Done
3	2	1	All actors are responsible for their own props. The Prop Crew will be available to coordinate, help with difficult prop problems, and help with storage.	
3	3	2	Prop Crew general meeting with actors. Hand out prop forms.	
3	3	3	Provide Program Crew with Prop Crew list.	
3	4	4	Prop Crew collects prop forms and makes master list.	
4	1	5	Discuss additional ideas for props that would be appropriate and do-able for the show. Make lists of ideas to present to director and writers.	
4	1	6	Give updated Prop Crew list to Program Crew.	
4	1	7	Meet with director and writers about special prop needs for show.	
4	1	8	Use scene breakdown to plan/design props for each scene.	
4	2+	9	Provide racks, boxes, and storage for props for rehearsals and performances.	
4	2	10	Make chart with prop needed, time the prop is needed, and crew member responsible. Post in crew area.	
4	3	11	Help actors mark props.	
4	4	12	Assign prop jobs to individual crew members.	
4	4+	13	Construct props as needed.	
4	5	14	Plan extra-curricular prop work with director/sponsor if necessary.	
5	1	15	Give updated Prop Crew list to Program Crew.	

Prop Crew Possible Schedule, continued

Week	Day	Meeting	Activity	Done
5	2	16	Announce any special items necessary to show but not readily available to actors.	
5	2+	17	Acquire any special items necessary to show but not readily available to actors.	
5	3+	18	Help actors preset props for rehearsals and performances.	
5	3+	19	Make sure actors remove their props from acting area after rehearsals and performances.	
5	3+	20	Remove set props from acting area after rehearsals and performance.	
5	3+	21	Make final check for props left out after rehearsals and performances.	
6	5	22	Return borrowed props promptly.	
6	5	23	Discard/store props as appropriate.	
6	5	24	Write thank you notes to people who have lent or donated props.	

Prop Form

Actor's Name _____ Character's Name_____

Scene	Prop	Need	Have

Master Prop List

Cross Reference with Each Actor's Prop Form			Please list prop and check when prop is at theatre	
Actor	**Character**	**Scene**	**Prop**	**At Theatre**

Prop Worksheet

Scene	Actor	Character	Description	Source	Need	Have/date	OK

Scenery for Your Show

All scenery should be very basic and multi-functional. If you have small flats or three-dimensional pieces that can move to your performance space, great. If not, think three-dimensional scenic pieces based on appliance boxes and carpet tubes. You can use up to four sides of a box (six if you're really creative), giving you four to six looks. How about a group of boxes with one side of each painted neutrally? Those sides can work with the creatively painted sides of other boxes to give you multiple sets.

Hint:

Why not borrow from the Greeks? Remember the periaktoi the Greeks used that you learned about in theatre history? They were three-sided columns that rotated. Having three instead of four sides kept the other sides from being seen.

Materials that can make your scenery happen:
- Butcher Paper (white and colored) • Poster Paint •Appliance and Mattress Boxes
- Carpet/Flooring Tubing • House Paint (interior and exterior) *Use only water clean-up paint!*
- Construction Adhesive (Liquid Nails)

Cardboard: Did you know that you can purchase sheets of cardboard from box companies? Check your yellow pages.

Paint: Where to get paint? Of course, you can buy mixed-to-order paint at your local hardware store, but it's usually not in an ordinary budget. Remember, you are doing the show as a fundraiser.

Why not have a scavenger hunt for paint? Many families have paint sitting around from a do-it-yourself job. Suggest students check at home or with neighbors for paint they don't need anymore. If you are flexible about the colors you need, this can be your salvation. (Not to mention a way for folks to get rid of paint that's been hanging around.)

Paint that has been frozen won't stick well or for long. This is probably not a problem for you. Mis-mixed paint may be available at your local hardware store. It is paint that didn't come out as the paint chip or customer expected. And it's cheap. Ask.

Paint all scenery white with paint you have been given or purchased then use poster paint to cartoon in your scenic elements. Just make sure your paint doesn't rub off.

Buying white paint and tinting it yourself works, too. Hardware stores sell universal tinting colors right there in the paint department. Or you can purchase single quarts of primary red, blue, and yellow and use those to create your own colors.

Always add colors to white a little at a time and mix thoroughly. It's easier to darken than to lighten paint. Try your mixed color out on a scrap and let it thoroughly dry if matching colors is important.

Backgrounds: That staple of "let's put on a show" backgrounds are at a premium these days, so we can use old white sheets, white and colored butcher paper that the school already has, or purchased muslin. How about hanging your background from volleyball standards that your school may also already have?

Scenery Crew

Job Description: Design, build, paint, and move the scenery for the play.

- Work with the writers to design/plan scenery that serves and enhances the plot.
- Use scene breakdown to plan scenery for each scene.
- Acquire and build scenery.
- Paint scenery.
- Move the scenery as needed during the play.
- Strike (remove) scenery from performance area at end of show.
- Take scenery apart, discard, salvage, and store appropriately.

Scenery Crew Possible Schedule

NOTE: "Day" column indicates day of the week based on a five-day week and 35-minute work period. "Meeting" column indicates the work period and jobs to be accomplished. If a plus (+) follows the day, then activity begins on the day noted and continues until it is completed.

Week	Day	Meeting	Activity	Done
3	2	1	Discuss ideas for scenery that would be appropriate and doable for the show. Make lists of ideas to present to director and writers.	
3	2	2	Provide crew list to Program Crew.	
3	3	3	Meet with director and writers.	
3	4	4	Measure performance space.	
4	1	5	Provide updated and accurate crew list for program.	
4	1	6	Meet with director and writers. Get scene breakdown.	
4	1	7	Use scene breakdown to plan/design scenery for each scene.	
4	1	8	Assign scenic jobs to individual crew members.	
4	2+	9	Make chart with scenic element needed, time the element is needed, and crew member responsible. Post in crew area.	
4	3	10	Arrange for storage of scenic elements.	
4	4+	11	Acquire scenic elements.	
4	4+	12	Construct scenic elements as needed.	
4	5	13	Plan extracurricular scenic work with director/sponsor if necessary.	
5	1	14	Provide updated and accurate crew list for program.	
5	1+	15	Acquire, construct, and paint scenery.	
5	2+	16	As necessary, set up and remove scenery in acting area before and after rehearsals.	
6	1	17	Provide updated and accurate crew list for program.	
6	5+	18	As necessary, set up and remove scenery in acting area before and after performances.	
6	5+	19	Return borrowed scenic items promptly.	
6	5+	20	Take scenery apart and discard/store it.	

Scenic Breakdown for Scenery Crew

Scene	Location	Description

Scenic Needs

Scene	What	Description	Location	Responsible

Scenic Element Needs

We Need (scenic element)	Scene	To (function)	Have	Need	Source	Person in Charge

Costume Crew

Job Description: Coordinate, acquire, and manage costumes for the play.

Important: Actors should use their own clothing or acquire their own costumes whenever possible.

- Work with the actors to determine what their characters would wear.
- With actors, create a costume sheet for each character.
- Create a master costume plot for the production.
- Provide storage and costume racks for all costumes and accessories for rehearsal and performances.

Costume Crew Possible Schedule

NOTE: "Day" column indicates day of the week based on a five-day week and 35-minute work period. "Meeting" column indicates the work period and jobs to be accomplished. If a plus (+) follows the day, then activity begins on the day noted and continues until it is completed.

Week	Day	Meeting	Activity	Done
3	1+	1	All actors are responsible for their own costumes. The costume crew will be available to coordinate, help with difficult costume problems, and help with storage.	
3	3	2	Work with actors to decide what characters will wear. Hand out costume forms.	
3	3	3	Provide crew list to Program Crew.	
3	3+	4	Help actors fill out individual costume forms as needed.	
3	4	5	Collect costume forms.	
3	4	6	Meet with director and writers about special costume needs of show.	
3	4	7	Collect costume forms, make master plot for production, and post plot.	
4	1	8	Provide updated crew list to Program Crew.	
4	1	9	Assign costume jobs to individual crew members. Post jobs in crew area.	
4	1+	10	Provide racks and secure storage for costumes for rehearsals and performances.	
4	2+	11	Help actors mark costumes as they bring them in.	
5	1	12	Provide updated crew list to Program Crew.	
5	1+	13	Acquire any special items necessary to show but not readily available to actors.	
5	1+	14	Plan extracurricular costume work with director/sponsor if necessary.	
5	3+	15	Help actors preset costumes for rehearsals and performances.	
5	3+	16	Make final check for costumes left out after rehearsals and performances.	
6	1	17	Provide updated crew list to Program Crew.	

Costume Form

Actor's Name _____ Character's Name_____

Scene	Costume element	Need	Have

Costume Master List

Cross Reference with Each Actor's Costume Form.   Please check when costumes are at theatre.

Actor	Character	Scene	headgear	underwear	top: shirt/blouse	jacket	outerwear	bottom: skirt, trousers	socks/hose	shoes	accessory 1	accessory 2	Complete (Date)

Costume Worksheet

Actor's Name _____   Character's Name_____

	Scene	Source	Color	Size	Need	Have/date	OK
Headgear							
Underwear							
Top: shirt/blouse							
Jacket							
Outerwear							
Bottom: skirt, trousers							
Socks/hose							
Shoes							
Accessory 1							
Accessory 2							
Notes:							
Headgear							
Underwear							
Top: shirt/blouse							
Jacket							
Outerwear							
Bottom: skirt, trousers							
Socks/hose							
Shoes							
Accessory 1							
Accessory 2							
Notes:							

Electrics Crew

Lighting

Job Description: Coordinate, design, and operate the lighting cues and effects for the play.

- Work with the writers to design/plan lighting that serves and enhances the plot.
- Assure appropriate lighting for audience safety.
- Use the scene breakdown to plan lighting for each scene.
- Acquire, connect, and control all lighting elements.
- Using the script, create a master lighting plot for the production.
- Run the lighting for the play.
- Strike (remove) lighting from performance area at end of show.
- Store equipment appropriately.

Sound

Job Description: Coordinate, acquire, record, and play back sound effects and background music for the play.

- Work with the writers to choose sound that enhances the production.
- Provide appropriate music for before the show, intermission, and after the show.
- Using the script, create a master sound plot for the production.
- Instruct MCs in the use of microphones.
- Run the sound for the play.
- Strike (remove) sound equipment from performance area at end of show.
- Store equipment appropriately.

Special Effects

Job Description: Coordinate, acquire, and operate any special effects for the show.

- Work with the writers to choose special effects that enhance the production.
- Using the script, create a master special effects plot for the production.
- Ensure that any desired special effects are legal and operated safely.
- Run the special effects for the play.
- Strike (remove) special effects equipment from performance area at end of show.
- Store equipment appropriately.

Electrics (Lighting, Sound, FX) Crew Possible Schedule

NOTE: "Day" column indicates day of the week based on a five-day week and 35-minute work period. "Meeting" column indicates the work period and jobs to be accomplished. If a plus (+) follows the day, then activity begins on the day noted and continues until it is completed.

Week	Day	Meeting	Activity	Done
3	2	1	Discuss ideas for lighting, sound, and special effects that would be appropriate and doable for the show. Make lists of ideas to present to director and writers.	
3	2	2	Provide crew list to Program Crew.	
3	3	3	Meet with director and writers about the electrical needs of the show.	
3	3+	4	Arrange for secure storage of lighting, sound, and special effects elements.	
3	3+	5	Inventory existing equipment. Make list of equipment that may be borrowed and from whom.	
4	1	6	Provide updated and accurate crew list to Program Crew.	
4	1+	7	Use the scene breakdown to plan lighting, sound, and special effects for appropriate scenes.	
5	1	8	Provide updated and accurate crew list to Program Crew.	
4	1+	9	Acquire lighting, sound, and special effects elements.	
4	1+	10	Store equipment appropriately.	
4	3+	11	Ensure actor and audience safety for all rehearsals and performances.	
4	1+	12	Acquire prerecorded background sound and special effects as needed.	
4	1+	13	Record background sound and special effects as needed.	
4		14	Plan extracurricular electrics work with director/sponsor if necessary.	
5	2	15	Using the script, create master lighting, sound, and special effects plots for the production.	
5	3+	16	Connect and control all lighting, sound, and special effects elements for rehearsal and performance.	
6	1	17	Provide updated and accurate crew list to Program Crew.	
6	5	18	Set up and run lighting, sound, and special effects for performances. Ensure audience safety.	
6	5	19	Strike (remove) lighting, sound, and special effects from performance area at the end of the show.	
6	5+	20	Store equipment appropriately.	
6	5+	21	Return borrowed or rented equipment.	

Scene Breakdown for Electrics Crew

L=Lights, S=Sound, E=Special Effects

Scene	Effect	L	S	E	Description

Electrical Effects Needs

We Need (effect)	In Scene	To (function)

Electrical Physical Needs

We Need (equipment/CD/etc.)	Scene	To (function)	Have	Need	Source	Person in Charge

Week Four Possible Schedule

Day	Class Business 5 min	Activity 1 10 minutes	Activity 2 15 minutes	Activity 3 10 minutes	Class Business, Handouts, & Homework 5 min
1		Game: Happy Hands	Writing Crew, Scenery Crew, and Electrics Crews meet with adult director. Use scenic breakdown to coordinate crew activities with the needs of the play.	Writing Crew, Costume Crew, and Prop Crew meet with adult director. Use scenic breakdown to coordinate crew activities with the needs of the play.	
			Costume Crew and Prop Crew meet individually to refine master lists.	Scenery Crew and Electrics Crews meet individually to plan work.	
			Program Crew, Prize Crew, Publicity Crew, Ticket Crew, and Hospitality Crew meet individually to plan their drives. Program Crew: basic design for program. Work with Publicity Crew on cover design. Arrange to print posters and flyers. Prize Crew: create sign-up for prize solicitation and prize kit. Publicity Crew: plan posters and flyers. Start writing press releases for radio and newspapers. Start writing school announcements. Get permission for school announcements and policies for releases to radio and newspapers. Ticket Crew: plan type of tickets to use, find source of tickets, or start ticket design. Plan ticket sales contest. Make and post sign-up sheet for ticket sales.		
		(AFTER SCHOOL) Writing Crew: Make plan/schedule to create dialogue for entire play before Friday. Begin dialogue work.			
2		Game: TMATTY	Program Crew: basic program design. Prize Crew: construct prize request kit for each class member. Publicity Crew: create posters and flyers. Write announcements and press releases. Ticket Crew: post sign-up for tickets with student name and quantity (multiples of 5) needed for each performance.		
		Writing Crew: Dialogue.			
		(AFTER SCHOOL) Writing Crew: Dialogue.			
3		Game: Frozen Pictures	Scenery, costumes, and props.	Program Crew: ask directors and crew heads for names and roles. Prize Crew: construct prize request kit for each class member. Publicity Crew: create posters and flyers. Write announcements and press releases. Ticket Crew: make master list for ticket sales with student name and quantities. Count and bundle tickets. Make ticket sales graph. Number tickets if necessary.	
		Writing Crew: Dialogue.			
		(AFTER SCHOOL) Writing Crew: Dialogue.			

Week Four Possible Schedule, continued

Day	Class Business 5 min	Activity 1 10 minutes	Activity 2 15 minutes	Activity 3 10 minutes	Class Business, Handouts, & Homework 5 min
4		Game: Talk Show	Program Crew: continue program design. Prize Crew: finish and print prize solicitation forms and plan role-playing prize requests for next day. Publicity Crew: have posters ready to distribute by next day. Ticket Crew: count tickets out for packets for class. Note ticket numbers and quantities.		
4		Writing Crew: Dialogue.			
4		(AFTER SCHOOL) Writing Crew: Suspense and characterization through dialogue and action. Prize Crew, Publicity Crew, and Ticket Crew may want to meet to get ready for the next day's distributions.			
5		Game: Word Tennis	Role-play prize request. Role-play ticket sales speech.	Prize Crew: distribute prize request kits. Publicity Crew: distribute posters. Each person gets a poster for each parent who works outside the home, one for each poster location signed up, and one souvenir poster for each person. Ticket Crew: check tickets out for class to sell. Keep track of quantity and ticket numbers of tickets checked out to each seller.	Homework: EVERYONE: Using prize kit, request at least one prize. Place posters in designated places. Sell tickets.
5		Writing Crew: Suspense and characterization through dialogue and action.			
5		(OVER WEEKEND HOMEWORK) Writing Crew: Meet with adult director for help with problems and suggestions. Then, finish script. Arrange to copy script before next class meeting. Create tentative rehearsal schedule deciding which writers will rehearse which scenes. Ideally, more than one scene will be rehearsed at a time for blocking and basic dialogue.			

Hospitality Crew

Job Description: Coordinate all personnel, equipment, supplies, and refreshments needed for a positive audience experience.

- Post sign-ups for refreshments.
- Follow up to assure refreshments will be at the performance space when needed.
- Acquire refreshment supplies including plates, napkins, flatware, cups, and tablecloths.
- Arrange for ice, coffee pots, hot plates, Crock-Pots, platters, and serving pieces for the performances.
- Acquire pencils and pads of paper for the audience members to record their clues and questions.
- Assure cleanliness and appropriate temperatures of performance space.
- Provide change, cash box, and ticket sellers if any tickets will be sold at the door.
- Provide ushers to take tickets, hand out programs, and seat audience members.
- Provide staff to serve refreshments.
- Provide a clean-up crew for performance space for both before and after performances.

Hospitality Crew Possible Schedule

NOTE: "Day" column indicates day of the week based on a five-day week and 35-minute work period. "Meeting" column indicates the work period and jobs to be accomplished. If a plus (+) follows the day, then activity begins on the day noted and continues until it is completed.

Week	Day	Meeting	Activity	Done
3	2	1	Make sign-up sheet for ushers, refreshment servers, and clean-up crew. Post in crew area, encourage sign-ups.	
3	2	2	Provide crew list to Program Crew.	
3	3+	3	Arrange for cold storage of refreshments needing refrigeration.	
3	3+	4	Arrange for secure storage of refreshments.	
3	3+	5	Make master list of ushers, refreshment servers, and clean-up crew. Post in crew area. Encourage sign-ups.	
4	1	6	Provide accurate and updated crew list to Program Crew.	
4	1	7	Make master list for refreshments, post in crew area, and assign crew members to keep track of each donation.	
4	1+	8	Arrange for ice, coffee pots, hot plates, Crock-Pots, platters, and serving pieces for the performances.	
4	2+	9	Acquire pencils and pads of paper for the audience to record their clues and questions.	
4	5	10	Plan extracurricular hospitality work with director/sponsor if necessary.	

Hospitality Crew Possible Schedule, continued

Week	Day	Meeting	Activity	Done
5	1	11	Provide accurate and updated crew list to Program Crew.	
5	1+	12	Meet with director or adult sponsor to ensure all necessary work is being done.	
6	1	13	Provide accurate and updated crew list to Program Crew.	
6	2	14	Meet with servers to describe duties: prepare plates and cups with refreshments, serve refreshments, provide additional paper and pencils as needed, and clean up accidental spills.	
6	2	15	Meet with ushers to describe duties: take tickets, hand out programs, and seat audience members.	
6	2+	16	Remind those providing refreshments about what they have signed up to bring and when they have signed up for.	
6	5	17	Have someone on the crew available to accept refreshments before school, after school, and at final call before the first performance.	
6	5	18	Ensure cleanliness and appropriate temperatures of performance space.	
6	5	19	Have someone from the crew available to accept refreshments at final call before the second performance.	
6	5	20	Write thank-you notes to those who have helped with facility and organization. Provide thank you notes to students to thank everyone who donated refreshments.	
6	5	21	Ensure that performance and refreshment storage and prep places are completely clean and restored.	

Hospitality Server Sign-Up

Name	Performance 1	Performance 2

Hospitality Refreshment Sign-Up

Name	Refreshments Promised	Performance 1	Performance 2

Hospitality Crew Supplies

Item	Qty	Source	Who	Have	Date

Weeks Five and Six Materials

Ideas and Assessment for Week Five

Room Configuration

Continue with room configuration the same as Weeks Three and Four with emphasis on the duplication of the performance space taped onto the floor.

Atmosphere

Excitement and stress will build. It's important to outline what the day's responsibilities and goals will be every day. Respect, civility, clarity in communication, and openness to ideas are most important in these decisive days. If the adult director has favorite relaxation exercises, now is the time to employ them.

Equipment and Materials

Now, you're accumulating all the stuff for the production. Appropriate storage and tidiness are mandatory. Props and costumes can become a liability at this point if everyone is not extremely careful.

_____ Ticket money and prize collection paperwork (Beginning of every class)

_____ Basic lighting equipment and control

_____ CD player and basic sound equipment

_____ Basic special effects projectors and equipment

_____ Electrics Crews will have to strike (remove) and secure everything they use after each rehearsal

_____ Scenery and props will be added daily (And probably will have to be struck daily, too)

_____ Pencils and paper provided by students

Assessment

Is everyone following the master schedule? Has everyone learned their lines and blocking on time? Are all the crews up-to-date with their duties? (Keep referring to those schedules and duties.) The adult director needs to stress that there will be time to perfect everything in the next weekend and week. A good plan today is good enough.

Week Five Possible Schedule

Day	Ticket Money, Class Business 5 min	Rehearsal and Discussion • Crew Work 35 minutes	Class Business, Handouts, & Forms 5 min
1	Writing Crew picks up scripts if necessary. Prize Crew makes note of acquired prizes on master list.	Writing Crew presents script and scene-by-scene rehearsal schedule. Actors read script as written in their characters, but without stage directions. Actors take notes specific to their characters and to plot in general. Crew heads take notes specific to their jobs. Class discusses script and, with leadership of adult director, designates appropriate changes.	
		(AFTER SCHOOL) Writing Crew: make script changes as approved in class. Tentatively block action.	
2	Prize Crew makes note of acquired prizes on master list.	Actors read script as written in their characters, but without stage directions. Actors take notes specific to their characters and to plot in general. Crew heads take notes specific to their jobs. Class discusses script and, with leadership of adult director, designates appropriate changes.	
		(AFTER SCHOOL) Writing Crew: make script changes as approved in class. Tentatively block action.	
3	Prize Crew makes note of acquired prizes on master list.	Rehearsal by scene. Minor script changes as appropriate. Actors not rehearsing should memorize lines or work with their crews. Crews meet, even as actors in those crews are rehearsing.	
		(AFTER SCHOOL) Writing Crew: make script changes as approved in class. Tentatively block action.	
4	Prize Crew makes note of acquired prizes on master list.	Rehearsal by scene. Script changes as appropriate. Actors not rehearsing should memorize lines or work with their crews. Crews meet, even as actors in those crews are rehearsing.	
5	Prize Crew makes note of acquired prizes on master list.	Rehearsal by scene. Script changes as appropriate. Actors not rehearsing should memorize lines or work with their crews. Crews meet, even as actors in those crews are rehearsing. Last day of script changes.	

Ideas and Assessment for Week Six

Room Configuration

Continue with room configuration the same as Weeks Three, Four, and Five. You may have to adjust the tape (and the performance space it represents).

Atmosphere

Relax. Be positive. Be excited. How could the show be anything but wonderful? Nothing negative should ever be said. Helpful comments from anyone except the adult director may not be so helpful, so be aware of what everyone is doing and saying. Keep on letting everyone know just what they are supposed to be doing. Walk among the student directors as they work on scenes. Make sure the crews know you are a resource.

Equipment and Materials

Now, you're adding all of the hospitality and front of house equipment to the mix. A place for everything, and everything in its place.

_____ Final scripts

_____ Ticket money and prize collection paperwork (Beginning of every class)

_____ All electrical equipment

_____ All props and costumes labeled and stored

_____ Crews must strike and secure everything they use after each rehearsal

Assessment

Is everyone following the master schedule? Has everyone learned their lines and blocking on time? Are all the crews up-to-date with their duties? (Keep referring to those schedules and duties.)

Week Six Possible Schedule

Day	Ticket Money, Class Business	Rehearsal and Discussion • Crew Work • Hospitality			Class Business, Handouts, & Forms
	5 min	25 minutes	5 minutes	5 minutes	5 minutes
1	All Crews submit updated lists to Program Crew. Assemble props and costumes, place scenery, lighting, FX, and sound	Full dress rehearsal by scene with all available costumes, props, and scenery. Actors not rehearsing should work with their crews.			Secure props, costumes, scenery, lighting, FX, and sound.
2	Assemble props and costumes, place scenery, lighting, FX, and sound. Program Crew posts updated program for proofing.	Full dress rehearsal by scene with all available costumes, props, and scenery. Actors not rehearsing should work with their crews. Rehearsal starts where last rehearsal left off.			Secure props, costumes, scenery, lighting, FX, and sound.
3	Assemble props and costumes, place scenery, lighting, FX, and sound.	Full dress rehearsal by scene with all available costumes, props, and scenery. Actors not rehearsing should work with their crews. Rehearsal starts where last rehearsal left off.	Speed through of first half of play.	Interview 1/2 of characters.	Secure props, costumes, scenery, lighting, FX, and sound.
4	Assemble props and costumes, place scenery, lighting, FX, and sound.	Full dress rehearsal: second half of play.	Speed through of second half of play.	Interview 1/2 of characters.	Secure props, costumes, scenery, lighting, FX, and sound.
	Assemble props and costumes, place scenery, lighting, FX, and sound.	(OUTSIDE CLASS TIME) 2 hours. Rehearse at adult director's discretion.			Secure props, costumes, scenery, lighting, FX, and sound.
5	Assemble props and costumes, place scenery, lighting, FX, and sound.	Rehearse at adult director's discretion.		Interview characters as indicated by adult director.	Secure props, costumes, scenery, lighting, FX, and sound.

A Sample Schedule for Performance on a School Day

Time	Directors/ Actors	Hospitality	Refreshments	Scenery	Electrics	Props and Costumes
7:00 AM		Collect desserts.				
7:30 AM						
8:00 AM		Secure desserts.				
8:30 AM						
Regular School Day						
3:00 PM	Rehearse.	Set tables: cover, plates, napkins, flatware, pencils, paper, programs, cups.	Set up dessert table.	Put up set.	Set up lights, sound, and effects.	Set up prop table. Set up costume chairs.
3:30 PM						
4:00 PM			Collect and organize desserts.			Bring in and organize props and costumes with actors' help.
4:30 PM	Choose suspects/rehearse.					
5:00 PM						
5:30 PM						
6:00 PM					Electrics checks.	
Cast and crew eat.						
6:30 PM		Ushers ready.	All desserts in place.			All props and costumes in place.
6:50 PM	Choose murderer/places.			Places.	Places.	Places.
7:00 PM	**Performance**					
7:30 PM						
8:00 PM	Questioning of suspects — the murderer revealed. Prizes awarded. Refreshments finished. The audience leaves.					
8:30 PM						
9:00 PM	Clean up. Everything pre-set for next show.					

A Sample Schedule for a Weekend Performance

Time	Directors/ Actors	Hospitality	Refreshments	Scenery	Electrics	Props and Costumes
3:00 PM	Rehearse.	Collect desserts. Set tables: cover, plates, napkins, flatware, pencils, paper, programs, cups.	Set up dessert table.	Put up set.	Set up lights, sound, and effects.	Set up prop table. Set up costume chairs.
3:30 PM						
4:00 PM			Collect and organize desserts.			Bring in and organize props and costumes with actors' help.
4:30 PM	Choose suspects/rehearse.					
5:00 PM						
5:30 PM						
6:00 PM					Electrics checks.	
Cast and crew eat.						
6:30 PM		Ushers ready.	All desserts in place.			All props and costumes in place.
6:50 PM	Choose murderer/places.			Places.	Places.	Places.
7:00 PM	**Performance**					
7:30 PM						
8:00 PM	Questioning of suspects — the murderer revealed. Prizes awarded. Refreshments finished. The audience leaves.					
8:30 PM						
9:00 PM	Clean up. Everything cleaned up and put away.					

119

The Adult Director Thinks about Theatre Terms and Practices

Stage Directions:

Stage Right — the actor's right.

Stage Left — the actor's left.

Downstage — the part of the stage closest to the audience.

Upstage — the part of the stage farthest from the audience.

Off-stage — anywhere not seen by the audience.

Body Positions:

Open — most of the actor's front is facing the audience. ("Open up" is one of the director's most frequent pleas.)

Closed — most of the actor's front is facing away from the audience.

More Helpful Theatre Jargon:

Places — the announcement that lets everyone know that they should be in the place where they start the show.

Call — when everyone should be at the theatre and ready to go.

Notes — observations of the director (or other person whose opinions are valued) that are written during a rehearsal or performance and shared with the appropriate people afterward in order to improve the next session. Notes should always be framed positively: "Will you try _____ next time?" or "What if you _____ next time you rehearse?" Often simply asking someone how they would like to do it next time will make the corrections needed.

Helpful Rehearsal Tools:

Line Bash — Do actor's know their lines? Find out by sitting in a circle and just saying lines in order as fast as possible. Just the lines, ma'am, just the lines.

Speed Through — A line bash with blocking. Often actors get caught up in "meaning," and "thought," and "pauses" and forget to work on lines and flow. The speed through is the answer to this problem. The single goal of the speed through is to go as fast as possible and get all lines right while doing all of the blocking.

Dry Tech — While the actors are working on something else, the tech crew takes over the performance area and makes all shifts as quickly as possible. A student director may be there to say cue lines only.

Hint:

Use a shallow set to force the actors to be in front of the set, being more visible and audible to the audience. If the audience is eight feet in front of the front of the set, all actions happens "up close and personal." (This gives you more room for those revenue-generating tables, too!)

The Maui Murders – A Sample Show

How It Might Have Happened:

- In Week One, the class chooses an island theme and presents excellent plot ideas for a play called *The Maui Murders*. There is a good balance of kid characters and adult characters.

- In Week Two, the students write interesting character biographies with enough detail to easily place their characters in the plot. They effortlessly come up with motivations to murder their fellow characters.

- Throughout class discussion, students show interest in the possible jobs for the play and are already thinking of potential costume and scenic elements.

- The teacher carefully chooses the Writing Crew: Bill Blore, Vera Claythorne, Tony Marston, and Tom Rogers. These four have an excellent feel for the dramatic, work well with other students, are delightfully creative, and are dependable. They will also act as student directors and stage managers in Weeks Five and Six and for the show. Here's a sample of what the writing committee came up with:

Writing the Script

- In Week Three (the first week of Writing/Acting/Tech) the Writing Crew creates an excellent scenario. The show is called *The Maui Murders* and is set at an exclusive celebrity resort on Maui where several families have won weeklong stays. Here is the beginning of the scenario the Writing Crew presents to the class at the end of Week Three.

Cast

Mr. Brown	Mrs. Brown
Brad Brown	Pete Brown
Jenny Brown	Mr. Green
Mrs. Green	Lesley Green
Anna Green	Bob Green
Management — Pilar	Management — Laird
Strange waiter	Maître d'
Waiter 1	Waiter 2

Scene 1: Connecticut, Scene 2: Oregon — Two families from different parts of the USA discover that they have won weeklong, all expenses paid trips to an exclusive resort on Maui. One family has never traveled before and accepts this trip enthusiastically. The other is very suspicious and assumes it's a scam to sell timeshares. Their teenage children talk them into going.

We open with two short scenes, one for each family: the Brown home in Connecticut and the Green home in Oregon. In these scenes, we introduce the situation and family members and establish each character's unique personality.

Scene 3: LAX — The families meet at the airport and board the plane.

The airport scene allows for further introduction of characters. Not just as they are in their families but as they appear to others.

Scene 4: Maui Airport — There is some problem on the flight, but they arrive safely where the resort management meets them.

Scene 5: Corridor at Resort — At the resort, they go to their respective rooms. Some of the kids decide to check out the pool area. They meet a strange waiter who tries to tell them to get help before he disappears behind a door. Following him, they discover a secret passageway.

The first mysterious events occur: a mysterious person AND a secret passageway!

Scene 6: The Browns' Room — Meanwhile, back in the rooms, the adults are discovering the hotel's amenities. Someone shows up at the window and then disappears leaving a cryptic message on a napkin saying, "help me."

The second mysterious events occur: a cryptic message and a sudden disappearance!

Scene 7: Dining Room — The two families meet in the dining room for dinner. The tour directors join them and ask how things are going. One of the kids starts to ask about the waiter, but no one claims to know who he is. Mrs. Brown starts to ask about the napkin but is stopped by her husband. The rest of the dinner is tense. The management leaves and everyone asks each other what they think the message means. They decide it's probably some sort of a joke.

The tension mounts as questions aren't answered and people don't act the way we anticipate.

Scene 8: Hotel Corridors — Jenny and Bob are not so sure. They decide to meet after everyone goes to bed.

Scene 9: Hotel Corridors — So do Pete and Lesley.

Here the four teenagers start out acting like kids: inquisitive and sociable. (Do you dare add romance?)

Scene 10: Hotel Corridors — The four run into each other wandering the corridors when they discover the dead body of the "waiter." Terrified, they try to run back to their rooms, but run into the management who claim to have heard a noise they are checking out. When the kids tell them about a dead body, the body has mysteriously disappeared.

MURDER! Our kids end up finding a body — or do they? The adult tour sponsors are "conveniently" there, and the body disappears.

Scene 11: Hotel Corridor outside the Browns' and the Greens' Rooms — The next morning the two families meet for an orientation tour of the property. The parents can't understand why the kids are so upset. On the way to the meeting, a scream is heard. The families return to the Browns' room and decide to leave. Then Mr. Brown reveals that he is an FBI agent on the trail of mysterious doings at the hotel.

An Off-stage scream punctuates the families' morning meeting. Who is it? Where did it come from? Will the answers to the questions clarify or deepen the mystery?

Et cetera ...

As you can see, we have two murders, and they are obviously linked. We have suspects in all the hotel staff and, perhaps, the Green family. Depending on time constraints and class decisions, scenes can be added with meals, recreational activities, and introductions of other hotel guests, personnel, or perhaps even a scene in the spa or the gym. It all depends on the number of students and the amount of rehearsal time for the play. One of the dead bodies can turn up not dead at all, or another guest may disappear.

A Note on Scene Changes and Continuity

You may notice that there are many, many scenes, perhaps more than seem necessary. Please also notice that few of these scenes require much in the way of set pieces.

Scenes and scenery depend on your performance space, how you visualize the show, what you have on hand, and the technical background and skills of your students. You may choose to set up your playing area with simultaneous settings in numerous areas (as we do when performing in the school cafeteria) or play transitional scenes in front of a stage curtain. Alternately, you may choose to write a script with a limited number of scenes. Just remember that you do not want to have "dead time" so beware of set changes and plan for smooth transitions from one scene to the next scene.

After the writers have sketched out the scenes, they do a simple actor/scene breakdown that tells what the roles are, who they have selected to play those roles (based on character bios from Week Two), and where the scenes take place. All of the crews as well as actors will use this breakdown, though everyone understands that it will be fluid until the final week of rehearsal. Scenes may be added or deleted and even characters changed. On the next page is a sample of the actor/scene breakdown the writers have devised. Note that they included a character that no one wrote a character bio for. It was a small part and the writers are confident that it can easily be filled.

Actor/Scene Breakdown for the First Ten Scenes of
The Maui Murders

Actor	Character	Where	1 Connecticut	2 Oregon	3 LA International Airport	4 Maui Airport	5 Corridor at Resort	6 Brown's Room	7 Dining Room	8 Hotel Corridors	9 Hotel Corridors	10 Hotel Corridors	11 Corridor outside Brown and Green Rooms
Ed Armstrong	Mr. Brown		x		x	x		x	x				x
Lucy Combes	Mrs. Brown		x		x	x		x	x				x
Larry Wargrave	Brad Brown		x		x	x	x		x				x
Ted Seaton	Pete Brown		x		x	x	x		x		x	x	x
Emily Brent	Jenny Brown		x		x	x	x		x	x		x	x
Bill Blore	Mr. Green			x	x	x			x				x
Bea Taylor	Mrs. Green			x	x	x			x				x
Liz Henry	Lesley Green			x	x	x	x		x		x	x	x
Caroline James	Anna Green			x	x	x	x		x				x
Cyril Hamilton	Bob Green			x	x	x	x		x	x		x	x
Louisa Clees	Pilar					x			x			x	
Phil Lombard	Laird					x			x			x	
	Strange waiter						x					x	
Art Richmond	Maitre d'								x				
John McArthur	Waiter 1								x				
Ethel Rogers	Waiter 2								x				

While the writers are writing, the actors are talking about acting, talking about mysteries, and playing improv games. The students are also committing themselves to the work that must go on to present the play. It's a busy time.

Suggested Improv Games to Build Acting Skills for Weeks Three and Four

The entire class plays improvisation games to improve their acting skills. The teacher may mix and match games to suit class time and interest. The writers may be excused at the teacher's discretion.

Week Three

M *Murder in the Dark* (quick thinking)
   Headline Prompts (plot)

T *If I Were (Metaphor) Game* (character)

W *Suspense* (plot)

R *Park Bench* (quick thinking)

F *Motivations* (character)

Week Four

M *Word Tennis* (quick thinking)
   Happy Hands (character)

T *CSI: Your Home Town* (plot)

W *Frozen Pictures* (plot)

R *Talk Show* (characterization)

F *Tell Me About The Time You …
   (TMATTY)* (quick thinking)

Crew Work in Weeks Three and Four

Below is a sample roll sheet with roles and jobs filled in for our mythical *Maui Murders*. Notice that lighting and effects (FX) have been combined, as have box office and ticket sales, and hospitality and ushers. It's easy enough to create a spreadsheet customized to your needs. Once you have it, you can adapt it to many uses such as actor and crew sign-in, and a double check for the Program Crew.

Two parent volunteers, Annette Henry (Elizabeth's mom) and Tom Rogers (Ethel and Tom's dad) have graciously offered to help with box office, ticket sales, scenic construction, and lighting and effects. Frances Flyingfingers (Middleton Middle School's office manager and a whiz with desktop publishing) has graciously offered to help with the programs. Hopefully, later in the process, more parents will offer to help.

L Name	F Name	writer	director	scenic design	lighting design	stage manager	role	scenic construction	stage crew	lighting/FX	costume/hair	prizes	props	sound	graphics	publicity	box office/ticket sales	hospitality/ushers
Armstrong	Edward						Mr. Brown				■					■	■	
Blore	William	■					Mr. Green		■			■						
Brady	Jennifer						Mrs. Brown	■								■		■
Brent	Emily						Jenny Brown				■					■		
Claythorne	Vera	■				■		■										
Clees	Louisa						Pilar		■			■	■					
Combes	Lucy								■								■	
Hamilton	Cyril						Bob Green		■								■	
Henry	Elizabeth						Lesley Green	■							■		■	
James	Caroline						Anna Green		■	■								
Landor	Stephen							■						■		■		
Lombard	Phillip				■		Laird		■	■								
Macarthur	John						Waiter 1						■			■		
Marston	Anthony	■						■	■							■		
Ogilvie	George								■		■		■					
Richmond	Arthur			■			Maitre d'	■				■						■
Rogers	Ethel				■		Waiter 2			■					■			
Rogers	Thomas	■		■			Strange Waiter	■				■		■				
Seton	Ted						Pete Brown		■								■	■
Taylor	Beatrice						Mrs. Green	■				■						
Wargrave	Lawrence						Brad Brown					■						■
Henry	Mrs. Annette																■	
Rogers	Mr. Thomas							■		■								

The Maui Murders Prize Crew

The Maui Murders
Prize Crew
Bill Blore
Emily Brent
Louisa Clees
Art Richmond
Tom Rogers
Bea Taylor
Larry Wargragve

Jobs
Post Prize Deadlines
List Potential Donors
Assemble
Solicitation Kits
Keep Track of Prizes
Store Prizes

Each student in the class is responsible for getting at least one prize for the play. The Prize Crew coordinates everything. They take donor suggestions from the class and make a list of potential donors. They then fill out an assignment list and check it daily to see who has gotten prizes and who may need some encouragement. When they aren't in a scene, they're working on prizes or on their other crews, but they set aside time during class, during the school day, or on their own to coordinate their activities.

The class brainstorms prize solicitation techniques. The teacher chooses one student and the teacher and student model a prize solicitation. Then each student role-plays a prize request. Students may role-play in small groups or for the entire class. The class summarizes good solicitation techniques. The teacher looks at prize acquisition as a speech project.

Each student gets a "prize kit" of a manila folder with prize solicitation hints, a list of where the student will solicit prizes with the name of the person to ask, a prize form (in duplicate) printed on school letterhead, a piece of carbon paper, and a pen. Perhaps a local business or bank will donate the pens. A clipboard is a nice luxury.

The Prize Crew posts the prize solicitation deadline prominently and makes sure the prizes are tabulated when the forms come in (see example on page 127). They arrange for secure places to store prizes that are brought in, and if students need help, they assign someone to pick up prizes when and where the donor chooses.

Soliciting Prizes

Each student soliciting prizes should be ready to discuss the following with potential prize donors:

- School Name.

- That your drama class (name of group if you have one) is presenting an original interactive murder mystery.

- Know how to describe the interactive murder mystery.

- Performance date(s).

- That part of the success of the show depends on donation of prizes for those who correctly guess the murderer.

- That you hope the business will donate a prize.

- That the business gets recognition in the program and when the prize is presented.

- Number in anticipated audience.

- Reiterate that it will be good publicity for the business.

- The donation is tax deductible as the school and program is nonprofit.

- Be ready to talk about the teacher, what the money from this show will be used for, and a little about the show. (Without giving anything away!)

126

Hints for Students

- Know what you are going to say.
- Be ready with answers for questions. If you don't have an answer, know where to get one.
- Respect the potential donor's time. If they want to talk more, that's OK.
- Dress in "nice" school clothes.
- Be well-groomed.
- No gum.
- Use your company manners.
- Introduce yourself.
- Have donation form and duplicate printed on school letterhead ready to fill out.
- Have pen to fill out form.
- Be ready to make arrangements to get prize to school before the performance.

Student		Prize	Prize Source	Prize Contact and Phone	Prize at Theatre	Prize in Program	Thank You
Armstrong	Edward	$25 Savings Bond	Middletown National Bank	Mr. Wells, xxx-xxx	■		
Blore	William	4 coups for CD's ($15 ea)	First Street Books and Music	Mr. Gordon, xxx-xxx	■		
Brady	Jennifer	2 tickets	Middleton Cinema	Mrs. Deal, xxx-xxx			
Brent	Emily	10 $5 coups	Dollar Day	Mr. Smith, xxx-xxx	■		
Claythorne	Vera	coup for 1 dozen doughnuts	Fourth Street Catering	Mr. Stephens, xxx-xxx			
Clees	Louisa	6 climbing wall coups	Middletown YMCA	Mrs. Day, xxx-xxx	■		
Combes	Lucy	1 framing ($25 value)	Village Arts	Mrs. Walker, xxx-xxx			
Hamilton	Cyril	1 quart local honey	Hometown Market	Mr. Jones, xxx-xxx			
Henry	Elizabeth	2 coups for a dozen eggs each	Shop Right	Mr. Grothus, xxx-xxx	■		
James	Caroline	One 1-hour gig, coup	Joe the DJ	Mr. Allen, xxx-xxx	■		

Prize Solicitation Kit

- Manila folder
- Prize donation form(s) in duplicate: original on school letterhead (donor copy), carbon paper (school copy)
- Ballpoint or roller ball pen (provided by student)
- Clipboard (optional)

Sample Prize Solicitation Interview (in person)

Hello! Thank you for giving me a moment of your time. My name is Bill Blore and I am a student at Middleton Middle School. My first period drama class is presenting an original interactive murder mystery as a fundraiser. (If your potential donor is interested, you could explain a bit abut the plot and format here.) It will be performed on January twenty-first and twenty-second, and we will be awarding door prizes to those in the audience who correctly guess the murderer. We hope your business will be interested in donating a door prize to us for this enterprise. In return, your name will be printed prominently in the program as well as being announced when the prize is awarded. We anticipate approximately one hundred and fifty people will attend, many of them adults, and we feel that your donating a prize will be good publicity for your business as well as supporting our school's drama department. Your donation will be tax-deductible since our school is a nonprofit organization. Do you have any questions? I have a form here you can fill out. I can take the prize with me now or you can call me to let me know when to pick it up. Thank you so much for your time.

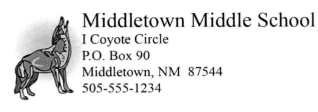

Middletown Middle School
I Coyote Circle
P.O. Box 90
Middletown, NM 87544
505-555-1234

Maui Murders Prize Donation

To encourage the amateur detectives in our audience to do their very best sleuthing, we will offer prizes to those who correctly deduce the murderer's identity. You are invited to join in the fun by donating a prize to the show.

Business or Organization _____
(please write name as it should appear in the program)

has donated (item) _____

to be given as a prize at a performance of **The Maui Murders**, at Middletown Middle School on January 21 and/or 22, 2000.

Donors' names will be featured prominently in the play program as well as being mentioned as the prize is awarded.

Representative of Donating Business: _____

Business Address: _____

Business Phone: _____

Approximate value of donation: _____ Date _____

Student Representative of Maui Murders: _____

The Maui Murders, An Interactive Mystery, is a production of The Rebels Without Applause, Middletown Middle School's first period drama class
Questions about The Maui Murders or prize donations
should be directed to Mrs. Jones at 505-555-1234 x 123.

Please keep this copy for your tax records.

www.middletownms.net   Home of the Coyotes   A Baldrige School
John Ducksinarow, Principal   Miriam Ontopofit, Assistant Principal

Prize Thank You Notes

Every donated prize deserves a handwritten note from the person who solicited it. Ms. Frances Flyingfingers, the very helpful school office assistant, turned the show's logo into notepaper using Photoshop and some ingenuity. The notepaper printed up two to a sheet and photocopied beautifully. Below are samples of the notepaper and the note.

Of course, the note was sent after the show so a reference to the success of the show and of the prize can be included, but students may make rough drafts of their notes before the event.

Envelopes for the four-and-one-quarter inch by five-and-one-half inch size are readily available at your stationery or warehouse store. Regular postage applies or you can hand deliver it.

Remember when you are laying notepaper out to put the graphics on the right side of the paper, when it's printed and folded, it comes out.

> Dear Mr. Smith,
>
> The *Maui Murders* were a great success. The audience loved the show and all of the class had a great time working on it. *Maui Murders* made enough money that we can go ahead with our plans for a spring musical.
>
> I don't have to tell you that we couldn't have done it without the support of First Street Books and Music. Our amateur sleuths loved the First Street CD coupons. It really made their detective work pay off!
>
> Having you serve as our ticket outlet was perfect. You helped us get tickets to people who don't know cast members and the bookkeeping was flawless.
>
> On behalf of all of the Rebels Without Applause, Thank You!
>
> Very sincerely yours,
>
> William Blore

The text of the note. Notice it doesn't start with "thank you," includes why it was important to have prizes, that the donated prizes made a difference to the show, the audience response to the donated prizes, and ends with a sincere "thank you."

Cover   Inside

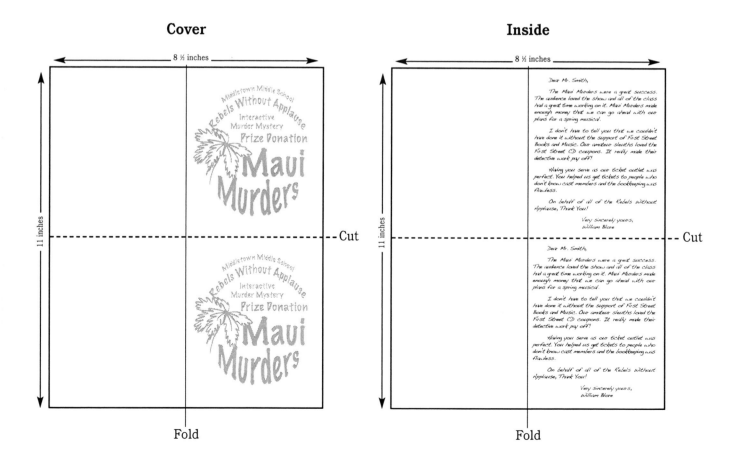

The Maui Murders Scenery Crew

Remember KISS: Keep it Simple and Sensible? This one rule is *vital* for the Scenery Crew. Most of the crew members must also act and get prizes; they don't have time to design and construct an elaborate set. Fortunately for *The Maui Murders,* Ethel and Tom Rogers' dad, Tom Rogers, Sr., has offered to help the class. He's even manipulated his work schedule so he can be available during first period for four days during the next two weeks. Mr. Rogers will bring his own hand tools to the class, and the crew promises to treat his tools with care and respect. He will pre-cut lumber so no power cutting tools will be necessary.

● ● ● ● ● ● ● ●

The Maui Murders
Scenery Crew
Jennifer Brady
Vera Claythorne
Liz Henry
Steve Landor
Tony Marston
Arthur Richmond
Tom Rogers
Bea Taylor
Advisor
Mr. Thomas Rogers

Jobs
Measure/Draw Acting Space
Create Scene Breakdown
Plan Scenery
Schedule Scenery
Construction
Acquire Scenic Materials
Construct/Assemble Scenery
Paint Scenery

● ● ● ● ● ● ● ●

Preliminary Scene Work

The Scenery Crew uses the planning that was done in Weeks One and Two to make a preliminary scenery plan. They know there will be scenes in the homes of the two families, at the airport, and at the resort in Maui. The Writing Crew will keep them up to date on any additional scenes they might decide to use. By the end of the third week, the writers present the play to the class and the Scenery Crew will adjust their work to include any scenes that have been added. If the writers have gotten too fanciful, the Scenery Crew will ask them to rethink the scene to make the set requirements manageable.

With Mr. Rogers' help, the Scenery Crew measures the acting space in the cafeteria where the play will be presented. They draw the space to scale on graph paper. They note all doors and obstacles in the playing space. The Scenery Crew will use these measurements to plan the set and use the preexisting features to their advantage. The measurements will come in handy when the class rehearses the show in the classroom where they will mark out the playing space on the floor with masking tape.

Notice that Mrs. Jones has not been too proud to ask for help, and she has developed a good enough rapport with fellow teachers, parents, and community actors that they are delighted to be asked.

The Scene Breakdown

After all scenes are listed by the location, the crew starts planning. They work to minimize the scenery needed in each scene. Less truly is more with scenery.

Less scenery = more time to rehearse the show.

Less scenery = more time to make individual scenic pieces wonderful.

Less scenery = more sanity.

Working on the principle, "If you say it, you don't have to show it; if you show it you don't have to say it," the Scenery Crew encourages the Writing Crew to include descriptions of what the actors are seeing in the dialogue. "What a beautiful sunset." "I didn't realize how far I could see from the eleventh floor." "This dining room is huge. There must be a hundred tables."

They make a scene breakdown for the show with what they need for each scene. Cleverly, Mr. Rogers has only left five spaces to fill out for each scene (see chart on page 131).

After making their list, they schedule the work and volunteer for/assign jobs. They post their job list prominently in the classroom. Each day, crew members mark on their breakdown what they have done.

The Plan

The crew and Mr. Rogers decide to build palm trees out of carpet tubing, heavy wire, and butcher paper over plywood and two-by-four foot bases and create the masking they need from appliance boxes. They figure they need a neutral white background, a natural tan background, and a beach scene. The appliance boxes will come from Central Avenue Appliances, owned by Louisa Clees's family. The appliance store will deliver the boxes to the school. The actors will modify the Greek idea of periaktoi for three-sided rotating masking.

The local flooring store, Floor Art, has graciously promised the class seven carpet tubes that the shop teacher, John Henry, will pick up and deliver to the drama room. Steve Landor, who takes shop, has asked Mr. Henry for plywood and lumber scraps that the crew is confident will be sufficient for their construction needs. Mr. Henry agrees. The Middletown Players, of which Mrs. Jones is a member, has generously agreed to lend stock scenery to the Rebels and even provide the transportation for the pieces. In this case, the borrowed scenery consists of a door on a rolling platform that will be used for all scenes requiring a door (affectionately called the "skateboard door," a stand-alone railing, and a pair of club chairs.

The crew and Mr. Rogers create a preliminary construction schedule that breaks all jobs down into small parts and gets everything ready for rehearsal by Week Five. Scenery Crew members volunteer for projects that suit their time and talents. Vera and Bea, the artists in the group, take on the complicated tasks of scene and sign painting. The schedule allows crew members to work on small projects as time permits. Mr. Rogers is a great help as he pre-cuts all the wood and makes diagrams of how to build the palm trees. It was he who (thinking ahead to moving scenery) suggested that the trees share common bases.

	Place	Element 1 - Masking	Element 2	Element 3	Element 4	Element 5
1	Connecticut	Periaktoi A - tan	club chair 1	club chair 2	skateboard door	
2	Oregon	Periaktoi C - white	club chair 1	club chair 2	skateboard door	sheets for chairs
3	LA International Airport	Periaktoi A	sign palms	sign	free standing railing	
4	Maui Airport	Periaktoi B&C - beach and white	sign palms	sign	palms 1, 2	palms 3, 4, 5
5	Corridor at Resort	Periaktoi C - white				
6	Brown's Room	Periaktoi B&C - beach and white	club chair 1	club chair 2	skateboard door	palms 3, 4, 5
7	Dining Room	Periaktoi B&C - beach and white	folding tables - 2	folding chairs - 12	palms 3, 4, 5	free standing railing
8	Hotel Corridors	Periaktoi A - tan				
9	Hotel Corridors	Periaktoi C - white				
10	Hotel Corridors	Periaktoi A & B - tan and beach	palms 1, 2	palms 3, 4, 5	free standing railing	palms 6 & 7
11	Outside Brown and Green Rooms	Periaktoi C - white	skateboard door			

Maui Murders   Scenery - Scenes 1 - 11

1	2	3	4	5	6	7	8	9	10	11	Element	Person in Charge	Notes	Treatment	Deadline
											Connecticut / Oregon / LA Int Airport / Maui Airport / Corridor at Resort / Brown's Room / Dining Room / Hotel Corridors / Hotel Corridors / Hotel Corridors / Corridor/Rooms				
■	■			■							club chair 1	Mrs. Jones	from Middletown Players		
■	■			■							club chair 2	Mrs. Jones	from Middletown Players		
		■								■	palm trees 1 & 2	Bea Taylor	Jennifer, Tony, Art -paint tubes, Tom, Bea - cut and wire leaves	brown trunk, fixed green leaves, curved, all on same base	
		■	■	■						■	palm trees 3, 4, 5	Bea Taylor	Jennifer, Tony, Art -paint tubes, Tom, Bea - cut and wire leaves	brown trunk, fixed green leaves, curved, all on same base	
	■	■								■	palm tree/ post 6 & 7	Bea Taylor	Jennifer, Tony, Art -paint tubes, Tom, Bea - cut and wire leaves	brown trunk, straight, leaves may be removed to make sign	
■	■			■						■	skateboard door	Steve Landor	Steve will paint (OK with Middletown Players)	neutral off white	
	■										sheets for ccl 1 & 2	Arthur Richmond	Art will bring two full-sized flat sheets from home. Green print		
					■						folding table 8' x 2.5' - 2	Mr. Al; MMS custodians	Mr. Al's crew will deliver tables and chairs to classroom.		
					■						folding chairs - 12	Mr. Al; MMS custodians	Students will move them to the cafeteria for final rehearsals		
		■		■							free-standing railing	Mrs. Jones	from Middletown Players, Steve will paint	neutral off white	
	■	■									airport sign LA/Maui	Bea Taylor	Bea will paint one side to say, "Welcome to Los Angeles," the other to say "Welcome to Maui"	LAX on one side, Maui on other, sign fits on palm tree bases	
■	■					■	■				periaktoi 1, A	Liz Henry	Mr. Rogers will cut, Liz will paint	neutral light tan	
											periaktoi 1, B	Vera Claythorne	Mr. Rogers will cut, Vera will paint	painted with beach scene, sand and water	
	■	■	■	■			■			■	periaktoi 1, C	Steve Landor	Mr. Rogers will cut, Steve will paint	neutral off white	
■						■					periaktoi 2, A	Liz Henry	Mr. Rogers will cut, Liz will paint	neutral light tan	
				■	■						periaktoi 2, B	Vera Claythorne	Mr. Rogers will cut, Vera will paint	painted with beach scene, sand and water	
	■	■	■				■			■	periaktoi 2, C	Steve Landor	Mr. Rogers will cut, Steve will paint	neutral off white	
■	■										periaktoi 3, A	Liz Henry	Mr. Rogers will cut, Liz will paint	neutral light tan	
				■	■						periaktoi 3, B	Vera Claythorne	Mr. Rogers will cut, Vera will paint	painted with beach scene, sand and water	
	■	■	■				■		■		periaktoi 3, C	Steve Landor	Mr. Rogers will cut, Steve will paint	neutral off white	
■						■					periaktoi 4, A	Liz Henry	Mr. Rogers will cut, Liz will paint	neutral light tan	
											periaktoi 4, B	Vera Claythorne	Mr. Rogers will cut, Vera will paint	painted with beach scene, sand and water	
	■	■	■				■		■		periaktoi 4, C	Steve Landor	Mr. Rogers will cut, Steve will paint	neutral off white	

Paint is a problem. It's expensive and the class would rather not buy paint if they don't have to. After all, the whole project is a fundraiser for the spring musical. Several of the students offer to bring paint from home do-it-yourself projects. Mr. Rogers says that's great as long as it's water-based paint and has been kept inside.

A scavenger hunt?
What a cosmic idea! When the word gets out that the Scenery Crew is having a scavenger hunt, the other crews piggyback their needs onto the list. Everybody works together and has a great time — not to mention coming up with almost all the scenery, props, and costumes the group needs.

This gets the Scenery Crew's creative juices flowing and they devise a scavenger hunt/competition for the class. They need:

- paint — greens, blues, tropical colors, browns, white
- paint brushes (marked indelibly with the owner's name so they can be returned)
- newspapers or plastic tarps for ground cloths
- masking tape
- duct tape (Mr. Rogers added this multi-purpose aid)
- artificial tropical flowers and plants (marked with permanent ink for easy return)
- luau-type decorations: tiki masks, grass skirting, etc.

Planning for the scavenger hunt takes a bit of time, but it's worth it in both the items the class finds, and in the enthusiasm it engenders. After all, who wouldn't want to buy a ticket for a show they've had a part in?

The Maui Murders Electrics Crew — Lighting

Mrs. Jones has wisely suggested that there should be very little special lighting for *The Maui Murders* and she set up the lighting crew accordingly. As the lighting in the cafeteria can be controlled by sections, it will light the acting area nicely while the audience area is not lit.

A simple lighting plan is appropriate to the space as well as the show. Because Middletown Middle School is older, it doesn't have many electrical outlets and all of them are on the same two 20-amp circuits. There are no places to hang lights in the cafeteria.

● ● ● ● ● ● ● ●

The Maui Murders
Electrics Crew –
Lighting
Ethel Rogers
Phil Lombard
Jobs
Inventory Equipment
Check Equipment
Create Scene Breakdown
Create Lighting Looks
Light Plan to Create Looks
Set Up Lighting for
Rehearsal

● ● ● ● ● ● ● ●

Ethel and Phil inventory their equipment. They find:

- two 8' tall tripods with a bar for lights at the top
- ten 500W halogen work lights
- four additional 500W halogen bulbs
- old 6" 500W Fresnel
- lighting control board with eight channels
- 10 15A 50' extension cords
- 10 15A plug strips
- color media (gel), full sheets, in amber, lavender, light blue, red, purple, and dark blue

Using a scene breakdown from the Scenery Crew/writers, Ethel and Phil create their own light plot. First they decide on the look they want for each scene. Next, they decide how they will achieve that look.

Ethel and Phil choose to put four work lights on each tripod and place them at the edge of the audience area near the stage. Those lights will add the atmosphere and versatility they need. The work lights will plug into plug strips that plug into extension cords that in turn plug into the control board. They choose amber and lavender as the colors for front light and decide to add dramatic side lighting with the two remaining work lights — one from each side gelled with red and purple. They put this into a simple light plot.

All goes well until Ethel's father, Mr. Rogers, supervising the lighting setup, notices that the work lights exceed the capacity for the plug strips and extension cords. Ethel and Phil use additional extension cords on each side and create four 1000W circuits instead of two 2000W circuits. This gives them the potential for more versatility and control. They can modify their plot later to reflect the changes or simply use the same settings as before.

	Place	Look	Overhead Lights	Warm - Amber (R)	Cool - Lavender (L)	side special 1 - Red (R)	side special 2 - Purple (L)
1	Connecticut	Winter, snow outside, cool inside and out. Gloomy.	on	5	10	(R)	
2	Oregon	Winter, cool but green outside. Sunny.	on	10	5		
3	LA International Airport	Interior lighting.	on	5	5		
4	Maui Airport	Outside the airport, Warm, balmy.	on	10	5		
5	Corridor at Resort	Interior but warm feeling	on	5	5		
6	Brown's Room	Interior with balcony overlooking ocean. Warm, Sunny.	on	10	5		
7	Dining Room	Interior with wall opening onto the beach. Later in the day. Sunset.	on	10	10	5	
8	Hotel Corridors	Interior. Darker than earlier, but not threatening.	off	10	10		
9	Hotel Corridors	Interior. Darker than earlier, but not threatening.	off	10	10		
10	Hotel Corridors	Interior. Unfamiliar. Kind of spooky. Not well lit. Shadows on walls. (Bump up when staff arrives)	off	3	8	3	10

The Maui Murders Costume Crew

Fortunately, everyone has chosen a character to play and has an idea of how to dress that character. All the Costume Crew has to do is coordinate all the costumes, provide secure storage, supply dressing space, and encourage the cast to bring in their costumes in a timely manner.

Mrs. Jones stresses that the show is not about costumes and that the class should plan to costume the show out of their own and their friends' and families' closets. No one should feel obligated to purchase costumes for the show, though many students will want to buy a fun island shirt or shorts and use the show as an excuse. After deciding that Mr. Brown should wear a business suit and a fedora, the crew adds the fedora to the scavenger hunt. They get three!

Using the filled out Costume Worksheets for individual actors (there is space for two different ensembles/scenes on each worksheet, some actors have one sheet, some more), the Costume Crew makes the Costume Master List and posts it prominently in the classroom. It has a space for each scene and each actor. All of the costume worksheets are kept in a three-ring binder in the costume area of the classroom.

The Costume Crew may work during class time or on their own. A reasonable homework assignment is for the actors to fill out their Costume Worksheets and bring them to class. It's surprising how often thinking about how a character will look will nudge an actor into more thoughtful characterization. The crew approaches Mrs. Jones for money to buy leis that they have found on sale at a local party store. She agrees.

Costume Master List

Cross Reference with Each Actor's Costume Form.   Please check when costumes are at theatre.

Actor	Character	Scene	headgear	underwear	top: shirt/blouse	jacket	outerwear	bottom: skirt, trousers	socks/hose	shoes	accessory 1	accessory 2	Complete (Date)

Costume Worksheet

Actor's Name _____   Character's Name _____

	Scene	Source	Color	Size	Need	Have/date	OK
Headgear							
Underwear							
Top: shirt/blouse							
Jacket							
Outerwear							
Bottom: skirt, trousers							
Socks/hose							
Shoes							
Accessory 1							
Accessory 2							
Notes:							
Headgear							
Underwear							
Top: shirt/blouse							
Jacket							
Outerwear							
Bottom: skirt, trousers							
Socks/hose							
Shoes							
Accessory 1							
Accessory 2							
Notes:							

The Maui Murders Prop Crew

Like costumes, props can often help actors complete their characterization. The crew gives actors a Prop Form to list their props by scene. Again, Mrs. Jones emphasizes that the play isn't about props; it's about characterization and plot. (To that end, each actor's Prop Form has space for only twelve props.) Usually school rules preclude weapons, so those won't be an issue, and as the play stops for audience scrutiny before the perpetrator(s) is/are revealed, there is no need for handcuffs or other restraint.

The Maui Murders props are relatively simple. Suitcases for the families, clipboards for resort staff, the mysterious note, and tablecloths and table wear for the dining room pretty much cover all the prop needs. Individual actors are responsible for the first two. Remembering that if you talk about it you don't have to see it, the actors can leave their surfing and diving equipment outside.

The Prop Crew organizes a closet in the classroom for props. They find that plastic crates and photocopier paper boxes are great for storing individual actors' props. They label the boxes with the actors' names and put a copy of the actors' Prop Form on the outside of the box.

The crew uses the individual forms to create a Master Prop List for the entire class. They post the form prominently and use it to keep track of what props have been brought in. The crew makes a list of props that belong to the show rather than a specific actor, add them to the Master Prop List, and work to find those. The tablecloths were the trickiest item to find until the crew realized that the school office has a number of tablecloths that they can borrow.

Actors will be responsible for their own props throughout the rehearsals and performances.

The Maui Murders Prop Crew
John Macarthur
Louisa Clees
George Ogilvie
Jobs
Have Actors Fill out Individual Prop Worksheets
Create Master Prop Form
Monitor Prop Acquisition
Provide Safe Storage
Offer Prop Suggestions to Actors
Make List of Set Props That Crew Must Acquire

Prop Form

Actor's Name ___ Character's Name ___

Scene	Prop	Need	Have

Master Prop List

Actor	Character	Scene	Prop	At Theatre

● ● ● ● ● ● ● ●

The Maui Murders
Electrics Crew

Ethel Rogers

Tom Rogers

Stephen Landor

Jobs

Create Master Sound Plan

Acquire Sound Cues

Record Cues

Burn Two Copies to CDs

Show Assistant Directors

How Sound Works

● ● ● ● ● ● ● ●

The Maui Murders Electrics Crew — Sound

Again, Mrs. Jones has suggested that the sound cues should be at a minimum. She suggests that a sound cue can start and end a scene but that no music/sound is necessary under the scene. The crew brainstorms and comes up with a sound plan that Mrs. Jones approves.

Steve Landor is a whiz with computers and at finding things on the Internet and finds several appropriate sound cues that may be downloaded and played for free. He also has a currently popular CD of music the class likes that will set the scene nicely for Scene Two. Ethel and Tom Rogers' dad, Tom Sr., has offered to help the crew if they have any glitches and will bring sound equipment from home to play back the sound in the cafeteria. For rehearsal, the class will use one of the class's CD players and the rehearsal CD the crew burns. They'll keep a second CD for the performances and Steve will keep all music on his computer "just in case."

Everyone (even Mrs. Jones) understands that things need to be kept fluid during the two weeks of crew work. As time goes on cues may be added or deleted. It's obvious that the crew works well by themselves or with Mr. Rogers and that sound effects may be layered (such as the sound of surf under Hawaiian music) by this able and hardworking crew.

● ● ● ● ● ● ● ●

The Maui Murders
Graphic Artist

Elizabeth Henry

(Mrs. Fitz, the art teacher, scans the image and provides it on several CDs for class use.)

● ● ● ● ● ● ● ●

The Maui Murders Graphics

Mrs. Jones, with the help of the school's art teacher, Mrs. Fitz, chooses the graphics for the show from those submitted. Elizabeth Henry, one of the excellent artists in the class has created the winning graphics for the unified look of the show. This includes: posters and flyers, programs, solicitation letters, tickets, publicity mailings, and thank you notes. Mrs. Fitz helps the class by scanning the image and providing it on disc to the crews who need graphics.

	Place	Sound **Maui Murders**	CD	Download	Tape	Playback	Notes
1	Connecticut	Winter Storm Sound	burn onto CD	x		CD	Free download
2	Oregon	Offstage music playing from bedroom	Steve has			CD	
3	LA International Airport	airport sound	burn onto CD	x		CD	Free download
4	Maui Airport	Hawaiian music	Mrs. Jones has			CD	
5	Corridor at Resort	none					may want tension builder
6	Brown's Room	none					
7	Dining Room	dining room ambience	burn onto CD	x		CD	Free download
8	Hotel Corridors	none					
9	Hotel Corridors	none					
10	Hotel Corridors	tension mounting sounds	burn onto CD	x		CD	Free download

The Maui Murders Publicity Crew

The Publicity Crew's work is immediate and important. They need to create publicity for the show and get it to the public's eye and ear soon. They are responsible for creating the publicity, but all class members must distribute posters and flyers.

They decide that they will concentrate on three audience sectors: students at the school, parents and friends of the class, and the public at large. They brainstorm possible ways to reach their audience. Mrs. Jones encourages the crew to offer as many ideas as possible and discuss and cull them later. They come up with the following list:

- Flyers/posters displayed in the school and community
- Print ads in the local newspaper — B
- Press releases to the local papers
- Radio ads — paid — B
- Radio ads — public service announcements
- School marquee
- Postcards mailed to friends and family — B
- Mini flyers in utility bills — B/T
- Mini flyers to everyone at school — B
- E-mailed announcements to family friends
- Magnets — B/T
- Banner in front of the school
- Table tents in local restaurants — B
- Small flyers attached to delivered pizza boxes — B
- T-shirts worn by the cast — B/T
- Preview performances in community
- Preview performance in school assembly

● ● ● ● ● ● ●

The Maui Murders Publicity Crew
Ed Armstrong
Jennifer Brady
Emily Brent
Steve Landor
John Macarthur
Tony Marston
Ted Seaton
Jobs
Brainstorm and Choose Publicity Avenues
Assign a Crew Person to Be in Charge of Each Avenue
Do Assigned Tasks in the Time Allotted

● ● ● ● ● ● ● ●

Notice that they only rejected ideas as not possible for *The Maui Murders*. This leaves the idea as a possibility for their spring show when they have more time and money.

After creating their list, they looked at it in view of their budget and time. They marked "B" for Budget or "T" for Time next to the items that were not possible for *The Maui Murders*. That left them with the following list to pursue. They put the initials of the person who will look into the possibility of the advertising avenues they keep. They agree to have the information by the next day. Mrs. Jones approves the list.

- Flyers/posters displayed in the school and community EB
- Press releases to the local papers SL
- Radio ads — public service announcements TS
- School marquee JM
- E-mailed announcements to family friends JM
- Banner in front of the school TM
- Preview performances in community EA
- Preview performance in school assembly JB

The Publicity Crew meets with Mrs. Jones and shows her the list that has charted their progress. She looks it over and makes suggestions.

		Maui Murders Publicity Ideas		
Idea	Who	Notes/Contact Person
flyers/posters displayed in the school and community	EB	The school will let us photocopy 100 8 1/2 x 11 flyers for free. We can pay $3.00 for an additional 100. Mrs. Flyingfingers
press releases to the local papers	SL	The Middletown Monitor will print two stories for us and will send a photographer to take photos for the second one that will appear in the Sunday paper before our show opens. They want a brief story with the who, what, when, where and how much as well as the cast names for the first. For the second they want more about the class and how we created Maui Murders. Mr. Kent. The Middletown Guardian only wants one standard press release and will try to get it in the week before the show. Miss Lane.
radio ads - public service announcements	TS	They really want to help us. We need to get two or three cast members to the radio station to record the announcements. They also offered to interview Ms. Jones and the writers live on the Monday morning before the show opens. Mr. Burns
school marquee	JM	Mrs. Flyingfingers has put us on the calendar for the marquee to go up two weeks before opening. Mrs. Flyingfingers.
e-mailed announcements to family friends	JM	Mrs. Flyingfingers suggested that we get permission from Mr. Ducksinarow to send an e-mail announcement about Maui Murders to all school parents. She can do that from her office if it's OK. Mr. Ducksinarow said OK, but he wants to see the announcement. Mrs. Flyingfingers. Mr. Ducksinarow.
banner in front of the school	TM	Mrs. Flyingfingers said if we had the marquee for two weeks, we don't need a banner. Mrs. Flyingfingers.
preview performances in community	EA	Mrs. Hamilton from the Arts Council says that she will ask the Arts Council board if we can have a preview performance at a Brown Bag Lunch the week of the show. It would probably be on Wednesday. We'd have to get kids out of fourth period to go. Mrs. Hamilton.
preview performance in school assembly	JB	Mr. Ducksinarow said he will OK a preview performance on the Monday before the show during first period. Teachers who want their students to come can sign up for their classes to attend starting tomorrow. Mr. Ducksinarow. Teachers.

The meeting yields the following:
- Flyers — they will only get 100 as the group can't think of more than 100 places to put flyers. Emily will work with Liz Henry to have a copier-ready flyer by the end of the week. Mrs. Flyingfingers will make the copies and put them in Mrs. Jones' mailbox by Monday morning of the next week.
- Press releases — Steve will assemble all facts necessary to help Mr. Kent and Miss Lane with their stories. He will write a release suitable for publication in case they want to print his story as is. Mrs. Jones suggests that he put all of the most important information in the first paragraph as most editors cut from the bottom up to make stories fit available space.

- Radio ads — Ted Seaton will work with Mr. Burns at the radio station to coordinate an after-school recording session with a few cast members. Mrs. Jones sadly points out that they won't be able to do a live broadcast during school time as they can't take time off from school. She suggests that Ted ask if they could pre-record the interview at the same time they make the radio spots. Ted will report back.

- School marquee — John Macarthur has already done everything he needs to as he and Mrs. Flyingfingers set up the marquee information at his first meeting. Mrs. Flyingfingers will put the marquee up on Week Five to run for two weeks. It's on her calendar.

- E-mail announcement to school population — John Macarthur will take the final poster to Mrs. Flyingfingers at the end of the week. The crew decides to have Mrs. Flyingfingers do the bulk e-mail at the beginning of Week Five. That will give the parents time to buy tickets but, hopefully, not enough time to forget the event.

- Preview performances in the community — The crew and Mrs. Jones realize that they can't get out of school or pay for school transportation for a midday preview. Mrs. Hamilton didn't give a possible evening date. Ed Armstrong will get back to Mrs. Hamilton about an evening date.

- Preview performance at school — Jennifer Brady asks Mrs. Jones if the 100 flyers cover all school advertising, as she'd like to have posters for the in-school assembly posted around the school to build up anticipation. Mrs. Jones agrees to spend three dollars more for publicity before and during the assembly. Jennifer figures that she can print 50 half-sheet flyers to put on lockers and 300 quarter-sheet flyers to hand out at the assembly for that three dollars. 300 will cover half the school population. Jennifer will get together with graphic artist Liz Henry about flyer design. Ed Armstrong will work with Jennifer and Liz as it looks as if there will not be a community preview. They plan to meet with the writing committee to plan the preview.

The Maui Murders Ticket Crew

Edward Armstrong
Lucy Combes
Cyril Hamilton
Liz Henry

Advisor
Mrs. Annette Henry

Jobs
Design Tickets
Print Tickets
Number Tickets
Distribute Tickets
Teach Class How to
Sell Tickets
Encourage Ticket Sales
Keep Track of Ticket Sales

The Maui Murders Ticket Crew

The crew meets with their advisor, Mrs. Henry, to decide:

• What the tickets should look like

• How they will print them

• When they will go on sale

• How to keep track of them

Fortunately, the drama club has been using the same ticket technique for quite a while, so they don't have to reinvent the format. In fact, they even have blank perforated ticket paper in two colors on hand. The tickets have two stubs that facilitate selling tickets in advance and keeping track of who sold them. Liz Henry's artistic abilities are called on and she and her mom, Annette Henry, offer to make the sample ticket. The ticket is simple, as it needs to be clearly understood.

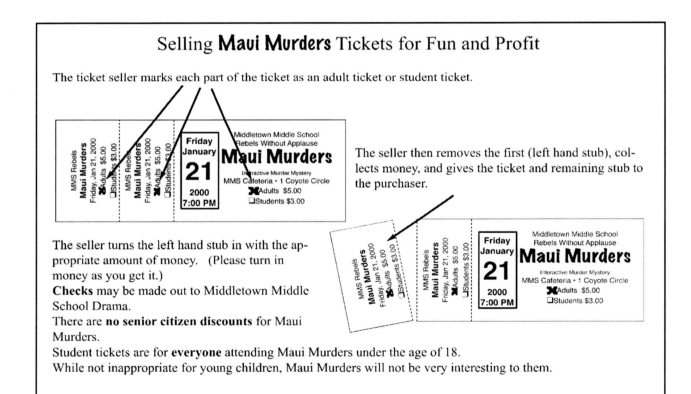

Selling **Maui Murders** Tickets for Fun and Profit

The ticket seller marks each part of the ticket as an adult ticket or student ticket.

The seller then removes the first (left hand stub), collects money, and gives the ticket and remaining stub to the purchaser.

The seller turns the left hand stub in with the appropriate amount of money. (Please turn in money as you get it.)
Checks may be made out to Middletown Middle School Drama.
There are **no senior citizen discounts** for Maui Murders.
Student tickets are for **everyone** attending Maui Murders under the age of 18.
While not inappropriate for young children, Maui Murders will not be very interesting to them.

It occurs to the crew that they don't know how many seats they can sell tickets for. They get permission from Mrs. Jones to go to the cafeteria to count seats. They get a tentative ground plan for the set and go off to the cafeteria.

There is room in the cafeteria for the set and ten twelve-person cafeteria tables, plus two long tables that are eight feet long by two and a half feet wide that will be used for refreshments. The audience will be limited to 120 people per performance.

Some quick figuring tells the crew that if they sell 120 tickets a night for two nights, there is a potential of 240 audience members. If they sell their tickets for three dollars for students and five dollars for adults and the audience is half and half, there is a possible 960 dollars to be made. With just slightly more adults than students, and careful control of expenses, the class can clear 1,000 dollars. Two full houses is the class' goal. Ed Armstrong asks his mom, Jan Armstrong, who is a potter, if she will make a special award for the person who sells the most tickets. Mrs. Armstrong readily agrees to custom make small first, second, and third place plaques for ticket sales winners plus another plaque for First Street Books and Music. She also generously offers to supply four of her locally famous coffee mugs as prizes.

The crew decides that, as the tickets are so reasonably priced, there will be no price break for senior citizens and that the student price will be for everyone under the age of eighteen.

With twenty-one students in the class, and having First Street Books and Music as the ticket outlet, each student needs to sell approximately fifteen tickets. Some students will not be able to sell that many; others will want to sell a great many more. The crew thinks a ticket sale contest will motivate the class.

The crew sets the goal of having tickets and ticket sale information in student hands before the weekend between Weeks Three and Four so they will have as long as possible to sell tickets. Then disaster strikes. Their lovely ticket paper has been ruined in storage and they don't have time to reorder. What will Plan B be? They'll ask the Parent Teacher Organization if they have 240 roll-tickets with stubs left over from their last raffle. Each ticket seller will mark the backs with A for Adult and S for Student so they can make sure the tickets sold match the money collected.

The ticket sales may seem a bit complicated at first, but it is the only way they can be sure they don't oversell the event. When students sell tickets, they bring in the stub with the money collected for each ticket. A quick check of stubs against money makes bookkeeping easy. With the tickets already numbered and a good checkout system, it's even possible to know who sold which ticket. This comes in handy when students lose tickets or, worse yet, have them stolen.

Tickets will go to First Street Books and Music on Monday of Week Five, giving student ticket sellers a head start.

The crew decides to create a sales thermometer to keep track of ticket sales and motivate the class. Lucy Combes takes butcher paper home to work on it there. They ask Mrs. Jones for a place to put the thermometer so it will always be visible in the classroom.

They modify the ticket sales form from past productions and photocopy one for each student. It shows how to sell tickets and will accompany an envelope with tickets. Mrs. Flyingfingers gives the class a box of envelopes that have the school's old logo on it. They will be perfect for tickets and money for individual students.

Mrs. Jones sets aside a few minutes at the beginning of class in Weeks Four, Five, and Six for the Ticket Crew to collect tickets stubs and money. They use a form to keep track of each student's sales and another to report money and stubs collected. Having students turn in money and stubs from tickets sales daily makes recordkeeping easier and keeps the school bookkeeper happy, too.

Ticket Sales Master List

Seller		Mon		Tue		Wed		Thur		Fri		Total	
		Qty	Amt	Qty	Amt	Qty	Amt	Qty	Amt	Qty	Amt	Qty	Amt
	AD												
	CH												
	AD												
	CH												
	AD												
	CH												
	AD												
	CH												
	AD												
	CH												
	AD												
	CH												
	AD												
	CH												
	AD												
	CH												
	AD												
	CH												
	AD												
	CH												
	AD												
	CH												
	AD												
	CH												

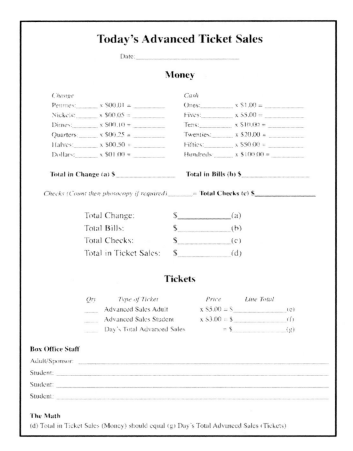

Today's Advanced Ticket Sales

Date:_____

Money

Change
Pennies:_____ x $00.01 = _____
Nickels:_____ x $00.05 = _____
Dimes:_____ x $00.10 = _____
Quarters:_____ x $00.25 = _____
Halves:_____ x $00.50 = _____
Dollars:_____ x $01.00 = _____

Cash
Ones:_____ x $1.00 = _____
Fives:_____ x $5.00 = _____
Tens:_____ x $10.00 = _____
Twenties:_____ x $20.00 = _____
Fifties:_____ x $50.00 = _____
Hundreds:_____ x $100.00 = _____

Total in Change (a) $_____   **Total in Bills (b) $**_____

Checks *(Count then photocopy if required)*_____ = **Total Checks (c) $**_____

Total Change: $_____ (a)
Total Bills: $_____ (b)
Total Checks: $_____ (c)
Total in Ticket Sales: $_____ (d)

Tickets

Qty	*Type of Ticket*	*Price*	*Line Total*	
_____	Advanced Sales Adult	x $5.00 = $	_____	(e)
_____	Advanced Sales Student	x $3.00 = $	_____	(f)
_____	Day's Total Advanced Sales	= $	_____	(g)

Box Office Staff
Adult/Sponsor: _____
Student: _____
Student: _____
Student: _____

The Math
(d) Total in Ticket Sales (Money) should equal (g) Day's Total Advanced Sales (Tickets)

The Maui Murders **Hospitality Crew**

It's time for the Hospitality Crew to jump into action and plan everything they will need for the refreshments for the show, plus line up all of the "detecting" items. The crew chooses what type of refreshments they want to serve and what a serving of that refreshment consists of.

After a sobering trip of pricing supplies, the crew decides to use brownies and cookies (refreshments that need no plates, spoons, or forks) as the main refreshments and to serve only drinks that are made from a mix — no soft drinks or coffee. Mrs. Jones agrees to use ticket sale money for necessary supplies if they cannot be donated.

They decide that a serving is one twelfth of a nine inch by thirteen inch baking pan of brownies or two cookies. They choose to use twelve ounce cups in which they will put ice and eight ounces of liquid. They plan on an average of one and a half drink servings per patron for a total of 15 gallons. They will need twenty pans of brownies or forty dozen cookies for the two performances or a combination of the two.

Ideally each student brings in home-baked goodies to serve to the play's guests. It works out to be either one pan of brownies or two dozen cookies per student. The crew announces this and posts a sign-up sheet for refreshments. The same may be done for drinks or they might get drinks donated. The crew decides to explore drink donation options before they ask for students to bring drinks. They will report back about beverages at the end of Week Three.

When Art Richmond asked, Middletown National Bank graciously agreed to provide ten dozen pens for the play. The crew decides to use binder paper for the detectives to write on, providing two sheets per person for a total of a 500-sheet package. The crew will shop prices for supplies at a warehouse store and report back. The cafeteria will supply ice for the refreshments at no charge to the Rebels. They also will give the class space in a walk-in refrigerator for refreshments.

The Hospitality Crew posts a sign-up sheet for cookies and brownies. Because of the offer of walk-in refrigerator space, they decide to make the refreshment deadline the day before the show. Crew members will each be responsible for the refreshments for four students plus themselves. They will remind students at the end of Week Five about their promised refreshments and again the day before they are due.

As Middletown serves a reasonably affluent part of town, it isn't a hardship for most students to be assigned to bring in cookies or brownies. Here's where sensitive guidance from Mrs. Jones is crucial. In no way should it ever look as if a student is graded on his or her resources rather than abilities. Mrs. Jones knows which of her students might not be able to provide refreshments and makes other arrangements with them individually, perhaps suggesting that they ask for the donation of baked goods from a local bakery or grocery. She may also decide not to worry about one or two students not bringing in refreshments, as many families will send in a recipe's-worth of cookies, often as many as six dozen, which will nicely cover for the missing refreshments. It is her experience that there are always more than enough baked goods for the show, plenty for the kids to eat during clean-up, and enough leftovers for the custodial break room and staff lounge.

Sample Program for *The Maui Murders*

Everything fits on one eight and a half by eleven inch paper printed horizontally. Note that the cover (first page) is at the right. When it folds, it all works out correctly. A single page program is easy to photocopy.

The Program Crew starts with a cast list provided by the writer/directors, crew lists provided by the crews themselves, donor information from those who got the prizes, and acknowledgements from everyone. They get updated and corrected lists every Monday in Weeks Four, Five, and Six. They post their version of the updated lists on Tuesday. Everyone is expected to initial their entry every time if it's correct or correct and initial if it's not.

The Program Crew starts with just lists and formats the program in the beginning. Gradually, they format and add Liz Henry's graphics.

What the crew can't do, Mrs. Flyingfingers in the school office can, and graciously will do.

Sample Flyer for *The Maui Murders*

Everything fits on one eight and a half by eleven inch paper printed vertically. The Publicity Crew has gotten all of the information on it and used Liz Henry's graphics well.

Posters Include:

Who – school, drama class period, their class' name

What – name of play, that it's an interactive murder mystery

When – day(s), date(s), time

Where – not just the school but where at the school

How much – adults, students/retired, *how to get tickets*

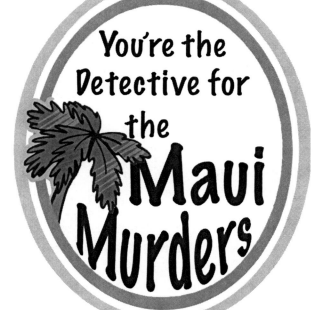

The Middletown Middle School First Period Drama Class
Rebels Without Applause
Say

You're the Detective for the Maui Murders

An Original Interactive Murder Mystery
7:00 PM   January 21 and 22, 2000
Middletown Middle School Cafeteria
Tickets Advanced Sales Only **$3.00** Students & Retired **$5.00 Adults**
Available from Cast Members and at
First Street Books and Music

More Sample Scenarios

Following are cast lists, scenarios, and comments on five of the plays created by eighth grade students at Los Alamos Middle School from 1994-2004. I decided to include cast lists and scenarios instead of scripts for several reasons. First of all, these were all collaborative efforts. Some of them were scripted entirely by a committee while others were written scene-by-scene, each scene by different students. But all of them belong to the specific class that produced them, and I did not feel that it was my place to publish others' works. Secondly, specific slang seems to change on a monthly basis. I found that dialogue from 1994 was greatly different from that used in 2004. I didn't want to have to revise this since by the time the scripts are published they will have changed again. Next, each group of young people has its own personality. It is very important that any script developed reflect this. Different parts of the country will have different stereotypes, values and interests, perhaps even local urban legends that may be incorporated.

Finally, these scenarios may be used and adapted, and each group will come up with different types of characters, victims, and perpetrators. Perhaps only the setting will be used and an entirely different plot will emerge. Maybe only the characters will inspire a group.

By providing these as examples, I expect that the basic structure of the scripts will emerge and suggest hundreds of other ways for your group to proceed. Remember that this is not supposed to be a work of high art, but a process in which all the students can participate.

Middle School Murder Mysteries 1994-2004

1. *Camp Minnehaha.* Summer camp setting. Different activities.
2. *Celebrity Survivor Island.* Well-known celebrities trapped on an island.
3. *Graduating to Murder.* A high school graduation week and its activities.
4. *The Halloween Murders.* Costumes, disguised identities.
5. *Mama Said Murder.* Film screening.
6. *The Middle School Murders.* A staff member is "murdered" and all staff and students are suspects.
7. *Murder among the Tombstones.* Graveyard setting. Supernatural, locked room.
8. *Murder at the Chocolate Factory.* The return of Willy Wonka!
9. *Murder at the Mall.* Clichés, mall stuff. Varied set.
10. *Murder in the Museum.* Middle school class field trip. Teacher and students in a wax museum.
11. *Murder on the High Seas.* Celebrities on a cruise. Academy Awards.
12. *A Rehearsal for Death.* Theatre setting, supernatural, musical. Inspired by *The Phantom of the Opera.*
13. *A Reunion with Death.* High school conflicts at a reunion.
14. *The Subway Murders.* Unit set. "Locked room." Variety of characters.
15. *The Talent Show Murder.* Short acts. Easy to stage.
16. *A Very Brady Murder.* Well-known and well-loved TV characters recast into a different situation.
17. *A Willful Murder.* Stereotyped characters and motives. A big house.

A Willful Murder
Characters

Edgar Cunningham
A rich old man dying of a mysterious illness. 80.

Scarlett Cunningham
Cunningham's granddaughter. Raised by Cunningham and is his only heir. 25.

Dr. Robbins
Family physician. 60s.

Mr. Pembroke
Cunningham's family attorney. 60s.

Jonathon Winston
Scarlett's fiancée.

Robert Patterson
Scarlett's true love, a student.

Nurse Rogers
A formidable dominating woman, in charge of Cunningham's medical care in the home.

Chef LeBlanc — A persnickety French chef.

Yves Roucel — The wine master.

Dotty — Kitchen maid.

Doris — Kitchen maid.

Bennison — The butler.

Maisie — A servant.

Molly — A servant.

Mr. Brown — The mayor.

Count Orloff — Newcomer to town.

Countess Orloff — Newcomer, the count's wife.

Jack — Band member.

Thom — Band member.

John — Band member.

Nick — Band member.

Mr. Black — The undertaker.

Townspeople

A Willful Murder

Scenario

Rich old Edgar Cunningham is dying — or so he thinks, and no one can tell him otherwise. Convinced he has little time left, he instructs his attorney to change his will.

No one is happy in this household! Cunningham's granddaughter, Scarlett, has been "engaged" to Jonathon in a marriage of convenience since his father is a business associate of Cunningham's. But she is in love with Robert, a young man studying at the local community college in town. The servants are all aflutter, not knowing how much longer they will be employed. And, to top it all off, Mr. Cunningham has just informed everyone that he intends to throw a magnificent ball, a sort of "send-off" party.

The day of the ball arrives. Not all is well. The servants seem unusually touchy. The chef has made some strange dishes. The sommelier/bartender has chosen odd wines and designed personalized drinks that do not sound tasty in the least. As the guests arrive, much confusion and suspicion is revealed. Scarlett has a fight with Jonathon and tells him the she does not love him and never has.

Some "important" people arrive in a limousine, and more intrigues are introduced. Who are the Count and Countess, really? Where are they from? Why is the mayor so overly eager to please? Why is Edgar's nurse so very eager that he takes his newly prescribed medication? And why is the undertaker there?

Before Edgar can announce the changes in his will, an odd band shows up allegedly replacing the string quartet that had been hired. With their arrival, the servants seem especially nervous. Why? Suddenly Edgar collapses, dying before he can read the changes in his will.

> *Comments:* We added the band so that the cast would have a chance to dance the Macarena, a dance craze. Alternatively, that could be an excuse for an already existing middle school band to play or for some class members to mime and lip-synch currently popular music. This was the only mystery that had a somewhat hardwired plot with a mostly "adult" cast. As the years went by, fewer and fewer classes wanted to portray adults, the only exception being celebrities.

Murder at the Museum
Characters

Museum Staff

Natasha Tarkovsky — The strong, seemingly sadistic museum director. A Russian spy.

Jesse — A Vietnam veteran in need of a job, has constant flashbacks to combat.

Jason — An out-of-work slacker, wants a job. Any job.

School Staff

Sister Mary Margaret — Principal of Our Lady of Constant Sorrow Middle School, about to retire, just wants peace.

Joy — Chemistry teacher. Disapproves of "alternative" behavior, paranoid.

Terra — English teacher. Flies off the handle. Has a reputation for not controlling her students.

Dominique — Music teacher. Very critical.

Students

Andy — Very sensitive. Mooning after Kate.

Iris — Sarcastic. Very "alternative" in appearance and attitude.

Kate — An airhead cheerleader.

Theo — A nerd who does other's homework so he will be liked.

Jeff — Surfer dude. Agreeable.

Bryan — Surfer dude.

Derek — Spacey.

John — An athlete. Thinks he's cool.

Christine — Shy.

Raven — A goth poet. Psychic.

Loren — Critical.

Grace — Boy crazy.

Bob — A prankster.

Justin — Slow.

Fantastic Predators

Humans —
Lizzie Borden
Jack the Ripper
Jeffrey Dahmer

Animals —
Shark
Tiger
Bear
T-Rex
(Whatever costumes you have)

Concept —
War
Death
The Plague

Fantasy —
Frankenstein
The Mummy
The Wolfman
Dracula

The Murder at the Museum

Scenario

Sister Mary Margaret, principal of Our Lady of Constant Sorrow Middle School, has decided that the eighth graders will take their annual field trip to the newly opened Museum of the Predators. This museum has a rather strange concept — it is a museum exploring four kinds of predators: human, animal, fantasy, and concept. The other teachers are less than enthusiastic about this decision. Some feel that the museum is inappropriate while others squabble over which students they will need to be responsible for. The staff seems much divided.

Meanwhile, Natasha Tarkovsky, the new director of the museum, is just finishing the hiring process. Part of the museum's attraction is that some of the exhibits are actually actors portraying the actual predators. She has just finished hiring two rather odd young men to portray Death and War. While they seem to be most satisfactory, she herself seems suspicious and unduly nervous. The students are excited about the field trip and eagerly get on the bus. While riding to the museum, each student reveals his/her personality as they interact in small groups and react to events on the bus.

Arriving at the museum, the students are assigned in groups of five to each of the four teachers. Some of the groups get along. Others are immediately unhappy with their assignments.

Each group visits a different part of the museum, interacting with each other and reacting to the exhibitions. Some find the exhibits interesting and engage in discussions on the aspect of the times/historical significance. Others are simply interested in their peers and how they can bully, bother, or impress the others.

The groups meet up in the cafeteria to discuss the exhibits and to have lunch. Much disagreement occurs with the teachers doing a lot of infighting and the kids mocking each other and the teachers. At the end of the lunch, someone discovers that the museum's doors are all locked. Then someone is found dead under the table.

The museum staff disclaims all responsibility but starts acting strangely. Accusations fly back and forth. Finally, the police arrive. One of the students tries to solve the crime. Blame is assessed.

Comments: This play can utilize a very large cast. When we performed it, we used volunteers from the other classes to be the "wax" figures. This was especially fun because the volunteers got to wear interesting costumes which made the set much more colorful.

The students all loved to play stereotypical eighth graders as well as making fun of "types" of teachers.

The only challenging part of the set was the school bus, and we made use of a spotlight and freezes to stage this scene.

The Halloween Murders
Characters

Family

Allen Michael — Father of the girls. An accountant. Tennis player. A softy.

Michelle Michael — A socialite. Tries to be strict.

Alisa Michael — The oldest sister. Hates her annoying parents.

Marie Michael — Annoying little sister.

Linda Michael — A nerd. Dependable. Tries to keep order. A worrywart.

Grandma Michael — Lives with her son and daughter-in-law. Old but tries to be young.

Staff

Brad — A studly security guard. Hates Linda.

Callie — A caterer. Hates teens.

Alf — An employee of the caterers. Foreign. Doesn't speak English well.

Lynch — Musician. Tries to be cool.

Guests

Cindy — Cheerleader.

Francesca — Hates Cindy.

Andrea — Sweet.

Belle — Poor.

Karen — Talkative.

Stan — Jaded.

Mac — Skater.

Others

Mrs. Black — Neighbor. Likes to spy on the kids.

Mr. Black — Henpecked husband.

Sergeant Brown

The Halloween Murders

Scenario

The Michael family is known for their annual Halloween party. Mr. and Mrs. Michael are always extravagant, hiring bands, and caterers. This year, however, the oldest of their three daughters has convinced them to leave while she and her responsible sister, Linda, host a group of their friends. The only catch is that their grandma and little sister have to be included. The parents have hired a security staff, so they are quite sure that nothing will get out of hand at this teenage party.

From the time they leave, however, things go wrong. Stephanie doesn't want her little sister anywhere around, and Grandma starts acting like a teenager. The security staff has a bad history with certain members of the band, and the invited guests have conflicting agendas. Some want to rollerblade in the house, others want to push rivals into the pool.

Meanwhile, the next door neighbors have had it. They have never liked the Michael family as they feel that the older girl is a bad influence on their oldest son, David. They decide to spy on the party to see if there is some behavior they can report to the police. Ideally, they would like to have the party shut down altogether. Then, they discover that their son is missing. Using this as an excuse to crash the party, they demand to see their son whom the others claim is not there.

Comments: This play is good especially if you have a local band or even a group of students who can play a few songs. If not, a DJ can replace the idea of a live band. It also has room for dancing and even showing off rollerblading or skateboarding kids. Halloween costumes can figure as colorful additions to a simple living room set.

Murder among the Tombstones
Characters

Kids
Billy

Brad — Can't read. A football hero.

Katie — Cheerleader. Stuck up.

Nassria — A foreign exchange student living with Katie's family.

Sammy — An intellectual.

Timmy — Billy's little brother.

Frankie — A prankster.

Cindy — A socialite.

Sophie — Drama girl. Poet.

Colleen — Drama girl. Dramatic.

Selina — Tarot card reader.

Jane — Afraid of everything, superstitious.

Bobby — Computer nerd.

Johnny — Hates violence, a nerd.

Tanya — Valley girl.

Brittney — Valley girl.

Sheila — Bookish.

Adults
Howard — Gravedigger.

Francesca — Gravedigger's wife.

Drake — Caretaker of cemetery.

Murder among the Tombstones

Scenario

It's getting towards Friday the Thirteenth, and a group of kids get mysterious invitations to a party at an unknown address. Most are thrilled to be invited, but a cautious few consult the local psychic to see if doom is foreseen. It is, but then, who believes in psychics?

Meanwhile, back at the cemetery, the evil gravedigger and his cohort chortle over the gullibility of teenagers and anticipate another exciting time scaring the teens half to death. But why? What do they really want?

Undeterred, the teens arrive at the unknown address that turns out to be the local cemetery. Sensing an adventure, small groups enter the park only to find the gates slammed and padlocked behind them. They decide to split up to try to find an exit, vowing to meet at a certain spot in an hour.

Each group then experiences various problems. One group discovers that the tombstones carry the names of certain members of their group. Another starts losing group members. Another argues so much that they split up. And each group starts getting clues from the gravedigger on how to find the way out. Is this just a game, or is it something more sinister? And is there someone or something evil lurking in the crypt? Are zombies real?

Comments: The graveyard setting complete with tombstones was really lots of fun to make. Transitions were easy as lights were turned out and the different groups went their respective ways through the graves by flashlight, adding an eerie look and an interesting focus. The blend of mystery and the supernatural is always something that appeals. Instead of ghosts, we used zombies. A good reference for this show was *The Zombie Survival Guide* by Max Brooks.

A Talent for Murder
Characters

Students

JD — An earnest student government representative.

Kyle — A "hottie."

Mandy — Cheerleader.

Michelle — Cheerleader.

Miranda — Cheerleader.

Amber — Wannabe cheerleader.

Vanessa — Wannabe cheerleader.

Natalia — Foreign exchange student.

Skip — Boy band wannabe.

Matt — Boy band wannabe.

Michaele — Band member.

Kristin — A shy poet.

Kitty — A snobbish poet.

Bob — Juggler.

Paul — Juggler.

Stephanie — Drama jock, MC.

Josh — Drama jock, MC.

Adam — Student director.

Cynthia — Techie.

Riley — Techie.

Alice — A mime.

Adults

Gladys — A stage mother.

Mr. Butler — School drama teacher.

Elizabeth — Student teacher, assistant director.

A Talent for Murder

Scenario

It's audition time for the annual high school talent show, the event of the year at good ole West High! As tryouts are announced, we are introduced to all the potential performers, many of whom have histories of interpersonal and intergroup conflicts.

Before the audition, we meet the crew-to-be and the teacher/director, Mr. Butler. No one seems to be very experienced or to really know how to go about it. In addition, they do not seem to get along very well.

The day of the audition arrives. As each act gets ready to display his/her talent, much anxiety and competitiveness is displayed. Unfortunately as well, several acts have failed to show up and props and costumes have disappeared. Sabotage is suspected.

Each act auditions as the techies strive valiantly to get the sound and lights to work properly. An electrical short happens just as one of the contestants is standing near the light and when the lights come back on, he/she is found dead.

Chaos reigns as each contestant accuses another. Luckily, the police arrive in time to gather the suspects!

Comments: This was a particularly fun project since the students all had "acts" to perform, both in groups and individually. Since shows such as *American Idol* and *X Factor* are all the rage, even those less comfortable with their "talent" were eager to perform. Being bad could be good, in this case!

In this particular class, we had several cheerleaders, but you could have lip-synchers or dancers instead. Any budding stand-up comedians? Anyone for another performance of "Who's on First?"

The sky's the limit for the acts, and this format is particularly easy to stage!

Titles

Sometimes when you hear a title, you just know it will be a good mystery. You might want to talk about how these titles by well-known mystery writers evoke a feeling.

Let's start with titles from the first lady of mystery, **Dame Agatha Christie** (1890-1976). Some are literary allusions, some sound sinister, and others sound completely innocent. From over one hundred and fifty titles, here are some of the most evocative:

4.50 from Paddington
A.B.C. Murders, The
Absent in the Spring
After the Funeral
Afternoon at the Seaside
Alibi
Alphabet Murders, The
Appointment with Death
Black Coffee
Blood Will Tell
Body in the Library, The
Burden, The
By the Pricking of My Thumbs
Cards on the Table
Cat Among the Pigeons
Daughter's a Daughter, A
Dead Man's Folly
Dead Man's Mirror
Death in the Air
Dumb Witness
Easy to Kill
Endless Night
Evil Under the Sun
Five Little Pigs
Funerals are Fatal
Go Back for Murder
Hickory Dickory Death
Hidden Horizon

Holiday for Murder, A
Hound of Death, The
Innocent Lies
Listerdale Mystery, The
Man in the Brown Suit, The
Mirror Crack'd , The
Mousetrap, The
Moving Finger, The
Mrs. McGinty's Dead
Murder After Hours
Murder Ahoy!
Murder at the Vicarage, The
Murder for Christmas
Murder in Retrospect
Murder in the Mews
Murder in Three Acts
Murder Is Announced, A
Murder Is Easy
Murder Most Foul
Murder She Said
Murder with Mirrors
Mystery of the Blue Train, The
Nemesis
Ordeal by Innocence
Overdose of Death, An
Pale Horse, The
Partners in Crime
Patient, The

Patriotic Murders, The
Peril at End House
Pocket Full of Rye, A
Remembered Death
Rule of Three
Secret Adversary, The
Sleeping Murder
So Many Steps to Death
Sparkling Cyanide
Spider's Web
Taken at the Flood
Tea for Three
Ten Little Indians
The Rats
There Is a Tide
They Do It with Mirrors
Third Girl
Thirteen at Dinner
Three Blind Mice
Towards Zero
Under Dog, The
Unexpected Guest, The
Unfinished Portrait
Verdict
Wasp's Nest
What Mrs. McGillicuddy Saw!
While the Light Lasts
Why Didn't They Ask Evans?

Sir Arthur Conan Doyle
(1859-1930) gave us Sherlock
Holmes and the following titles:
(Notice that many of his titles are
"The Adventure of —." Today one
would be inclined to leave that off.)

The Adventure of:
the Blue Carbuncle
Silver Blaze
the Bruce-Partington Plans
the Dancing Men
the Devil's Foot
the Empty House
the Final Problem
the Musgrave Ritual
the Priory School
the Reigate Squire
the Second Stain
the Six Napoleons
the Speckled Band

Five Orange Pips, The
His Last Bow
Hound of the Baskervilles, The
Red-Headed League, The
Scandal in Bohemia, A
Sign of Four, The
Study in Scarlet
Valley of Fear, The

Rex Stout
(1896-1975) gave us detectives
such as Nero Wolfe and titles that
often left us eager to discover
how the title worked with the
story:

Assault on a Brownstone
Before I Die
Bitter End
Black Orchids
Cop-Killer, The
Cordially Invited to Meet Death
Counterfeit for Murder
Death of a Demon
Die Like a Dog

Disguise for Murder
Door to Death
Easter Parade
Eeny Meeny Murder Mo
Fourth of July Picnic
Frame-Up for Murder
Gun with Wings, The
Hand in the Glove, The
Help Wanted, Male
Home to Roost
Immune to Murder
Instead of Evidence
Invitation to Murder
Kill Now — Pay Later
Man Alive
Method Three for Murder
Mountain Cat Murders, The
Mr. Cinderella
Murder Is Corny
Murder Is No Joke
Next Witness, The
Not Quite Dead Enough
Omit Flowers
Poison à la Carte
President Vanishes, The
Rodeo Murder, The
Squirt and the Monkey, The
This Won't Kill You
Too Many Cooks
Too Many Detectives
When a Man Murders…
Window for Death, A
Zero Clue, The

Dashiell Hammett
(1894-1961) wrote of detective
Sam Spade and gave us one of the
most famous mysteries of all
time, The Maltese Falcon. Other
Hammett titles include:

Adventures of Babe Lincoln, The
Black Bird, The
Charlie Wild, Private Eye
House in Cypress Canyon, The
Kandy Tooth Caper, The
Satan Met a Lady

Strange Case of the End of
   Civilization as We Know It, The
They Can Only Hang You Once
Too Many Have Lived

Jeffery Deaver
(1950) gives us several
protagonists and some juicy
titles:

Bloody River Blues
Blue Nowhere, The
Bodies Left Behind, The
Bone Collector, The
Broken Window, The
Coffin Dancer, The
Cold Moon, The
Devil's Teardrop, The
Empty Chair, The
Garden of Beasts
Hard News
Lesson of Her Death, The
Maiden's Grave, A
Manhattan Is My Beat
Praying for Sleep
Roadside Crosses, The
Shallow Graves
Sleeping Doll, The
Speaking in Tongues
Stone Monkey, The

Dorothy Sayers
(1893-1957) sleuth, the
aristocratic Lord Peter Wimsey,
is featured in the following
mysteries (don't the titles make
you want to know more?):

Busman's Honeymoon
Clouds of Witness
Five Red Herrings
Gaudy Night
Hangman's Holiday
Have His Carcase
In the Teeth of the Evidence
Lord Peter Views the Body
Murder Must Advertise

Nine Tailors, The
Presumption of Death, A
Striding Folly
Strong Poison
Thrones, Dominations
Unnatural Death
Unpleasantness at the
   Bellona Club, The
Whose Body?

In light of the many titles that contain numbers, it's probably time to mention **Janet Evanovich** (1943):

One For the Money
Two for the Dough
Three to Get Deadly
Four to Score
High Five
Hot Six
Seven Up
Hard Eight
To the Nines
Ten Big Ones
Eleven on Top
Twelve Sharp
Lean Mean Thirteen
Fearless Fourteen
Finger Lickin' Fifteen

Sequential numbering might work if a drama club or little theater group decided to create a series of interactive mysteries.

And while we're talking about series and sequential titles, we should mention **Sue Grafton's** (1940) alphabetically ordered Kinsey Milhone novels. What wonderfully evocative titles!

"A" Is for Alibi
"B" Is for Burglar
"C" Is for Corpse
"D" Is for Deadbeat

"E" Is for Evidence
"F" Is for Fugitive
"G" Is for Gumshoe
"H" Is for Homicide
"I" Is for Innocent
"J" Is for Judgment
"K" Is for Killer
"L" Is for Lawless
"M" Is for Malice
"N" Is for Noose
"O" Is for Outlaw
"P" Is for Peril
"Q" Is for Quarry
"R" Is for Ricochet
"S" Is for Silence
"T" Is for Trespass
"U" Is for Undertow
"V" Is for Vengeance (as of 2011)

Occasionally a mystery writer has a theme. Often titles from themed mysteries use word play to draw the reader in. This is true with mysteries from the dog world. **Lee Charles Kelley** (1951) takes time out from training dogs to write mysteries about them and their owners:

Like a Dog with a Bone
Murder Unleashed
Nose for Murder, A
To Collar a Killer

Laurien Berenson also writes dog mysteries:

Best In Show
Chow Down
Dog Eat Dog
Doggie Day Care Murder
Hair of the Dog
Hot Dog
Hounded to Death
Hush Puppy
Jingle Bell Bark
Once Bitten

Pedigree to Die For, A
Raining Cats & Dogs
Underdog
Unleashed
Watchdog

If you're looking for tasty titles, try **Diane Mott Davidson's** (1949) Goldy Schultz novels. Goldy is a caterer and the books even include recipes:

Catering to Nobody
Cereal Murders, The
Chopping Spree
Dark Tort
Double Shot
Dying for Chocolate
Fatally Flaky: A Novel
Grilling Season, The
Killer Pancake
Last Suppers, The
Main Corpse, The
Prime Cut
Sticks and Scones
Sweet Revenge
Tough Cookie

Aligning Mystery Class to the National Standards for Theatre Education

About the National Drama Standards

This list may act as a reference indicating drama skills addressed in the lessons and also help with lesson plans, as many state theatre standards reflect the national standards. Please see Resources at the National Alliance for Theatre and Education's website at www.aate.com.

Content Standard #1: Script writing by the creation of improvisations and scripted scenes based on personal experience and heritage, imagination, literature, and history.

Achievement Standard:

a) Students, individually and in groups, create characters, environments, and actions that create tension and suspense.

b) Students refine and record dialogue and action.

Content Standard #2: Acting by developing basic acting skills to portray characters that interact in improvised and scripted scenes.

Achievement Standard:

a) Students analyze descriptions, dialogue, and actions to discover, articulate, and justify character motivation and invent character behaviors based on the observation of interactions, ethical choices, and emotional responses of people.

b) Students demonstrate acting skills (such as sensory recall, concentration, breath control, diction, body alignment, control of isolated body parts) to develop characterizations that suggest artistic choices.

c) Students in an ensemble interact as the invented characters.

Content Standard #3: Designing by developing environments for improvised and scripted scenes.

Achievement Standard:

a) Students explain the functions and interrelated nature of scenery, properties, lighting, sound, costumes, and makeup in creating an environment appropriate for the drama.

b) Students analyze improvised and scripted scenes for technical requirements.

c) Students develop focused ideas for the environment using visual elements (line, texture, color, space), visual principles (repetition, balance, emphasis, contrast, unity), and aural qualities (pitch, rhythm, dynamics, tempo, expression) from traditional and nontraditional sources.

d) Students work collaboratively and safely to select and create elements of scenery, properties, lighting, and sound to signify environments, costumes, and makeup to suggest character.

Content Standard #4: Directing by organizing rehearsals for improvised and scripted scenes.

Achievement Standard:

a) Lead small groups in planning visual and aural elements and in rehearsing improvised and scripted scenes, demonstrating social, group, and consensus skills.

Content Standard #5: Researching by using cultural and historical information to support improvised and scripted scenes.

Achievement Standard:

a) Apply research from print and non-print sources to script writing, acting, design, and directing choices.

Content Standard #6: Comparing and incorporating art forms by analyzing methods of presentation and audience response for theatre, dramatic media (such as film, television, and electronic media), and other art forms.

Achievement Standard:

a) Describe characteristics and compare the presentation of characters, environments, and actions in theatre, musical theatre, dramatic media, dance, and visual arts.

b) Incorporate elements of dance, music, and visual arts to express ideas and emotions in improvised and scripted scenes.

c) Express and compare personal reactions to several art forms.

d) Describe and compare the functions and interaction of performing and visual artists with audience members in theatre, dramatic media, musical theatre, dance, music, and visual arts.

Content Standard #7: Analyzing, evaluating, and constructing meanings from improvised and scripted scenes and from theatre, film, television, and electronic media productions.

Achievement Standard:

a) Describe and analyze the effect of publicity, study guides, programs, and physical environments on audience response and appreciation of dramatic performances.

b) Articulate and support the meanings constructed from own and others' dramatic performances.

c) Use articulated criteria to describe, analyze, and constructively evaluate the perceived effectiveness of artistic choices found in dramatic performances.

d) Describe and evaluate the perceived effectiveness of students' contributions to the collaborative process of developing improvised and scripted scenes.

Content Standard #8: Understanding context by analyzing the role of theatre, film, television, and electronic media in the community and in other cultures.

Achievement Standard:

a) Describe and compare universal characters and situations in dramas from and about various cultures and historical periods, illustrate in improvised and scripted scenes, and discuss how theatre reflects a culture.

b) Explain the knowledge, skills, and discipline needed to pursue careers and vocational opportunities in theatre, film, television, and electronic media.

c) Analyze the emotional and social impact of dramatic events in own life, in the community, and in other cultures.

d) Explain how culture affects the content and production values of dramatic performances.

e) Explain how social concepts such as cooperation, communication, collaboration, consensus, self-esteem, risk taking, sympathy, and empathy apply in theatre and daily life.

National Drama Standards for 5th-8th Grades

Write		Act			Design				Dir	Res		Compare				Analyze				Understand				
1.a	1.b	2.a	2.b	2.c	3.a	3.b	3.c	3.d	4.a	5.a	6.a	6.b	6.c	6.d	6.e	7.a	7.b	7.c	7.d	8.a	8.b	8.c	8.d	8.e
										★	★	★	★				★	★		★		★	★	★
★		★			★				★				★										★	★
★																								
★																								
		★		★																				
													★			★								
													★										★	
★																							★	
									★															
★									★															★
		★																						
		★							★										★					
		★																	★					
		★																	★					★
		★	★																★					
★		★			★															★		★		★
										★														
★													★											
★		★							★				★											★
																						★		★
★	★				★	★				★	★												★	

163

National Drama Standards
for 5th-8th Grades, continued

Page	Mystery Activities
31	**Games and Activities to Strengthen Writing and Acting Skills**
31	*Games for Developing Plot*
31	Headline Prompts
31	Suspense
32	CSI: Your Home Town
32	Frozen Pictures
32	*Games for Developing Characters*
32	If I Were (Metaphor) Game
33	Motivations
33	Happy Hands
33	Talk Show
34	*Games for Thinking on Your Feet*
34	Park Bench
34	Murder in the Dark
34	Tell Me About the Time You (TMATTY)
35	Word Tennis
37	**Crews: Who Does What in the Murder Mystery**
37	Crew Selection
38-41, 43	Prize, Publicity, Program, Ticket, and Hospitality Crews plan and begin work.
41-43	Scenery, Costume, Electrics, and Props Crews plan and begin work.
45	**Weeks Five and Six — Reading and Rehearsal in Ten Days**
45	Actors, Directors, Writers (Goals)
46	Prize, Publicity, Program, Ticket, and Hospitality Crews scheduled work and performances.
46-47	Scenery, Costume, Electrics, and Prop Crews scheduled work and performances.

Write		Act			Design				Dir	Res	Compare					Analyze				Understand				
1.a	1.b	2.a	2.b	2.c	3.a	3.b	3.c	3.d	4.a	5.a	6.a	6.b	6.c	6.d	6.e	7.a	7.b	7.c	7.d	8.a	8.b	8.c	8.d	8.e
★			★	★															★					
★	★		★	★					★										★					
★	★	★	★	★					★										★					
★									★										★					
		★	★																★					
★		★	★	★															★					
★		★	★	★															★					
		★	★	★															★					
★		★	★	★					★										★					
			★						★										★					
★	★	★	★																★					
				★															★					
					★	★	★		★												★			★
									★															★
					★	★	★	★	★	★						★								★
★	★	★	★	★	★	★	★	★	★	★		★	★	★		★	★	★	★					★
									★															★
					★	★	★	★	★	★						★								★

About the Authors

Justine Jones and **Mary Ann Kelley** have collaborated on two drama and theatre curriculum guides for public schools in addition to *Improv Ideas: A Book of Games and Lists* and *Drama Games and Improvs: Games for the Classroom and Beyond* from Meriwether Publishing Ltd. They have also collaborated on numerous productions and drama festivals in their former home of Los Alamos, New Mexico.

Justine lives only a few minute's drive from Scotland Yard, but she swears she has never been involved in a murder investigation of any kind! That said, she has taken great advantage of the U.K.'s incredible crime fiction and is still in mourning for the loss of the last London crime fiction shop. Other than crime, Justine is a practicing Jungian sand play therapist working in a London school. She continues to delight in London's thriving theatre scene and has just finished *Improv Ideas 2*.

Now retired to a small Victorian town in north-central Florida, **Mary Ann** thinks it's just the place for Miss Marple to make an appearance at a garden club or a church bazaar. So far though, all the exciting mysteries are on stage or in the movies. Mary Ann lives on a farm that has been in her family for 100 years. She is involved in many civic activities, helps local groups with their theatre programs, and finds time to do lighting with a local community theatre group. She credits her friends, and her yoga teachers and group, with helping her get the most out of her life. Her most recent design and painting efforts have not been with stage scenery, but in her own 1891 Victorian farmhouse.

Order Form

TM

Meriwether Publishing Ltd.
PO Box 7710
Colorado Springs CO 80933-7710
Phone: 800-937-5297   Fax: 719-594-9916
Website: www.meriwether.com

Please send me the following books:

_____ **Staging an Interactive Mystery Play   #BK-B331**   **$23.95**
by Justine Jones and Mary Ann Kelley
A six-week program for developing theatre skills

_____ **Improv Ideas   #BK-B283**   **$24.95**
by Justine Jones and Mary Ann Kelley
A book of games and lists

_____ **Drama Games and Improvs   #BK-B296**   **$22.95**
by Justine Jones and Mary Ann Kelley
Games for the classroom and beyond

_____ **Short & Sweet Skits for Student Actors**   **$17.95**
#BK-B312
by Maggie Scriven
55 sketches for teens

_____ **33 Short Comedy Plays for Teens   #BK-B325**   **$17.95**
by Laurie Allen
Plays for small casts

_____ **275 Acting Games: Connected   #BK-B314**   **$19.95**
by Gavin Levy
A comprehensive workbook of theatre games for developing acting skills

_____ **112 Acting Games   #BK-B277**   **$17.95**
by Gavin Levy
A comprehensive workbook of theatre games

These and other fine Meriwether Publishing books are available at your local bookstore or direct from the publisher. Prices subject to change without notice. Check our website or call for current prices.

Name: _____ e-mail: _____

Organization name: _____

Address: _____

City: _____ State: _____

Zip: _____ Phone: _____

❑ **Check enclosed**
❑ **Visa / MasterCard / Discover / Am. Express #** _____

Signature: _____ *Expiration date:* _____ / _____ *CVV code:* _____
(required for credit card orders)

Colorado residents: Please add 3% sales tax.
Shipping: Include $3.95 for the first book and 75¢ for each additional book ordered.

❑ *Please send me a copy of your complete catalog of books and plays.*

CPSIA information can be obtained at www.ICGtesting.com
Printed in the USA
BVOW052022161212

308239BV00005B/7/P